Shakespeare and Disgust

RELATED TITLES AVAILABLE FROM THE ARDEN
SHAKESPEARE

The Anatomy of Insults in Shakespeare's World
Nathalie Vienne-Guerrin
ISBN: 978-1-3500-5549-0

Emotional Excess on the Shakespearean Stage: Passion's Slaves
Bridget Escolme
ISBN: 978-1-4081-7967-3

Shakespeare and Forgetting
Peter Holland
ISBN: 978-1-3502-1149-0

Shakespeare and the Politics of Nostalgia: Negotiating the Memory of Elizabeth I on the Jacobean Stage
Yuichi Tsukada
ISBN: 978-1-3501-7507-5

Shakespeare's Body Language: Shaming Gestures and Gender Politics on the Renaissance Stage
Miranda Fay Thomas
ISBN: 978-1-3502-2814-6

Shakespeare and Disgust

The History and Science of Early Modern Revulsion

Bradley J. Irish

THE ARDEN SHAKESPEARE
LONDON • NEW YORK • OXFORD • NEW DELHI • SYDNEY

THE ARDEN SHAKESPEARE
Bloomsbury Publishing Plc
50 Bedford Square, London, WC1B 3DP, UK
1385 Broadway, New York, NY 10018, USA
29 Earlsfort Terrace, Dublin 2, Ireland

BLOOMSBURY, THE ARDEN SHAKESPEARE and the Arden Shakespeare logo are trademarks of Bloomsbury Publishing Plc

First published in Great Britain 2023
This paperback published in 2024

Copyright © Bradley J. Irish, 2023

Bradley J. Irish has asserted his right under the Copyright, Designs and Patents Act, 1988, to be identified as author of this work.

For legal purposes the Acknowledgements on p. viii constitute an extension of this copyright page.

Cover Designer: Jess Stevens
Cover Image: *Still life with rotting fruit and nuts on a stone ledge*
© Abraham Mignon

All rights reserved. No part of this publication may be reproduced or transmitted in any form or by any means, electronic or mechanical, including photocopying, recording, or any information storage or retrieval system, without prior permission in writing from the publishers.

Bloomsbury Publishing Plc does not have any control over, or responsibility for, any third-party websites referred to or in this book. All internet addresses given in this book were correct at the time of going to press. The author and publisher regret any inconvenience caused if addresses have changed or sites have ceased to exist, but can accept no responsibility for any such changes.

A catalogue record for this book is available from the British Library.

A catalog record for this book is available from the Library of Congress.

ISBN: HB: 978-1-3502-1398-2
PB: 978-1-3502-1403-3
ePDF: 978-1-3502-1401-9
eBook: 978-1-3502-1400-2

Typeset by Deanta Global Publishing Services, Chennai, India

To find out more about our authors and books visit www.bloomsbury.com and sign up for our newsletters.

For Jenny

CONTENTS

Acknowledgements viii
Textual notes x

Introduction 1
1 What is disgust? 17
2 *Titus Andronicus:* The spectacle of disgust 37
3 Food disgust 63
4 *Timon of Athens:* The cycles of disgust 73
5 Disease disgust 99
6 *Coriolanus:* The circuit of disgust 111
7 Body envelope disgust 135
8 *Othello:* The disgusting outsider 147
9 Racial disgust 165
10 *Hamlet:* Death and disgust 173
11 Sex disgust 195
Conclusion 205

Notes 209
Index 262

ACKNOWLEDGEMENTS

A book is written with the help of countless others. I owe special thanks for the various forms of help and support I've received from Brandi K. Adams, Cristina León Alfar; Mira 'Assaf Kafantaris, Katie Barclay, Jonathan Bate, Rob Boddice, Paul Budra, Joseph Buenker, William C. Carroll, Jeffrey Cohen, Thomas Dixon, Holly Dugan, Jessica Early, Natalie Eschenbaum, Ruben Espinosa, Richard Firth-Godbehere, John Garrison, Stephen Guy-Bray, Mary Floyd-Wilson, Yasmine Hachimi, Nic Helms, Diana Henderson, Peter Herman, David Hershinow, Allison Hobgood, Peter Holland, Jonathan Hope, Colleen E. Kennedy, Emily King, Carol Mejia LaPerle, James N. Loehlin, Jeremy Lopez, Jordan Loveridge, Andrew Lynch, Eric Mallin, Christopher Martin, Susan Matt, David Mazella, Erin A. McCarthy, Paul Megna, Jeffrey Alan Miller, Ian Frederick Moulton, Aidan Norrie, Bunmi O. Olatunji, Gail Kern Paster, W. Gerrod Parrott, Nathan Pensky, Kyle Pivetti, Krista Ratcliffe, Benedict Robinson, Bradley Ryner, Seth Schein, Ian Smith, John Staines, Peter Stearns, Ayanna Thompson, Michael Tueller, Katherine Walker, Doris Warriner, Breanne Weber, Frank Whigham, Jeffrey R. Wilson, David Wood, Marjorie Curry Woods and the many friends and colleagues I've made on social media.

I am grateful to my colleagues and students at Arizona State University – especially the librarians, who work endlessly for us.

I am enormously indebted to the wonderful staff at Bloomsbury, especially Lara Bateman and Ella Wilson.

Over the years, many parts of this book have benefitted from the suggestions of various anonymous readers: thank you for making my work so much better.

An earlier form of Chapter 6 appeared as 'Coriolanus and the Poetics of Disgust', *Shakespeare Survey* 69 (2016): 198–215 (copyright CUP, reprinted with permission). An earlier form of Chapter 8 appeared as 'Racial Disgust in Early Modern England:

'The Case of Othello', *Shakespeare Quarterly* 73.3 (2022): 1–22. Thanks are owed to the readers, editors and staff of these journals.

I am especially thankful to Cora Fox, Lalita Pandit Hogan, Patrick Hogan and Lani Shiota, whose brilliant minds have made me a better thinker and whose friendships have sustained me.

Finally, I owe everything to my family. Thank you to Mom and Dad, Olivia, Penelope and Jenny, most of all.

TEXTUAL NOTES

Unless otherwise mentioned, quotations from Shakespeare (cited parenthetically) come from *William Shakespeare: Complete Works*, ed. Richard Proudfoot, Ann Thompson, David Scott Kastan and H. R. Woudhuysen (London: The Arden Shakespeare, 2021). I have also consulted the individual Arden 3rd editions of Shakespeare's plays throughout.

When quoting early modern documents, I have on occasion silently amended punctuation for the sake of readability.

Introduction

In the final days of 1811, a London newspaper reviewed a recent production of *Coriolanus,* starring the renowned actor John Philip Kemble. To conclude his report, the anonymous critic summarizes Caius Martius and his tragedy:

> He affects to bow down, in spirit, and succumb before the Gods; yet, when his hot nature bursts forth into a summary and fatal resolution, he vomits blasphemy, and challenges the wrath of Jove, by denying his homage to the will of Heaven! He affects to be a patriot of the sternest order, yet he places the pretensions of his own swelling vanity above the institutes and ancient ceremonies of the land.[1]

Though much could be said about this reading of the play, a particular image strikes me as most notable: that of Coriolanus vomiting, his curses encompassing not just a verbal violence, but a visceral one as well. Shakespeare, in fact, would have encountered a similarly eruptive Roman in his reading of Plutarch:

> So *Martius* being a stowte man of nature, that neuer yelded in any respect, as one thincking that to ouercome allwayes, and to haue the vpper hande in all matters, was a token of magnanimitie, and of no base and fainte corage, which spitteth out anger from the most weake and passioned parte of the harte, much like the matter of an impostume.[2]

In his rage, Coriolanus is here imagined as ejecting a diseased substance from his mouth: 'the matter' is the pus and filth of an infected abscess ('impostume'), perhaps from an impacted tooth or an inflamed bowel. His response to the Roman plebs thus becomes somatized, as his rejection of their moral failings becomes akin to the bodily rejection of offending effluvia.[3]

In characterizing this somatic and moral response, we might say that Coriolanus is a man consumed by the emotion of disgust, the target of my investigation in this book. Historians and literary scholars don't always think of the premodern world in its capacity to evoke revulsion, but many aspects of sixteenth- and seventeenth-century life were sources of visceral offence – and not just from the more sanitized perspective of a modern observer. As Roy Porter reminds us, this begins with the very bodies in which people existed:

> To a degree that is hard to imagine nowadays, visible, tangible flesh was all too often experienced as ugly, nasty and decaying, bitten by bugs and beset by sores; it was rank, foul and dysfunctional; for all of medicine's best efforts, it was frequently racked with pain, disability and disease.[4]

This is something that Shakespeare would have been acutely aware of: Thomas Dekker comments in several places on the disgusting stench of early modern theatre, grumbling that the contemporary playhouse 'stinckes [like] there was some carion not far off', because it 'smoakt euerye after noone with Stinkards, who were so glewed together in crowdes with the Steames of strong breath, that when they came foorth, their faces lookt as if they had beene perboylde'.[5] In early modern England, cesspits overflowed with human waste, foodstuffs were in constant threat of rot, disease-laden vermin scurried across the floors and the mangled bodies of criminals were publicly displayed in gruesome spectacles. And while it certainly seems likely that early modern subjects had a stronger disgust threshold than many of us do today, this doesn't change the fact that Shakespeare inhabited a disgusting world. Disgust, I will argue in what follows, informs much more than just *Coriolanus*: it is a sentiment that thoroughly captivated Shakespeare's attention, and one that helped shape his understanding of how people relate to both their own physical bodies and to the symbolic bodies of their social world.

Dubbed the 'gatekeeper emotion' by modern theorists in the psychological sciences, disgust is the vital affective process through which humans protect the boundaries of their physical bodies from material contaminants and protect the boundaries of their social bodies from moral contaminants. Because of this flexibility, the things that can trigger disgust – for example, food, disease and bodily injury, to name but a few – provided Shakespeare with a literary vocabulary to interrogate important thematic matters concerning the violation and preservation of such boundaries – things like compromised moral actors, unstable political arenas and changing social orders. *Shakespeare and Disgust: The History and Science of Early Modern Revulsion* makes the case that disgust offered Shakespeare a master category of compositional tools – poetic images, thematic considerations and narrative possibilities – that he consistently deployed to explore notions of physical and symbolic boundaries in his plays. Disgust thus played a crucial component in how Shakespeare understood the ways that people inhabit the world and interact with each other, with vital implications for his portrayal of social configurations like class, gender and sexuality, race and disability. My thesis in this book, it follows, is not modest: in the pages to come, I will attempt to convince you that disgust is one of the central engines of human behaviour, and that disgust is one of Shakespeare's central dramatic concerns.

There will be much more on the workings of disgust to come – but first, it is important to situate my project. As a study of literary emotion, this book is a product of what has been called 'the affective turn' (or sometimes, 'the emotional turn').[6] In the last thirty years, scholars in countless disciplines across the humanities and sciences have become increasingly interested in the workings of emotion and affect, subjects once taken more or less for granted. In English Renaissance studies, the stage for recent work on emotion was set in 2004, with the publication of Gail Kern Paster's *Humoring the Body: Emotions and the Shakespearean Stage*, her mutually edited (with Mary Floyd-Wilson and Katherine Rowe) collection *Reading the Early Modern Passions: Essays in the Cultural History of Emotion* and Douglas Trevor's *The Poetics of Melancholy in Early Modern England* – and in the intervening years, there has been a wealth of articles, monographs and collections published on the topic, including important volumes like Richard Meek and Erin Sullivan's *The Renaissance of Emotion: Understanding Affect in Shakespeare and His Contemporaries* (2015), R. S. White, Mark Houlahan and Katrina O'Loughlin's *Shakespeare and Emotions: Inheritances, Enactments, Legacies* (2015), Amanda Bailey and Mario DiGangi's *Affect Theory and Early Modern Texts: Politics, Ecologies, and Form* (2017) and Katharine A. Craik's *Shakespeare and Emotion* (2020).[7] *Shakespeare and Disgust* is deeply indebted to this foundational work and is designed to be a new entry in this ever-growing field.

Furthermore, I must note that disgust, broadly speaking, has been of considerable interest to scholars and thinkers working on emotion. In the last twenty-five years, a number of full-length treatments of disgust have been published, emerging from a variety of disciplinary fields. The first was William Ian Miller's *The Anatomy of Disgust*, a social and cultural history of the emotion that arrived before disgust research had taken much hold in the scholarly imagination. (Indeed, writing in 1997, Miller notes that 'disgust has elicited little attention in any of the disciplines that claim an interest in the emotions: psychology, philosophy, anthropology'.[8]) Other books soon followed. In *The Hydra's Tale: Imagining Disgust* (2002), Robert Rawdon Wilson argues that disgust is enormously varied in form and function – and it is this multiplicity that leads him to compare the emotion to the hydra, the book's governing metaphor.[9] Winfried Menninghaus, in *Disgust: Theory and History of a Strong Sensation* (2003), and Carolyn Korsmeyer, in *Savoring Disgust: The Foul and the Fair in Aesthetics* (2011), survey how disgust has become a paradoxical category of aesthetic judgement in the last 250 years.[10] In both *Hiding from Humanity: Disgust, Shame, and the Law* (2004) and *From Disgust to Humanity: Sexual Orientation and Constitutional Law* (2010), Martha C. Nussbaum influentially argues that disgust is an unethical basis for legal judgement, given how the emotion encourages the dehumanization of vulnerable others, as we have seen historically in the opposition to interracial and same-sex couplings.[11] More recently, Debra Lieberman and Carlton Patrick reach a similar conclusion in *Objection: Disgust, Morality, and the Law* (2018).[12] In *The Meaning of Disgust* (2011), Colin McGinn offers a philosophical account of disgust, arguing that what disgusts us is that which makes salient the transitory process between life and death.[13] Rachel Herz's *That's Disgusting: Unraveling the Mysteries of Repulsion* (2013) and Valerie Curtis's *Don't Look, Don't Touch, Don't Eat: The Science Behind Revulsion* (2013) offer broad introductions to the psychological dynamics of disgust.[14] Donald Lateiner and Dimos Spatharas's *The Ancient Emotion of Disgust* (2016) collects essays on revulsion in Greek and Roman culture.[15] In *A Politics of Disgust: Selfhood, World-Making, and Ethics* (2020), Eleonora Joensuu draws upon the work of feminist theorist and psychoanalyst Jessica Benjamin to develop what she calls 'a feminist politics of disgust'.[16] And most recently,

Zachary Samalin's *The Masses Are Revolting: Victorian Culture and the Political Aesthetics of Disgust* (2021) broadly historicizes the emotion in nineteenth-century British culture.[17]

Besides inspiring such full-length works, disgust has also shaped a growing number of essays, articles and chapters in literary and cultural studies. To consider, for example, a few that have been published in the last several years: Luke F. Johnson analyses 'the cannibalistic dimensions of racial disgust and desire' in Michel Houellebecq's novel *Submission*, Hannah Lee Rogers argues that Jane Austen's *Persuasion* depicts a world in which tolerance is displaced by 'a concept of disgust that abjects those who would corrupt the social norms of respectable English people' and Neetu Khanna suggests that 'the erotics of disgust' in the work of Ismat Chughtai enable us to explore how the female body becomes 'the focal object of violent subjection by both colonial and anticolonial nationalist regimes of discipline'.[18] In general, these offerings reflect the fact that disgust has captivated a number of prominent critical theorists. In their celebrated essay 'Shame in the Cybernetic Fold: Reading Silvan Tomkins' (1995), Eve Kosofsky Sedgwick and Adam Frank discuss the proximity of disgust and desire; Sianne Ngai concludes her *Ugly Feelings* (2005) with an afterword that considers the same topic.[19] Sara Ahmed, in *The Cultural Politics of Emotion* (2004), analyses how labelling something disgusting is a thoroughly performative act and outlines how disgust seems to 'stick' to some kinds of bodies more than others.[20] And perhaps most notably of all, Julia Kristeva offers an enormously influential theory of abjection in *Powers of Horror* (1980).[21]

In early modern studies, there has not been a tremendous amount of scholarship that specifically considers disgust – though some important work is proximate. There has, of course, been a decades-long interest in the Renaissance grotesque, inspired by Bakhtin's analysis of carnival.[22] While disgust is not the focus, the emotion is implicitly invoked by Paster in *The Body Embarrassed: Drama and the Disciplines of Shame in Early Modern England* (1993), her foundational study of bodily regulation; she notes that the discourses of both humoralism and the grotesque feature 'the bowels, the belly, the genitalia, the excretory organs, [and] the mouth', sites of the body that (we will see) are regulated by disgust.[23] Another example is Barbara Correll's *The End of Conduct: Grobianus and the Renaissance Text of the Subject* (1996), which treats Friedrich Dedekind's ironic neo-Latin conduct poem *Grobianus* – a work that, as a 'nightmarish inversion' of *The Book of the Courtier,* actually 'inspires disgust'.[24] But the first full-length, explicit analysis of Renaissance disgust did not come until 2016, with the publication of Natalie K. Eschenbaum and Correll's edited collection *Disgust in Early Modern English Literature*.[25] Like Benedict Robinson's important essay 'Disgust c. 1600' (2014), this landmark volume takes primarily a historicist approach, and is premised on the fact that tending to disgust provides a new view of early modern life: because (as we will also see later) the emotion only emerges in humans through a process of enculturation, the book argues that 'studying disgust in the literature of the period reveals another view, perhaps more raw and real, of what it meant to be an early modern subject'.[26] To this end, authors in the collection survey a wide range of literary and cultural texts from the Renaissance, exploring how 'early modern English writers used this aversive emotion to explore sexual behaviors, to describe encounters with foreign cultures, and to manipulate their readers' responses'.[27]

This historical approach to early modern disgust is representative of early modern emotion studies more broadly. In general, work on Renaissance emotion has been historicist in nature, elucidating how contemporary discourses of the passions – most notably, humoural physiology – shaped the ways that early modern subjects understood the relationship between bodies, selves and environments. More recent scholars have also widened their attention beyond humoralism, to interrogate the 'other systems of knowledge and representation that people used to conceptualise and articulate emotional experience'.[28] Emerging from this critical tradition, *Shakespeare and Disgust* is fundamentally a historicist project: the book surveys Renaissance cultures of revulsion, and the various chapters routinely analyse moments of Shakespearean disgust by situating them within their early modern English context. In this sense, *Shakespeare and Disgust* first reflects its genealogical debt to the wealth of brilliant historicist scholarship on emotion that has been published in the last two decades.

But the book that follows isn't only a historicist work. While the conditions of early modern England are never too distant from my thought, *Shakespeare and Disgust* draws its fundamental understanding of how disgust works not from the discourses of humours or passions that circulated during Shakespeare's life, but from a drastically different source: the theories and models of the modern affective sciences. Literary and cultural critics have sometimes engaged discrete strands of scientific thought in their discussions of disgust; Sedgwick and Frank, for example, famously engage the work of mid-twentieth-century psychologist Silvan Tomkins in their treatment of affect. *Shakespeare and Disgust* amplifies this approach, by grounding much of its analysis in the broad, developing discourse of the contemporary affective sciences. The affective sciences have fundamentally shaped how I understand the workings of disgust, and it is this broad understanding that I bring to my historically situated analysis of disgust in Shakespeare. In this way, *Shakespeare and Disgust* is a historicist book that is nonetheless deeply indebted to radically modern forms of knowledge; combining these modes of enquiry, I believe, provides the most thorough account of Shakespearean disgust, and offers exciting possibilities for new ways of seeing the emotion at work in the plays and poems.

A historicist treatment of Shakespeare hardly needs much theoretical explanation. But utilizing modern scientific models is not yet entirely common in the study of early modern emotion, so it will be useful to offer a few initial comments on my approach.[29] One of the major challenges of employing a science-based methodology to the study of literary and historical emotion stems from the fact that there is a point of broad philosophical difference in how the humanities and sciences generally understand emotion. Humanists, wary of essentializing and universalizing discourses, tend to see emotion (at its core) as a socially constructed phenomenon, an aspect of psychology that is brought online and only made meaningful through the workings of particularized cultural and historical contexts. While there is a minority of scientists who subscribe to such a fully constructivist account – and while these scientists have received widespread endorsement by humanists who work on emotion – the clear majority of those working in psychology and neuroscience, on the contrary, believe that certain aspects of emotion are indeed meaningfully 'universal'.[30] For example, in a recent survey of 148 researchers currently active in the affective sciences, 88 per cent agreed that there is 'compelling evidence for universals' in some aspect of emotions.[31] This presents an obvious problem: discourses of the universal tend to be anathema to most scholars in the humanities, and universalism and transhistoricalism have long been identified as particular enemies of the historicist project.[32] More to the immediate point, Rob Boddice (one of the most prominent historians of emotion working today) has argued in a number of venues that we must not consider disgust a 'universal' emotion, and I suspect that many humanists would intuitively agree with him.[33] How, then, can humanists utilize the science of disgust in historical analysis, if most scientists see the emotion in terms of human universality?

When it comes to interdisciplinary exchange, this difference in outlook may initially seem like an impasse – but I want to suggest, however, that it is not actually an impediment to research, for (at least) three reasons. First, the traditional opposition between extreme universalism and extreme constructivism is no longer taken seriously by many emotion researchers; both scientists and historians now regularly adopt some kind of biocultural model of emotion, which accounts for the fact that the human brain has certain stable biological properties that nonetheless must inevitably develop within a particular cultural framework.[34] The workings of biology and culture are thus inseparable, and a researcher who is choosing to relatively privilege one or the other in their work is simply viewing the emotion problematic from a particular perspective at that particular moment.

Second, as we will see, even the scientists who understand disgust as a species-typical universal mechanism acknowledge the tremendous role that enculturation plays in how the emotion actually manifests. Despite being theorized as a universal psychological process, disgust shows enormous variability, as its properties are drastically shaped by the social context in which an individual both develops and then subsequently inhabits the world. Because 'universality' has historically (and disingenuously) been deployed in the service of a normative male, heterosexual, Eurocentric hegemony, humanists tend to be understandably suspicious when the term is invoked – but the scientific understanding of 'universality' is importantly different than the bad-faith applications of the concept that humanists rightly reject.[35] When scientists talk of species-typical psychological universality, they generally do not mean that every human who has ever lived in every time and place experiences something in exactly the same way; rather, they are referring more broadly to the ubiquity of certain psychological mechanisms that seem to be a regular feature of human mental architecture.[36] Indeed, as we will see, there are many aspects of human behaviour that display what Richard A. Shweder calls 'universalism without the uniformity' – and thus the fact that most scientists view disgust as a psychological universal is in no way incompatible with the view that disgust changes considerably depending on historical and geographical context.[37]

Finally, as I have argued in a recent article, even if humanists want to maintain their rejection of emotional universality, it is still possible to learn from research on disgust that emerges from a universalist premise, because much of that research isn't actually concerned with establishing that the emotion is universal.[38] Accordingly, it is possible to appreciate many things about how disgust works from such scientific accounts, even if the issue of its alleged universality is bracketed, or denied entirely. As the work of psychologist Klaus Scherer demonstrates, there's reason to think that certain fuzzy kinds of emotional episodes are ubiquitous enough in human experience that we might speak of their broad *functional congruence* in our species – and engaging scientific analysis that groups such instances under a single convenient category (like the English word *disgust*) does not in turn demand that the emotion be understood as strictly universal.[39]

For these three reasons, I think that it is perfectly possible to incorporate a scientifically grounded account of disgust into a more traditional historicist framework: to speak of disgust as a 'universal' emotion with certain evolved, species-typical properties does not require embracing any kind of rigid biological determinism, nor does it undermine the view that manifestations of disgust are fundamentally shaped by the cultural and historical context in which they emerge.[40] Since the human disgust system is theorized as a species-typical psychological process that is integrally formed by the social context in which it develops, scientific models with a broad, universal outlook can co-exist comfortably with a historicist sensibility: rather than being in opposition, the scientific approach simply offers certain theories about the raw affective material that must inevitably be shaped by the specific parameters of any given culture. Accordingly, I agree with Eschenbaum and Correll's sense that tending to disgust gives insight into the particularities of early modern subjectivity, and much of what I say about Shakespearean disgust will reflect the circumstances of his cultural moment – it just so happens that my general understanding of how disgust works, in the broadest possible sense, has been shaped via the categorical properties of the emotion that have been identified by affective scientists. A benefit of this approach, I suggest, is that it demonstrates correspondences between the findings of the sciences and humanities: we will often find that Shakespeare intuitively made arguments about disgust that, four centuries later, have been independently replicated in the research laboratory. In general terms, literary and cultural studies are becoming ever-more interdisciplinary, establishing increasingly complex links with other fields both inside and outside the humanities; by bringing the insights of the affective sciences to bear on a historicist study of an early modern subject, this book aims to provide a further example of how such disciplinary exchange can benefit the study of Shakespeare.

A final comment about the body of science I engage in *Shakespeare and Disgust*. For good reason, humanists tend to be rightly cautious about the uncritical enshrinement of scientific findings, and there is no doubt that psychological accounts of disgust have their potential limitations. For one thing, much of this research emerges from a WEIRD (Western, Educated, Industrialized, Rich and Democratic) context, which raises reasonable questions about the broader applicability of its findings. (Though, as mentioned earlier, and as we will see more in Chapter 1, there is a wealth of cross-cultural data that suggests the human disgust system has certain stable properties.) Furthermore, and more importantly, in the last decade the psychological sciences have broadly faced a so-called replication crisis, which has cast doubt on the credibility of both research findings and experimental techniques. While I thus very much acknowledge the possible shortcomings of disgust research, I have in this book nonetheless taken an inclusive approach to covering the scientific discourse of disgust. When engaging such a wide body of research, certain things are inescapable: some studies are going to be more scientifically sound than others, some are going to produce more statistically significant results and some may even reach contradictory conclusions. But when presenting findings about disgust in this book, I will generally not quibble, and instead take the overall stance that research by professional scientists, vetted by professional reviewers and editors, and published in professional journals can at least be reported in terms of its contribution to an overall scientific *discourse* on disgust – even if, as we must well acknowledge, the conclusions of such research may be subsequently reframed, re-evaluated, or rebutted, in the normal process of scientific progression. Accordingly, I do not attempt the impossible task of giving a transcendental account of what disgust really *is*; rather, I try to offer a broad overview of the current state of scientific *understanding* on the emotion, however imperfect it undoubtedly is.

With that said, let me briefly describe what is to come. Chapter 1, 'What Is Disgust?', sets the stage for my analysis, by offering a brief historical account of early modern disgust, and then presenting a broad survey of how the emotion is currently theorized in the affective sciences. There is little about Shakespeare in this initial chapter, but that is also by design. I purposely titled this book *Shakespeare and Disgust*, rather than *Disgust in Shakespeare*, because I see both the playwright and the emotion as objects worthy of equal attention; it is my hope that readers will take just as much interest in the workings of disgust as they take in the workings of Shakespeare. To this end, the initial chapter outlines the scientific discourse of disgust: what the emotion is thought to be, how it is thought to work and what it is thought to do in the world. As we will see, the wide range of things that trigger disgust suggests that the emotion is implicated in the fundamental ways that we exist in the world; disgust helps shape how we survive, how we reproduce, how we co-exist with others. Shakespeare, I argue, intuitively understood this, and the portrayal of disgust in his drama anticipates the modern findings of the affective sciences. For a poet supremely interested in human behaviour, disgust thus proved tremendously generative to Shakespeare's imagination; this emotion, it turns out, is a way of organizing our personal and interpersonal experience.

This theoretical foundation sets the stage for the book's primary contents: extended readings of disgust in *Titus Andronicus*, *Timon of Athens*, *Coriolanus*, *Othello* and *Hamlet*. '*Titus Andronicus*: The Spectacle of Disgust' begins my analysis, by considering Shakespeare's most overtly disgusting play. This chapter is firmly historicist in nature, as I argue that the staged horrors of *Titus* reflect a larger set of social practices that comprise what I call the early modern culture of spectacular disgust – a culture in which ostensibly repulsive objects become sources of attention and fascination, a function of the ambivalent behavioural response that disgust (we will see) is thought to inspire. This chapter considers things like execution rites, public dissections, discourses of monstrosity and medicinal cannibalism; these aspects of early modern England reflect *Titus*'s undeniable ability to generate both aesthetic pleasure and revulsion. '*Timon of Athens*: The Cycles of Disgust' not only explores *Timon*'s extensive use of disgust-based imagery but also argues that the play's three central characters – Alcibiades, Apemantus and Timon himself – undergo narrative cycles that recall the regulatory workings of disgust more broadly. These men, who are either willingly or forcefully ejected from their city's walls, refashion themselves as agents of social purgation, tasked with expelling the sickness from the corrupted body of Athens. '*Coriolanus*: The Circuit of Disgust', argues that *Coriolanus* stages a competition of disgust, as the play's factions struggle to assert the extent to which they are disgusted by one another. Caius Martius and his allies are viscerally disgusted by the plebeians' physical forms, and morally disgusted by their cowardice, presumption and ingratitude – while the plebeians and their Tribune spokesmen are disgusted by Martius's arrogance and disregard for the citizens of the city he protects. '*Othello*: The Disgusting Outsider' argues that it is disgust, rather than envy or jealousy, that is at the affective centre of Shakespeare's great tragedy. Modern research reveals that disgust is integral to the workings of racial and ethnic discrimination, and I show in this chapter how Othello's undoing is underwritten by the extent to which he becomes construed as a disgusting object by his fellow Venetians. Finally, '*Hamlet*: Death and Disgust' accounts for the infamous rottenness of Denmark by drawing on the modern psychological model of Terror Management Theory. This theory, which links the human disgust response to our species' existential fear of death, offers a way to think about how Hamlet's characteristic feelings of revulsion align with his other preoccupations in the play – not only his obsession with mortality but also his infamously negative view of sex.

The book's even-numbered chapters contain the full analysis of these plays. But because disgust is so widespread in the Shakespearean canon – and because it takes on so many different forms – my longer readings of *Titus*, *Timon*, *Coriolanus*, *Othello* and *Hamlet* are punctuated by a series of shorter chapters, each devoted to a different kind of disgust elicitor: 'Food Disgust', 'Disease Disgust', 'Body Envelope Disgust', 'Racial Disgust' and 'Sex Disgust'. These interludes (the odd-numbered chapters) serve two purposes. First, they allow me to elaborate on the modern science of disgust, by surveying relevant research that contextualizes the specific forms of disgust that we find throughout the plays and poems. (My goal, it will be remembered, is to spark an interest not only in Shakespearean disgust but in the science of disgust more broadly.) More importantly, these interludes also provide the opportunity to briefly explore a sampling of how these different disgust elicitors operate in Shakespeare's other works. These sections are not full readings of individual plays – and they are not intended to be – but rather exist to give a snapshot of how Shakespearean disgust can be located and engaged beyond the works considered in the book's central chapters. It is my hope that these brief exercises will encourage readers to take up the analysis of disgust across Shakespeare – because there is, to be sure, far more work to be done on this front than what is contained in the pages to follow.

This overview, I hope, sheds some light on the project's design. As noted earlier, *Shakespeare and Disgust* relies on both historicist and scientific analysis, and I have tried to be purposeful in how it engages these two methods. Throughout the book, my understanding of disgust has been fundamentally shaped by the affective sciences, but this does not mean that at all times my treatment of Shakespearean disgust will be directly linked to a particular psychological theory or a particular research study – especially in the early chapters on Shakespeare, my debt to the sciences is diffuse and generalized, rather than strictly explicit. Indeed, as the book progresses, the analysis increasingly moves from the more familiar confines of historicist practice to the more novel approaches of the affective sciences, a move facilitated by the basis of scientific knowledge that accrues as we proceed from chapter to chapter. So the first major chapter, which considers *Titus Andronicus* and early modern cultures of spectacular disgust, is entirely historicist in nature, while the final major chapter, which reads *Hamlet* in light of the tenets of Terror Management Theory, is precisely bound to one specific scientific model of emotion. With this structure, it is my hope that readers will become both increasingly familiar and increasingly comfortable with the science of disgust – and, more importantly, its literary applications – as they make their way through the book. I fundamentally believe that humanistic and scientific approaches can be mutually informing, and *Shakespeare and Disgust* thus tries to demonstrate the benefit of combining such methods in a mixed-mode of analysis.

To conclude, I should briefly discuss the limitations of the project. The most obvious is that the book is necessarily incomplete: Shakespeare's engagement with disgust is so robust that I can't possibly account for it fully in the space I have available to me. I have attempted to range widely in my analysis, but there are things that I will have inevitably missed, and ultimately the book's contents reflect the aspects of Shakespearean disgust that seemed to me most relevant. Most notably, comedy is underrepresented, which can be accounted for in a couple of ways. I am not, for example, focusing on Bakhtinian notions of the carnivalesque and grotesque, which often (though obviously not always) centre the 'realm of exaggeration, gluttony, abuse and defiance' that we find in comic sequences; but it is also true, I think, that Shakespeare's more elaborate engagements with disgust generally occur within a sombre context, so my analysis thus skews towards the tragic.[41] I have also made little attempt to integrate the scientific discourse of disgust into the models of emotion already anchored in contemporary cultural studies, such as the writings of Ahmed and Ngai described earlier. This work, which belongs to a field that has been called affective post-structuralism, is outside my area of critical expertise; nonetheless, I do believe that this scholarship has many points of potential contact with the scientific models of disgust that I do engage, and it is my hope that subsequent research will consider these intersections further.[42] Finally, because my ultimate aim is to explore Shakespearean disgust, the interdisciplinary exchange in this book is fairly unidirectional: I borrow from the affective sciences to enrich my historicist analysis. But it is becoming increasingly apparent that humanist and scientific approaches should be mutually informing, and literary and social historians of emotion are becoming increasingly vocal about the fact that cultural and historical analysis can provide vital context and evidence for the work on emotion being done by affective scientists in research laboratories today.[43] As suggested earlier, Shakespeare's engagement with disgust anticipates many twenty-first-century scientific findings – but his insights into emotion aren't simply valid or interesting to the extent that they can secure an existing scientific imprimatur. Humanist approaches to emotion, in other words, have valuable things to offer the affective sciences – and while my purpose in this book is not to advance that argument per se, I nonetheless hope that my treatment of Shakespearean disgust will at least give some indication of how the results of literary analysis might prove interesting to a scientist thinking more broadly about how disgust works.

The takeaway from all of this, I think, is that there's still much more work to be done. *Shakespeare and Disgust* is designed to be a starting point for such future conversations, and I hope that the analysis that follows will make a convincing case for why Shakespearean disgust is worthy of our continued attention.

1

What is disgust?

Shakespeare never uses the word *disgust*, a term that makes its first printed appearance during his adult life. But Benedict Robinson, the scholar who has most thoroughly historicized the emotion in the English Renaissance, notes that 'early seventeenth-century England has long been associated with a pervasive disgust', and, as this book aims to demonstrate, there is no shortage of moments in Shakespeare's plays that both activate and interrogate the workings of revulsion.[1] That Shakespeare doesn't invoke the word shouldn't concern us; while a great deal of emotion history work is lexical in method, both experimental research and common experience indicate that there is no strict linguistic determinism that restricts the emotional repertoire of a culture, or of individual members of that culture.[2] (For example, English speakers are easily able to both understand and indulge in *schadenfreude*, despite the fact that we have no native synonym in our language.) Even without usage of the actual word, we are still able to find endless engagement with disgust in Shakespeare's work – especially when we consider more precisely how the emotion is thought to operate.

A cognate of the Middle French *desgoust* and Italian *disgusto*, the English word *disgust* ultimately emerges as a negation of the Latin *gusto* (taste) – and indeed, the first recorded uses of the term have it as a general synonym of *distaste*, a word of only slightly earlier origin. This gastric register is suggested by the lexicographer Randle Cotgrave, who in his English-French dictionary of 1611 refers to 'a queasinesse, or disgust of stomacke'.[3] But, as we know from common usage in modern English – and as we will importantly see herein – the feeling of disgust is not simply about an upset stomach, but can also entail a broader form of aversion; Cotgrave equally renders the French *Desaimer* (literally 'to cease to love') as to 'fall into dislike, or disgust'.⁴ John Florio's English–Italian dictionary similarly displays this range of meaning, defining the Italian *disgusto/sgusto* as 'disgust, distast, vnkindnes, dislike'.⁵ In fact, in the currently available EEBO-TCP corpus, the first printed appearance of *disgust* (from 1596) confirms that early modern usage can refer to both visceral, somatic appetite and more generalized targets of repulsion: speaking of the sacraments, Thomas Wright argues that the Eucharist contains 'all delight and sweetnes of taste', because 'by nourishing the soule . . . it shaketh off all the disgusts and griefes which our enemies by sinnes or temtations can impose vppon vs'.⁶ A few years later, we see a similar linkage of taste and disgust, when Anthony Copley attacks religious prophecy:

> So likewise of her Maiesties end how disasterously they haue prophecied, and do expect, I am sure you haue heard and do disgust as much as I. But what talke I of Protestants, seeing that also vpon very religious Catholikes they haue augured no lesse fatally, for being their known or but suspected distasters?⁷

There are many such examples in the period, confirming Robinson's sense that 'at heart early modern usage [of *disgust*] refuses to draw a line between the most visceral bodily processes and the largest horizons of human action'.⁸

Readers interested in further historicization of Renaissance disgust can find both primary and secondary sources documented on my website, earlymodernemotion.net. But for now, the important point for me to stress is that this fundamental account of early modern disgust – that is, as an emotional concept that entails both visceral, bodily rejection and more general forms of aversion – is very much substantiated by current thinking in the affective sciences. And disgust has been enormously compelling to modern scientists. In 2002, Richard J. McNally noted that while disgust has historically 'been the most understudied of all the emotions', it had in recent years 'arrived as a topic of study in its own right' – but even McNally, I suspect, couldn't have predicted the extent to which contemporary researchers have been captivated by the topic.⁹ This explosion of recent interest can be easily quantified by the APA PsycInfo database: a search for 'disgust' across the entire twentieth century returns 633 items, while the twenty-first century has already produced 4750.[10] This attention is well warranted. As we will see, the evidence suggests that the basic capacity to feel disgust is a typical component of the mental architecture of our species' mental architecture – and thus, given its fundamental role in both personal and interpersonal life, to investigate disgust is to investigate part of what makes us human.[11]

The father of modern psychological research on disgust is Charles Darwin, who treats the emotion in his enormously influential study *The Expression of the Emotions in Man and Animals* (1872). Reflecting the etymology we saw above, Darwin notes that the word *disgust*, in its 'simplest sense, means something offensive to the taste': it is curious, he continues, 'how readily this feeling is excited by anything unusual in the appearance, odour, or nature of our food', which leads him to conclude that 'disgust primarily arises in connection with the act of eating or tasting'.[12] Half a century later, the famed psychiatrist Andras Angyal agreed that the 'nucleus of the disgust reaction, the main threat against which disgust is directed, is the oral incorporation of certain substances', and the notion of a food-centric disgust became the cornerstone for modern research on the emotion.[13] (Freud, however, was a dissenter, locating the disgust response in sexual aversion; while sex is indeed a disgust elicitor, modern theorists generally do not see it as the emotion's originary purpose.[14]) In evolutionary terms, the food-governing origins of the human emotion of disgust seem to be rooted in the general mechanics of distaste that are ubiquitous in animals. As we will see in more detail herein, non-human animals express responses to distasteful prey (such as 'head shaking or bill wiping') that seem to indicate the presence of a proto-disgust system, and it has been theorized that eliciting disgust responses from predators conveys a survival advantage to toxic prey.[15] It is sensible enough that organisms have developed biological measures to safeguard against the incorporation of toxic substances, and human disgust emerges, in the most basic form, from this domain of food regulation. (In fact, this biological response is so basic that some theorists have suggested that disgust may be closer to a motivational state like thirst or hunger than an actual 'emotion'.[16])

But disgust, we all know, is about much more than food, and the modern research tradition has devoted considerable attention to developing an understanding of the emotion that accounts for the various ways that disgust has expanded beyond its original purview, and that accounts for how this expansion has occurred. Though several different models have been offered, it has recently been said that 'most of the major current theories of disgust agree on four points'.[17] The first, unsurprisingly, is that 'disgust originates in part or whole as a food rejection system'. The second is that 'pathogen avoidance has some fundamental role in explaining the origins and expansion of disgust'. This is a natural elaboration of the first point, as food is rejected because of its potential to introduce dangerous pathogens into the body; furthermore, it is agreed (as we'll see in a moment) that many of the non-food-related items that elicit disgust do so because of their proximity to disease-transmitting agents. This is once again an evolutionary legacy, as great apes have been observed to exhibit a suite of pathogen avoidance behaviours that 'extends beyond distaste to resemble a muted form of disgust'; accordingly, 'rather than being unique to humans', the disgust system is likely 'a continuation of the armory of disease avoidance behavior ubiquitous in animals'.[18]

Having said that, we must once again stop to note that disgust, as common experience reveals, isn't *only* about pathogen avoidance – especially when we begin to consider its more abstract articulations. To this end, the third and fourth points of widespread theoretical agreement on disgust address how the emotion has expanded the domains of human life that it regulates. The third observes that 'a process like preadapation . . . is involved in the expansion of disgust elicitors'. Preadaptation, also known as *exaptation*, is a process through which an organism's fitness is enhanced by features serving a purpose different from that for which it was evolutionarily designed – for example, the mouth originally evolved for the purposes of respiration and food consumption but came to benefit some species by becoming a site through which they could vocalize communicative sounds.[19] In terms of disgust, the food rejection mechanism of distaste was gradually co-opted by a much larger behavioural avoidance system, which not only helped humans guard against an array of physical contaminants but also came to shield them from symbolic contamination. This leads us to the final point of widespread agreement: that 'the disgust emotion program (facial and bodily expression, psychophysiological events, behavioral withdrawal, and feeling of revulsion) is relatively conservative as disgust expands, while the class of elicitors and their meanings is more plastic'. This is a vital point, as it helps account for what is perhaps the most notable feature of the emotion: while the human disgust *system* is relatively consistent as a species-typical universal mechanism, what actually *triggers* that system is subject to wide cultural variance. The full workings of the human disgust system are, in the early years of development, brought online through enculturation and social learning – this is why the things the elicit disgust can vary widely across time and place, despite the fact that disgust is (for all meaningful purposes) a universal psychological process.

With these four points of agreement in mind, we should consider how disgust has been theorized in more precise detail. Two major models have been proposed. The most prominent (developed primarily from the work of Paul Rozin, Jonathan Haidt and Clark McCauley) has been under consistent refinement since the 1980s, and was largely responsible for the boom in disgust research in the last three decades. The second, more recent theory, developed by Joshua M. Tybur and colleagues, covers much of the same ground, yet offers an alternate explanation of the disgust system's functional domains. Conveniently, however, both models fundamentally agree on the categories of stimuli that trigger disgust, so their alternative explanatory approaches are not insurmountable, especially when it comes to investigating literary disgust.

The Rozin, Haidt and McCauley approach tracks how the human disgust system slowly expanded its regulatory purview across a variety of increasingly abstract domains; for this reason, it has been referred to as the *cultural evolution model* of disgust.[20] Acknowledging food as the emotion's starting point, this account argues that the 'phylogenetically ancient capacity for distaste' was 'coopted via the process of biological evolution to [become] an avoidance response to poisonous, contaminated, or spoiled items'.[21] The researchers term the resulting mechanism *core disgust*: the revulsion we feel from *food*, *bodily products* or *animals* (especially animals associated with spoiled or rotten food, such as insects and rodents) is designed to stop us from orally ingesting potentially dangerous pathogens, a visceral warning for an omnivorous 'species living with the constant threat of microbial contamination'.[22] This attends to disgust's origins as a food rejection system – but food, we have noted earlier, is not the only domain of disgust. Rozin, Haidt and McCauley thus suggest that there is another set of elicitors that reliably trigger disgust, but that have little to do with orality: matters concerning *sex*, *hygiene*, *the body envelope* (i.e. perceived violations of the integrity of the human body, such as wounds, mutilation, deformity and obesity) and *death*. Stimuli from these domains, they theorize, have in common the ability to trigger an existentially threatening 'recognition of our animality' – and this category of *animal-reminder disgust* has thus evolved as an avoidance response designed to shield us from 'evidence of [our] animal nature'.[23] Though this proposition is controversial, lines of investigation independent of disgust research (such as, we'll see in Chapter 10, those from Terror Management Theory) suggest that humans have a psychological need to distance themselves from their animal nature, so the notion that disgust has evolved to be part of this process is at least plausible. And to conclude, the cultural evolution model maintains that the regulatory function of disgust developed even more abstractly, coming to govern two more categories of human behaviour: first, *interpersonal disgust* discourages us from social interaction with those who are deemed physically or symbolically undesirable, while finally, *moral disgust* is the affective means through which infractions against the social order itself are policed. Moral disgust, which we will see throughout Shakespeare's plays, is a particularly interesting case of exaptation, in the sense that a process that began as a somatic vehicle for food rejection is thought to have evolved into an abstract guardian of mores, morality and divinity. Indeed, this visceral linkage is shown through experimental evidence supporting the notion of *moral dyspepsia*: the consideration of a morally offensive act that has nothing to do with food (such as consensual sibling incest) has been shown to 'directly engender the phenomenological state of oral inhibition . . . comprised of nausea, gagging, and diminished appetite'.[24] As Haidt and colleagues put it, disgust 'evolved to help our omnivorous species figure out what to *eat* in the physical world', but 'now helps our social species figure out what to *do* in the cultural world'.[25]

It should hopefully be clear why the Rozin, Haidt and McCauley paradigm is called the cultural evolution model; in essence, it maintains that the food rejection system of distaste was continuously co-opted, in a process of exaptation, by an increasingly abstract behavioural avoidance system capable of guarding against a battery of physical and symbolic contaminants, all while maintaining a distinct affective profile. In the last decade, however, Tybur and his colleagues have developed an alternative account of how the human disgust system developed – one which ultimately ends up in a similar place, in terms of how the emotion manifests in the world, but which takes a different route to get there.[26] Grounded in evolutionary psychology, this approach has been called an *adaptationist model*; while it agrees that a distaste system was co-opted for other fitness needs, it focuses not on disgust's development as a process of cultural evolution but, rather, on it as an adaptive response to certain selection pressures. Building on the work of Valerie Curtis, Tybur suggests that the majority of things that cause disgust in humans do so because of their fundamental proximity to potential disease; accordingly, his model groups the elicitors of *food, body products, animals, hygiene, body envelope violations, death* and *contact with strangers* under the broad umbrella of *pathogen disgust*, a robust category reflecting the fact that 'no other factor in our evolutionary history has shaped human behavior more than the consequences of pathogen and parasitic infection'.[27]

At the same time, however, humans also face another giant adaptive challenge: the need to avoid sexual interactions with individuals that jeopardize their overall fitness. Because of this, Tybur's model theorizes another domain of the emotion, *sexual disgust*, which is designed to help us avoid 'sexual interest [in] individuals with poor genetic compatibility (kin) and with low mate value'.[28] This proposal offers one explanation for the apparent universality of incest taboos, as well as, for example, why someone in their early reproductive years might find themselves 'disgusted' at the thought of casual sex with a very elderly partner. (Tybur acknowledges, of course, that sex also poses the risk of pathogen transmission, so it is likely that the disease-avoidance pressure of pathogen disgust also plays a role in sexual disgust.[29]) Finally, the Tybur model agrees that the emotion's most abstract and culturally elaborated form is *moral disgust*, which it sees as emerging from the universal need of human social groups to coordinate the condemnation of those individuals who violate collective rules. This disgust once again has a regulatory function, as it allows 'moral cognition to endorse rules in a fitness-promoting manner'.[30]

The adaptationist model thus sees disgust elicitors as falling under the three domains of Pathogen Disgust, Sexual Disgust and Moral Disgust – as opposed to the cultural evolution model, which groups them under Core Disgust, Animal-Reminder Disgust, Interpersonal Disgust and Moral Disgust. But the important point, I think, is that both of the dominant theories of disgust fundamentally agree on the nine categories of general stimuli that tend to elicit disgust in humans: issues related to *food, bodily products, animals, sex, hygiene, body envelope violations, death, contact with strangers* and *moral violations*. As will be clear from the chapters that follow, I think that these categories of elicitors are also categories of intense interest for Shakespeare; verbal images, themes and dramatic moments related to such items fuel many of the most interesting moments in his work.

These accounts tentatively explain the long evolutionary development of the human disgust system – but what, more specifically, may be said about the features of the emotion? Based on cross-cultural evidence, researchers generally characterize disgust as an avoidance response that is a species-typical universal feature of human psychological architecture; studies have shown that disgust elicitors in a variety of cultural contexts generate relatively consistent facial response, physiological reaction and neuroanatomical activation. Darwin first theorized what is now called the 'disgust face'; he noted that 'extreme disgust is expressed by movements round the mouth identical with those preparatory to the act of vomiting. The mouth is opened widely, with the upper lip strongly retracted, which wrinkles the sides of the nose, as with the lower lip protruded and everted as much as possible.'[31] This facial response, rooted in a food rejection system, seems to be part of our evolutionary heritage, since mammals 'react to bitter and sour flavors with nose wrinkling, squinting, tongue protrusion, and frowning' – a response 'accompanied by spitting, face washing, and head shaking, which are designed to expunge the offending substance from the mouth and face'.[32] In cross-cultural investigation, this facial expression has been found associated with disgust 'at rates higher than predicted by chance in numerous studies, using varied methodologies and samples'; while the so-called disgust face is not recognized in all situations by all people, 'participants across cultures have consistently paired the disgust emotion with the disgust facial expression, which provides support for the universal experience of the disgust emotion.'[33] (It is important to note, however, that there is fierce debate about the validity of cross-cultural facial recognition experiments, and both constructivist scientists and humanist emotion scholars have strongly contested this evidence.[34]) Beyond the face, the somatic response to disgust includes 'lowered blood pressure and galvanic skin response, nausea and actions including stopping, dropping the object of disgust and shuddering' – and the 'few studies comparing the physiology related to disgust between cultures have suggested that the physiological reaction is similar across cultures'.[35] Finally, in terms of neuroanatomy, imaging research suggests that 'three interconnected brain areas activated when there is exposure to disgust faces, disgust-eliciting images, disgust-related odors, or thoughts about disgusting entities': the anterior insula, the basal ganglia and certain parts of the prefrontal cortex.[36] More specifically, a meta-analysis of over eighty imaging studies indicates that disgust is particularly connected to the anterior insula, stimulation of which has been shown to 'induce nausea and unpleasant sensations in the throat mouth and nose'.[37]

Several other features of the emotion warrant mention. Individuals, of course, vary in the degree to which they experience disgust, and a person's tendency to do so is measured by 'two distinct but related constructs: disgust sensitivity, or how strongly a person negatively appraises his or her experience of disgust and disgust propensity, or how frequently one experiences disgust'.[38] Recent research suggests that disgust sensitivity is associated with a heightened general perception of risk; accordingly, some believe that disgust may be 'part of a general risk aversion mechanism aimed at guiding behavior in uncertain situations'.[39] Disgust has also been implicated in a range of psychopathologies, including posttraumatic stress disorder, suicidal ideation and, most importantly, anxiety disorders such as contamination-related obsessive-compulsive disorder, spider phobia and blood-injection-injury phobia.[40] (There is even a growing body of research on 'self-disgust', the tendency of an individual to be repulsed by their own person.[41]) Finally, disgust has been linked to a variety of other emotions, such as fear, anger and contempt; while researchers disagree on precisely how these sentiments interact with one another, there is clearly some degree of overlap, as common experience demonstrates.[42]

This brings us to the question of variance. While the development of the disgust response is a typical feature of human psychological architecture, it is vital to also recognize that 'specific learning experiences and sociocultural influences . . . shape the scope and intensity of the disgust response over the life span'.[43] Indeed, it actually seems that disgust *requires* enculturation – a fact suggested by a 'review of some 50 feral humans, none of whom showed any sign of disgust'.[44] The roots of the disgust system are present shortly after birth; infants can be identified making the stereotypical 'disgust face' in reaction to bitter substances.[45] But it is largely agreed that this is closer to a distaste response, rather than genuine disgust – especially because infants generally show little aversion to faeces, which seem to be a near-universal disgust elicitor in adults.[46] (In fact, it has been suggested that 'toilet training may be the initial disgust-generating experience', as children are shaped by their caregiver's cues regarding bodily products.[47]) Even outside of infancy, children do not shy from many prototypical disgusting objects, and, 'much to the dismay of their parents and caregivers, bodily products (e.g. feces, urine, mucus, vomit) and certain animals (e.g. worms, slugs, spiders) may entice approach behavior and actually become the focus of play'.[48] As children get older, however, they slowly gain contamination sensitivity and learn cultural rules that nuance their understanding of disgust (including a symbolic awareness that certain violations of social norms are considered disgusting). For evolutionary reasons, the delayed onset of this emotion may be a function of what has been called *the omnivore's dilemma*:

> Generalist species benefit from access to a broad spectrum of possible nourishment, but many potential foodstuffs are hazardous, and the cost for guessing wrong can be steep. Thus, omnivores must balance a promiscuous feeding strategy with a wariness of the unfamiliar.[49]

But whatever the case, sometime within about their first eight years children 'experience disgust, develop a concept of disgust, acquire a word for disgust, and are able to infer disgust in another from the situation the other encounters or how that person reacts to that situation'.[50] In developmental terms, the disgust system may thus 'be likened to language, in that it is a human universal, is developmentally delayed, and displays a constrained amount of cultural variation'.[51]

And variation, both individual and cultural, is vital to understanding how this emotion works. I have suggested throughout that the avoidance mechanism of disgust is a species-typical feature – but the apparent universality of the basic disgust system does not, of course, mean that every individual human experiences the emotion in the same way. Women, for example, are consistently shown to have higher disgust sensitivity than men, perhaps for reasons of reproductive fitness: because women must invest a higher personal cost in the generation of offspring, they may be more alert to the dangers of pathogen cues, sexually transmitted infections and suboptimal mate choice.[52] (Though gendered differences in socialization also undoubtedly play a role.) On a different front, African-Americans generally report higher contamination aversion and seem to have higher disgust sensitivity than European-Americans.[53] Other demographic variables, such as 'religion, political view, education, and age . . . do not directly influence disgust's sensitivity' – but they still do importantly 'modulate the context in which disgust is elicited'.[54] The emotion, then, is universal but not rigid, and disgust sensitivity is even contextually flexible for individuals. Evidence suggest, for instance, that 'mothers regard their own baby's fecal smell as less disgusting than that from someone else's baby', while a recent study equally shows that cadets in military training become less sensitive to elicitors of pathogen disgust, presumably because 'in a harsh environment, where survival may be more difficult, pathogen disgust sensitivity may decrease to allow the consumption of available resources'.[55] (This aligns with other research showing that subjects who have been food deprived for fifteen hours recorded less disgust to pictures of unpalatable food than control subjects.[56]) There is thus a natural plasticity to disgust, which is an emotion universal in fundamental psychological availability but not in actual manifestation.

Cross-cultural research tells a similar tale of variance within a universal framework. To be sure, certain broad categories of disgust elicitors seem ubiquitous. In one study, Curtis and Adam Biran asked populations from America, Europe, Asia and Africa to list things that triggered their disgust; they found, in all the cultures surveyed, that disgust elicitors can be grouped in the broad categories of (1) *bodily excretions and body parts*; (2) *decay and spoiled food*; (3) *particular living creatures*; (4) *certain categories of 'other people'* and (5) *violations of morality or social norms*.[57] Nina Strohminger similarly notes 'bodily effluvia (especially vomit and feces) and [certain] animal products' are considered disgusting in countless cultural contexts.[58] But while 'findings suggest that the presence of disgust appears across cultures, some of the characteristics of disgust [are] vulnerable to cultural influence': the human disgust system 'may be a universal psychological and cultural process, yet the particular constellation of bodily and social meanings must be arranged or filled in by each culture'.[59] This cultural arrangement takes many forms, influencing both how disgust manifests and what precisely triggers it. For example: individuals from Ghana, a region that has been historically marked by relatively high level of infectious disease, show higher disgust and contamination sensitivity than individuals from America, where the threat of infectious disease is significantly lower.[60] But the cultural influence of disgust is made most apparent by the fact that specific disgust elicitors vary widely across time and place. Once again, while broad categories of items appear with great consistency across cultures, the things that populate these categories show a great deal of variety, shaped by the norms of a particular cultural context.

The operation of moral disgust is a case in point. An association between visceral repulsion and violations of the sociomoral order seems to be a regular feature of human psychology. As Haidt and colleagues record, the 'English language is not unique in linking core disgust, animal reminder disgust, and socio-moral disgust together under one word, and linking all these issues to nausea and revulsion'; countless languages, from a variety of language families, 'have a word with a compound semantic domain linking together bodily concerns (about food, faeces, cockroaches, sex) with social and moral concerns, for instance, French *degout*, German *ekel*, Russian *otvrashchenie*, Spanish *asco*, Hebrew *go-al*, Japanese *ken'o*, Chinese *aw-shin*, and Bengali *ghenna*'.[61] While we must indeed remember that each of these 'disgust' words is uniquely nuanced in their actual usage, they are notably similar in the broad linkage of visceral and moral offence.[62] But while humans may be universally prone to find sociomoral violations disgusting, what marks such a violation can be quite different – a commonsense notion that has empirical support. In one experiment, students in America were asked to list experiences in which they felt *disgust*, and students in Japan were asked to list experiences in which they felt *ken'o*. In each group, participants recalled moments involving both visceral disgust and sociomoral disgust – but, while the items that triggered visceral disgust were largely similar, there were some categorical differences in what constituted a sociomoral violation in each culture:

> Americans and Japanese did not differ in linking [visceral] disgust to certain social issues, but they differed in the kinds of social issues that they mentioned. Americans connected their feelings

about cockroaches and faeces to their feelings regarding racism and senseless murder, while the Japanese connected their feelings about cockroaches and faeces to their feelings about frustration, indignation, and failure.[63]

The researchers suggest that this variation may arise from the two cultures' different investments in individualism and collectivism – but whatever the case, the larger point is that the *content* of sociomoral disgust is clearly socially constructed, even if the mechanism of sociomoral disgust seems to be culturally universal.

And, of course, it is not simply moral disgust that shows such flexibility: even in the domain of food, the most fundamental and visceral category of disgust elicitor, we can easily acknowledge that what is regularly deemed repulsive by one culture may be considered a delicacy in another (such as the case of spiders, an animal considered disgusting in many parts of the world, but eaten in others).[64] Justin H. Park and colleagues elaborate:

> Evolutionary processes contributed to the pan-human tendency to salivate at the sight and smell of desirable foods, and to respond with disgust when presented with strange foul-smelling foods. Nevertheless, individuals spend years learning which foods are desirable and which are not – and so the same food may elicit strong salivary responses among individuals from one culture while eliciting disgust among those from another.[65]

As noted in the Introduction, the disgust mechanism may thus be thought to display what has been called *universalism without the uniformity*. Usha Menon and Julia L. Cassaniti explain what this means:

> From a cultural psychological perspective, what is universal are the abstract potentialities of the human mind – the ability to think and act, to feel and desire, to possess norms and values, to have purposes and goals, and to envision the social and natural worlds. Rather than existing *a priori* in some precultural space, these very basic traits are emergent, realizing their full potential only within the context of the symbolic and behavioral traditions of a community.[66]

To reframe this basic construct in terms of disgust, the emotion can be understood as having its origins in certain universal themes of human existence, but how it actually manifests in the world is wildly variable, owing to countless personal, cultural and historical factors. As Rachel Herz puts it, disgust is 'culturally malleable, and contextually capricious' – meaning 'our age, our personality, our culture, our thoughts and beliefs, our moods, our morals, whom we're with, where we are, and which of our senses is giving us the feeling, all shape whether and how strongly we are able to feel disgusted'.[67] And as a universal impulse that is contextually shaped, disgust can finally help us navigate the theoretical controversies that, we saw in the Introduction, challenge the study of emotion more broadly. In his brilliant recent survey *A Human History of Emotion*, Richard Firth-Godbehere describes how disgust is an emotion that valuably illustrates the 'way emotions can be understood from both the universalist and constructivist standpoints':

> A universalist scientist such as disgustologist Valerie Curtis will argue that disgust is an obviously evolved safety mechanism helping us avoid harm from pathogens and poisons. A constructivist might argue that the fact that every language has a word for disgust – and that these words mean something almost entirely different in each case – proves that revulsion is constructed. They couldn't both be right, could they? Well, yes, they could. It could easily be the case that there's a basic evolved feeling designed to stop us from poisoning ourselves and picking up parasites. That basic feeling is then adapted, shaped, and manipulated by culture, giving rise to unique variations on a disgusting theme.[68]

As far as the debate between universalist and constructivists, disgust is thus what Firth-Godbehere calls 'the great unifier' – and this, I think, is why we should read widely in the psychological discourse of disgust, and why we should have no qualms about bringing the insights of this scientific analysis to our humanistic study of Shakespeare.[69]

So while it seems like humans have a pretty typical tendency to recoil from physically and symbolically offensive material, what more specifically makes up any person's precise understanding of disgustingness is deeply shaped by the social context in which they are emersed. Disgust is a 'universal' emotion, but it is one that nonetheless wildly changes from place to place and time to time. And this is an important point to remember when considering the state of disgust in early modern England. In one sense, of course, Shakespeare's era belongs to the same Western, English-speaking tradition that generates most modern scientific research on disgust – and the same tradition that I, as the writer of this book, belong to – so there are likely some serious continuities between Renaissance concepts of disgust and the discourse of disgust established by twenty-first-century research laboratories. But in another sense, the unique cultural features of sixteenth- and seventeenth-century life assure that early modern English subjects experienced disgust in different ways than we do today. Richard Sugg, surveying the sensorial landscape of the time, argues that 'the inhabitants of pre-modern Europe generally had a considerably higher stink threshold' than most of us today, and he believes that they must also have had a broadly higher threshold of disgust.[70] 'When everything was so disgusting', he suggests, 'it was not really possible to be disgusted' – and while I wouldn't endorse this statement literally, it nonetheless captures a truth about the different way that Shakespeare and his contemporaries likely experienced their everyday world.[71] When thinking about disgust in Shakespeare, we must always remember that the contextual flexibility of the emotion ensures that our ability to grasp what it meant to him and his audience will always be only partial.

One final general characteristic of disgust warrants consideration. In an oft-quoted remark, Kant suggests that while art routinely offers beautiful portrayals of things that we dislike, 'there is only one kind of ugliness that cannot be presented in conformity with nature without obliterating all aesthetic liking and hence artistic beauty: that ugliness which arouses *disgust*'.[72] Though Kant's pronouncement is the most famous, the sentiment he expresses has been a commonplace in Western theories of art, which have regularly denied a place for disgust in the realm of aesthetic appreciation.[73] But such judgements seem to be at odds with the realities of how humans actually engage the world, especially in modern times: there are countless examples in which people actively seek enjoyment in ostensibly disgusting objects and media, such as contestants consuming outlandish food on 'gross out' reality television, the bloody violence of slasher movies, portrayals of sibling incest in romance novels or, more extremely, videos of actual death and mutilation on internet 'gore' sites.[74] How do we account for the apparent pleasure that many seem to get from certain kinds of disgusting things?

Experiments suggest that disgusting stimuli both capture our attention more quickly and retain it for a longer period than more emotionally neutral stimuli do.[75] This is likely because, 'from an evolutionary perspective, an attentional bias *toward* disgust – no matter how aversive – would better equip humans to avoid harmful substances'.[76] It has thus been argued that while disgust makes us feel bad, 'it has functionally evolved over time to compel our attention', so that disgust-eliciting content (including artistic works) are inclined to keep us 'engrossed and engaged'.[77] This aligns with what Carolyn Korsmeyer calls 'aesthetic disgust', a response that 'signals appreciative regard and understanding' – one that, 'no matter how unpleasant, can rivet attention to the point where one actually may be said to *savor* the feeling'.[78] In laboratory settings, people routinely smile in response to disgusting video clips, even as they acknowledge feeling psychological distress, and other experiments confirm what we know from everyday experience: disgust and mirth regularly co-occur.[79] But it remains a question of just how the paradox of aesthetic disgust – the fact that we might be attracted to that which is designed to repel us – actually functions.

Psychological research offers a tentative answer. In a series of experiments, Strohminger found evidence for what she calls *hedonic disgust*, or 'disgust that increases enjoyment of an activity'.[80] When participants were primed with disgusting cues, they subsequently reported finding cartoons more humorous and abstract art more enjoyable; when sitting in a dirty or smelly room, they reported more enjoyment of an 'adventurous eating' television show (a programme designed 'to shock and disturb').[81] She suggests that these pleasurable features of disgust may be an instance of what has been called *benign masochism,* the human tendency to seek out ostensibly negative experiences for the purposes of enjoying 'constrained risks' (such as riding a roller coaster, or eating extremely hot foods).[82] Because of this, it seems 'possible that any negative feeling has the potential to be enjoyable when it is stripped of the belief that what is happening is actually bad, leaving behind physiological arousal that is, in itself, exhilarating or interesting'.[83] In fact, some people are dispositionally inclined towards *sensation seeking*, a personality trait that involves the tendency to pursue 'varied, novel, complex, and intense sensations and experiences'; in terms of disgust, for example, horror film researchers distinguish one category of audience member as *gore-watchers*, those who seek 'high arousal originating from graphic portrayals of blood, death, and even physical torture'.[84] But while not all of us enjoy gore, most people generally have a bias towards 'novelty and sensation, which itself reflects a drive to learn about the world around us' – a trait that humans share with many other animals.[85] In the most basic sense, organisms 'must balance caution about possible dangers in the world (neophobia) with desire to find extant resources (neophilia)' – and, in terms of disgust, it 'seems that we watch this paradox play out in culture, where our aversion towards the strange and the odious is balanced with curiosity about these very objects'.[86]

In the final analysis, then, we must acknowledge Strohminger's observation that 'disgust reflects ambivalence':

> Organisms must balance the need for nutrition against the peril of toxic comestibles, the need to socialize against the threat of communicable disease, the need to reproduce against the risk of selecting a genetic dud. More generally, organisms must negotiate the value of exploration against the potential danger lurking beneath each unturned stone. Disgust is a gatekeeper emotion, policing the semi-permeable membrane between the self and treacherous unknown.[87]

And because, she continues, of the many overlapping domains that are implicated in the workings of this particular emotion, we must become comfortable with the fact that 'disgust is less a monolith than it is a psychological nebula, lacking definite boundaries, discrete internal structure, or a single center of gravity'.[88] Appropriately enough, disgust is a messy emotion, and that messiness will be readily apparent in the analysis that follows. It is my hope, however, that the introduction in this chapter will have provided a valuable background for thinking about how this emotion works in general – a background, we will see, that underwrites my treatment of it in the plays of Shakespeare.

* * *

I began this chapter by reviewing the usage of disgust in the early modern period, and I need to conclude it by coming full circle. This is because one final bit of background is necessary before I can begin my analysis of individual plays: a brief consideration of how the emotion of disgust manifests lexically in Shakespeare's works. As noted earlier, Shakespeare never uses any variant of the word *disgust*, but he does employ a constellation of related words to describe what more modern English speakers mean when they call something *disgusting*. Talking about synonyms in history of emotion work is very tricky, because historians and literary scholars are usually more interested in delineating the precise, contextually situated uniqueness of specific emotion words – by examining the nuances in usage between, say, terms like *fury*, *rage* and *wrath* at some particular historical and cultural moment. And to be sure, this kind of taxonomical work is both interesting and important. But, with that said, it is also vital to think about how certain kinds of similar (but not necessarily identical) emotional experiences can be grouped together in broad categories, and I have indeed argued elsewhere that there is a good theoretical basis for working with such general categories.[89] So when turning now to Shakespeare's lexicon of disgust, I am not attempting to track the subtle distinctions between each word, or how each does or does not precisely align with our modern understanding of the emotion – rather, I aim to establish that there was a category of roughly analogous *disgust-like* experiences that Shakespeare signalled by using a cluster of synonyms.

And Shakespeare certainly had many ways to indicate that something is (what we could consider to be) disgusting. The most common is *foul*, which Shakespeare uses over 250 times.[90] Emerging from the Germanic tradition of *fúl*, the word *foul* originally carried a visceral meaning of 'grossly offensive to the senses, physically loathsome; *esp.* having a disgusting smell or taste; stomach-churning'; before long, however, it also came to adopt a symbolic sense of 'evil, sinful, wicked; morally or spiritually polluted; abominable', in a process that recalls the evolution of disgust's regulatory purview.[91] Shakespeare routinely employs both senses of the word, as when in *Hamlet* he describes 'a foul and pestilent congregation of vapours' (Q2, 2.2.268-9) and 'foul crimes done in my days of nature' (Q2, 1.5.12). He also adopts compound terms that activate both visceral (such as *foul cank'ring* [*Venus and Adonis*, 767] and *foul-reeking*

[*Rape of Lucrece*, 799]) and symbolic (such as *foul-defiled* [*Rape of Lucrece*, 1029] and *foul-tainted* [*Much Ado,* 4.1.144]) registers of disgust.

Because the concept of *disgust* can refer to violations of both our physical and moral senses, it is unsurprising that *foul* also does such double duty; indeed, several other terms that pre-date the English arrival of *disgust* function in a similar manner. One such example is *vile*, which Shakespeare uses over 100 times. By the fourteenth century, the word had come to mean both 'physically repulsive, esp. through filth or corruption; horrid, disgusting' and 'despicable on moral grounds; deserving to be regarded with abhorrence or disgust'; Shakespeare, to this end, speaks of both 'the vile contagion of the night' (*Julius Caesar,* 2.1.264) and 'vile outrageous crimes' (*1 Henry VI*, 3.1.11).[92] Another is *loathsome*, which in the sixteenth century could mean 'in the physical sense: exciting nausea; offensive to the senses; noisome, sickening' and 'in the moral sense: hateful, distasteful, odious, repulsive, shocking'; though Shakespeare uses the term relatively less frequently, he still writes of both the 'loathsome smells' of the Capulet tomb (*Romeo and Juliet,* 4.3.46) and Tarquin's 'loathsome enterprise' (*Rape of Lucrece,* 184).[93]

Finally, other words seem to indicate that something is a potential source of revulsion, but do so by more limited reference to a specific category of disgust elicitors – and just as importantly, such words are equally able to indicate that a target is compromised physically or morally. I'm thinking, for example, of the range of meanings associated with *filth/filthy*. As we will see later, dirtiness has long been theorized as an elicitor of disgust, and since its origins in modern English the term *filth* has meant both 'dirt, unclean matter, [especially] when especially disgusting or offensive' and 'moral corruption, depravity, or impurity; sinfulness; obscene, offensive, or disgusting behaviour'.[94] Shakespeare thus equally refers to the 'filth and dirt' of a puddle (*2 Henry VI* 4.1.71) and to 'the filth and scum' who rebelled against their king (4.2.115) – and in some cases, as when Macbeth's bloody hands are deemed 'filthy witness', the usage is simultaneously material and symbolic (2.2.48). *Rotten* is another such term, which in early modern usage signalled both physical matter that is 'in a state of decomposition; decayed; putrefied, putrid' and behaviours that are 'morally, socially, or politically corrupt'; Coriolanus, then, denounces his Roman enemies by invoking the 'reek o' the rotten fens' (3.3.120), while Hotspur, defending his brother-in-law Mortimer, declares that 'never did bare and rotten policy / Colour her working with such deadly wounds' (*1 Henry IV*, 1.3.107).[95] Though words like *filthy* and *rotten* are not exact synonyms for *disgusting*, their usage shares qualities with the broader cluster of disgust-like words, and it thus seems sensible to suggest that the affective consequence of their deployment involves the evocation of disgust.

I therefore suggest that words like *foul*, *vile* and *loathsome* – along with proximal terms like *filthy* and *rotten* – serve as functional synonyms describing an object that elicits disgust, available in English before the widespread usage of the term *disgusting*. And while there may indeed be nuances to how each word is precisely deployed in early modern English – Shakespeare, for example, uses *vile* much more commonly in the moral sense than the visceral – the fact remains that they account for a broad category of *disgust-like* experiences that can be valuably considered in tandem. These synonyms provide Shakespeare with a lexicon of disgust, apt to describe that which offends one's physical and/or symbolic boundaries; indeed, they often appear together, as when Old Hamlet's ghost describes the 'vile and loathsome crust' that covered his poisoned body (Q2, 1.5.72), the weary Henry IV wonders why sleep only 'liest . . . with the vile / In loathsome beds' (*2 Henry IV*, 3.1.15-16), or *The Taming of the Shrew's* unnamed Lord expresses his disgust at the 'foul and loathsome . . . image' of the drunken Sly (Induction, 1.34). Despite the fact that Shakespeare never uses any form of the word *disgust*, I am thus very much convinced that he had a vocabulary for indicating when objects trigger what we, as modern readers, know as the emotional experience of disgust.

With this said, I turn now to the analysis of Shakespeare's plays. As will become apparent, the categories of disgust elicitors described in this chapter were consistently mined by Shakespeare for poetic, thematic and dramatic content; indeed, some of the chapters that follow will explore certain disgust elicitors in much more detail. As I hope to show, Shakespeare took an enormous interest in the literary possibilities of disgust – one that, rather surprisingly, suggests that the emotion must be seen as an affective centrepiece of his dramatic universe.

2

Titus Andronicus

The spectacle of disgust

Decades ago, S. Clark Hulse attempted to quantify what makes *Titus Andronicus* an 'especially brutal' tragedy: the play, he calculates, stages '14 killings, 9 of them on stage, 6 severed members, 1 rape (or 2 or 3, depending on how you count), 1 live burial, 1 case of insanity, and 1 of cannibalism – an average of 5.2 atrocities per act, or one for every 97 lines'.[1] The very atrociousness of *Titus* has long made the play seem beneath the dignity of Shakespeare; Edward Ravenscroft, the Restoration adaptor, doubted its authorship, and (in a telling metaphor) deemed it 'the most incorrect and indigested piece' in the Shakespearean canon.[2] Of course, the notion of the cannibalistic *Titus* being indigested is quite apt, as the play's overwhelming and unrelenting violence, history has shown, renders it all too capable of eliciting a disgust response from viewers and readers. Indeed, William Hazlitt explicitly frames *Titus* as disgusting, dismissing it as 'an accumulation of vulgar physical horrors, in which the power exercised by the poet bears no proportion to the repugnance excited by the subject'.[3]

There is no doubt that the play's 'vulgar physical horrors' have made an impression on modern audiences. Since *Titus* began to be staged regularly in the mid-twentieth century, performances have generally 'tended to highlight in one way or another the play's preoccupation with the spectacle of violence', and theatregoers are often left reeling.[4] In 2006, Lucy Bailey's Globe production 'became famous for the number of people who fainted during the show';

a review of the 2014 revival notes that, during one performance, 'more than a dozen distressed theatregoers were helped out of the auditorium'.[5] A second report records that 'members of the audience have been fainting during the play's most violent scenes, with others reporting feeling sick and warning of sleepless nights'; one viewer said that she felt 'vaguely sick' throughout the entire performance, another reported that he had 'almost puked' by the intermission, while a third advised that 'you will definitely need a strong stomach' to tolerate the play.[6] (The violence inflicted upon Lavinia is often cited as a source of particular distress: 'the sight of her stumps, dripping with gore, and the uncontrollable trauma shakes that overwhelm her are almost unbearable to behold'.[7]) During Blanche McIntyre's 2017 Stratford run of *Titus*, the RSC collaborated with a marketing research firm to measure the audience's visceral response to the on-stage horror: the findings revealed that watching the play in both the theatre and the cinema could raise a stationary spectator's heart rate 'to the equivalent of a five-minute cardio workout'.[8] Recent productions thus seem to indicate that *Titus* can achieve 'a dramatic power that makes the stomach churn and the hands sweat' – but engagement with the play is contingent on having 'the stomach for it'.[9]

In 2002, Xavier Leret's *Titus* – a staging that has been said to evoke 'intractable disgust' – prompted one reviewer to observe that 'the production [could not] be described as enjoyable', in the sense that there can only be so much pleasure that is generated 'when there's a young girl wandering about the place with her arms and tongue cut off'.[10] But this statement, however sensible, does not quite align with the stage history of *Titus*: though there are certainly historical audiences that have found the play unpalatable, it has nonetheless enjoyed some periods of great popularity, including the recent past. And we know that it captivated early modern spectators: in 1614, Ben Jonson mocked those crude viewers who still, 'these fiue and twentie, or thirtie yeeres' later, 'will sweare, *Ieronimo*, or *Andronicus* are the best playes', and evidence from both early performance and textual history suggests that *Titus* spoke to the Elizabethan and Jacobean imagination.[11] So what do we make of this? In exploring the 'problematic appeal of this play's violence', we must, with Cynthia Marshall, ask, 'why would an audience, any audience, enjoy *Titus*'s reiteration of violence against the human body?'[12] Indeed, as Joel Elliot Slotkin notes, 'finding aesthetic pleasure in the consumption of dead bodies [and other horrors] is ultimately what the play's audience has to be doing if we are to regard *Titus* and many other early modern tragedies as entertainment that playgoers would voluntarily pay money to watch and not as some kind of psychological torture.'[13]

Critics have attempted to account for the complex pleasures of *Titus* in a number of ways. Marshall, for example, suggests that 'the brilliance of *Titus Andronicus* lies in the way it allows viewers to be scandalized and morally outraged by events portrayed on stage but also and at the same time to identify with characters who suffer and commit acts of horrific violence'.[14] This aligns with an anecdote reported by Pascale Aebischer, who, during the intermission of the Leret production, encountered two women who had been particularly bothered by Lavinia's rape and mutilation:

> They were debating about whether or not to miss the second part of the performance, not because they did not think the production was excellent, but because they felt unwilling to 'take more'. On the other hand, since they did not know the plot, they were eager to know where the story was heading and asked me to outline what was going to happen. When I told them that the play would end with the Andronici's revenge, they decided to stay: they wanted to watch the rapists die. Put off by the spectacle of violence, what they were craving was further violence.[15]

In Deborah Warner's famed 1987 RSC production, Aebischer similarly notes, 'spectators, who had a tendency to faint or leave the theatre at the sight of the Andronici's victimisation, seem to have experienced a reversal and actively craved graphic violence in the second part of the play'.[16] In fact, Brian Cox, who played Warner's Titus, recalled being 'aware as I played the scene with [Demetrius and Chiron], that members of the audience were thrilled that I had them, thrilled as I gripped their heads to expose their throats, thrilled at the revenge'.[17] Horror films, we saw in the last chapter, are a genre in which disgust can provoke aesthetic enjoyment, and Aebischer has argued that *Titus* can be read in terms of the 'rape-revenge narrative' prominent in modern horror cinema; 'the play demands that the audience identify first with the position of Lavinia as the victim', and 'then with her joint revenge with Titus'.[18] Given the popularity of revenge narratives on the early modern stage, and the genre's well-known tendency to depict bloody horrors, it seems that audiences must find some degree of pleasure in watching violence that can be framed as retributive.

But there are also other ways to talk about the appeal of a play like *Titus*. Elsewhere in her analysis, Marshall sees the play in terms of pornography, in the sense that it uses 'sexuality to activate a voyeuristic response'.[19] Alternately, Cox emphasizes the comic potential of the play, noting that *Titus* is a 'tightrope of absurdity between comedy and tragedy' that invites us to 'respond to its terrible laughter without diminishing its horror'.[20] This angle is explored by Adele-France Jourdan, who argues that there is 'overwhelming historical and textual support that suggests that humour, black or otherwise, plays an indispensable role in Shakespeare's revenge tragedy and its metaphysics of violence', and that *Titus* thus 'uses such hyperbolic carnage to question the permeability of the distinction between tragedy and comedy'.[21] And Slotkin, finally, has explored *Titus* in terms of what he deems *sinister aesthetics*: that is, 'poetic conventions that generate pleasure by representing things we are supposed to dislike, including deception and cruelty, filth and disease, deformity and monstrosity, destruction and punishment, and the demonic and infernal'.[22] While the kinds of poetic evils depicted by *Titus* can 'indeed be described as ugly, to the extent that they violate normative aesthetic principles', Slotkin insists that such 'artistic representations of evil are also aesthetic constructions, crafted according to principles and traditions analogous to those governing beautiful things'.[23]

Unsurprisingly, in this chapter I will attempt to account for the complex aesthetic appeal of *Titus Andronicus* by pointing to the dynamics of disgust. But I don't aim to demonstrate that *Titus* depicts certain stage material that is likely to evoke a disgust response; I'd like to think that most people would readily assent to that argument, and we saw a moment ago that there is both anecdotal and empirical evidence to substantiate the claim. Instead, I want to think more broadly about the somewhat bizarre fact that the play exists at all, by suggesting how properties of disgust can help us understand why audiences – particularly early modern audiences – may be willing, even glad, to expose themselves to the horrors depicted in a work like *Titus*. In Chapter 1, I reviewed research supporting the view that humans have an attentional bias *towards* disgusting objects, even as the emotion simultaneously warns us to withdraw ourselves from them; disgusting things can compel our imagination at the same time that they repel us, and this affective feature seems crucial to how repugnance works in an aesthetic context. *Titus*, I think, leverages such ambivalence, by gleefully embracing content that turns the stomach even as the eyes have trouble turning away. But it is not simply that the play stages disgusting events – more importantly, I will argue that, for Shakespeare's original audience, such events draw a large part of their theatrical power through their alliance with other social practices in Elizabethan England that similarly transform objects of ostensible disgust into objects of visual fixation. *Titus*, I believe, participates in what may be called the early modern culture of *spectacular disgust*: a nexus of related cultural fields in which disgusting content, usually in the form of traumas and violations inflicted on the human body, is fashioned into a site of social attention.

This chapter, then, is nominally on *Titus Andronicus*, but it is really about historicizing the early modern culture of disgust that frames the play's depictions of horrifying violence. My purpose is not to offer a reading of *Titus* – again, it wouldn't take much to establish its exploitation of disgusting content – but rather to document its relation to this broader domain of spectacular disgust, as a way of suggesting how the play emerged from a larger context of arresting revulsion. This framework, in turn, will support my readings of Shakespeare in the chapters that follow, by giving a partial sense of why engagement with disgust might prove an effective dramatic tool for a Renaissance playwright. By surveying some of the ways that early modern England made the disgusting, traumatized human body visible, and at times even appealing, I hope to elucidate not only the milieu from which *Titus* emerged, but also how the affective properties of disgust work more generally in the period. Renaissance England, Naomi Baker notes, 'was an age in which the human figure in all of its often repellent as well as potentially magnificent variety was an object of fascination' – and the notion of repellent fascination will be one that can help us not only achieve a better understanding of *Titus* but can usefully serve as a valuable starting point for a book on Shakespearean disgust more widely.[24] What follows in this chapter is thus a (partial) historical account of the disgusting body in early modern England, to show how the perverse allure of *Titus* reflects a larger set of affectively ambivalent, repulsive cultural practices.

* * *

To start with the beginning. *Titus Andronicus* opens in the aftermath of bloody conflict, but the tragedy's inciting incident is an event that, though a ritualized consequence of war, has the force of a peacetime judicial killing: Alarbus, 'the proudest prisoner of the Goths', is coldly dismembered, his 'limbs . . . lopped / And entrails feed[ing] the sacrificing fire' (1.1.99; 146–7). This action, of course, sets Tamora on her vengeful quest to 'find a day to massacre them all' – but it also introduces the play's important concern with the practice of legal (or perhaps, semi-legal) execution, one of the main ways that *Titus* engineers the death of its characters (455). Quintus and Martius are put to swift death, in a scene that perversely costs Titus a hand; an unfortunate clown, in a largely unnecessary sequence, finds himself sentenced to hang; Aaron, in the play's final moments, is set to be buried 'breast-deep in earth', where in his last hours he will 'stand and rave and cry for food' (5.3.178–9). Though much of the violence in *Titus* is extrajudicial, the play still has an interest in the legal machinations of death – and even those extrajudicial killings, in the scope of their horrors, likely reminded Elizabethan audiences of legal practices closer to home.

Long ago, with very good reason, J. Dover Wilson noted that *Titus Andronicus* seems 'to jolt and bump along like some broken-down cart, laden with bleeding corpses from an Elizabethan scaffold'.[25] It is thus not surprising that more recent assessments have linked the traumas inflicted on the play's characters to Elizabethan practices of judicial punishment and execution, and a generation of New Historicist scholars have broadly examined how 'cultural practices such as public executions and hangings at Tyburn' can explain the early modern theatre audience's 'fascination with the hanged man and the mutilated and dismembered corpse'.[26] Katherine Royer notes that justice had a spectacular quality in Renaissance England – and given the bloody violence that these practices could inflict on the human body, it is equally unsurprising that we may valuably think about them in terms of disgust.[27]

It is helpful to review the scope of capital punishment in early modern England. The English did not generally employ the more extreme forms of physical torture that were present on the Continent – Thomas Smith notes that 'breaking vpon the wheele, empaciling & such cruel torments, as be vsed in other nations by the order of their law, we haue not' – but the forms of punishment that were practised still would subject the criminal body to considerable trauma, in ways that most certainly had the capacity to elicit disgust.[28] The vast majority of English judicial killing was accomplished by hanging. But as Krista Kesselring reminds us, these executions were not quick and painless actions: the long drop that instantly broke the neck of the condemned did not emerge until centuries later, 'meaning that earlier hangings typically consisted of slow strangulations that could take half an hour or more to kill a person, unless someone tugged on the body as it hung'.[29] (Friends and family members would sometimes aid in this process, to try to relieve their loved one's suffering.) The gallows at Tyburn was a traditional place of hangings, while pirates and other maritime criminals were killed at Wapping; executions, however, could take place virtually anywhere, and were sometimes purposefully situated near the site of the crime in question.[30] Heretics were burned at the stake, as well as women convicted of petty treason. Though relatively rare in England, authorities did sometimes inflict forms of mutilation designed to stigmatize the living body and render it visibly criminal; this was accomplished by branding, slitting of the nose, or the dismemberment of hands or ears.[31] An epigram by John Harington, for example, refers to a criminal

> Adiudged, first to lye a yeere in fetters,
> Then burned in his forhead with two letters,
> And to disparage him with more disgrace,
> To slit his nose, the figure of his face.[32]

For those sentenced to death, Tudor authorities also innovated the punishment of publicly displaying criminal corpses by having them 'hanged with chaines while they rotte in the ayre', a sentence designed as an ominous warning to other would-be offenders.[33] (And particularly unfortunate criminals were actually 'hanged aliue in chaynes . . . till [their] bones consume to nothing'.[34]) This was obviously a rather disgusting practice, as the gruesome spectacle remained in place until 'the Carkase was consumed, or piecemeal rotted and fallen down'.[35] The logic, it seems, is that a body that decayed into nothingness was denied a proper burial; a midseventeenth-century poem, for example, exclaims that rebels should not 'have their corpse layd / in *Brittish* ground: Let them on Gibbets hang / Till th'aiery Foules consume them every one'.[36] (We may recall that Tamora's body is sentenced to be 'throw[n] forth to beasts and birds to prey' [5.3.197].) And a convicted traitor, of course, faced the foulest death of all: hanging, castration, disembowelment, beheading and quartering. Nobles convicted of treason usually found their sentence commuted to a more honourable beheading – but the full horror of a traitor's death was still inflicted on plenty of early modern subjects, and the disgusting bodily trauma it entailed seems naturally recalled by the mutilations and dismemberments portrayed in *Titus Andronicus*.

It is not simply that early modern capital punishment could entail repulsive practices – we must also note the ubiquity of judicial killings in the period. One scholar, for example, calculates that 'the English might have hanged more people between 1580 and 1630 than in *all* subsequent decades up to the virtual abolition of capital punishment in 1967'.[37] While many reading this book will never have been first-hand witness to one human killing another human, Kesselring reminds us that 'most people who lived in early modern England probably saw such an event... most likely through attending public executions'.[38] An elaborate series of conventions and rituals governed the Elizabethan public execution, and though modern scholars debate how to best interpret these events – with some seeing them in terms of the Foucauldian theatre of power, others in terms of carnivalesque revelry – there seems little doubt that they proved quite popular with early modern subjects.[39] It is vital, then, to appreciate the fact that the Elizabethan audience of *Titus Andronicus* would have had an intimacy with the last gasping breaths of dying men, with the sight and smell of rotting corpses being chewed on by birds, with the gory excrements of mutilations and dismemberments – an intimacy to the human body rendered disgusting that is rather unfathomable to many living in the modern world. In 1541, a Londoner reported that 'it is now no novelty among us to see men slain, hung, quartered, or beheaded . . . some for one thing, and some for another'; fifty years later, a Swiss traveller noted that 'rarely does a law day in London . . . pass without some twenty to thirty persons – both men and women – being gibbetted'.[40] Decapitated heads were so commonplace in the period that they casually feature in educational material: Robert Whittington's early-sixteenth-century Latin textbook uses the example of 'upon london bridge I sawe iii or iiii mennes heedes stande vpon poles'.[41]

That same Swiss visitor offers a remarkable account of witnessing this spectacle:

> At the top of one tower almost in the centre of the bridge, were struck on tall stakes more than thirty skulls of noble men who had been executed and beheaded for treason and other reasons. And their descendants are accustomed to boast of this, themselves even pointing out to one their ancestors' heads on this same bridge, believing that they will be esteemed the more because their ancestors were of such high descent that they could even covet the crown, but being too weak to attain it were executed for rebels; this they make an honor for themselves of what was set up to be a disgrace and an example.[42]

Elizabethans, then, were not shy about the ostensibly horrifying sights around them, which they would actively seek out and travel to see. Indeed, contemporary evidence suggests that hanging corpses could draw quite a crowd: in one case, local farmers petitioned to have a gibbeted body relocated, citing the 'spoile and depopulating the growing fields there abouts, stript of all fences; and the grasse trodden downe, and made levell by the infinite confluence of all sexes from all parts'.[43]

But it would be wrong, however, to suggest that this proximity to the broken, decaying human form meant that early modern subjects were simply desensitized and immune to its disturbing qualities. A character in the satire *The Parly of Beasts* (1660), for example, argues that 'after Man's death, ther's no carcase so gastly and noisom as his' – so much so 'that Toads and Serpents engender often in his scull'.[44] More pointedly, Montaigne – who admitted that he 'cannot endure to beholde [an] execution with an vnrelenting eye' – describes the horror with which an Italian crowd witnessed the dismemberment of a notorious criminal: 'when he came to be quartered, the Executioner gave no blowe that was not accompanied with a pitteous voyce, and heartie exclamation, as if every man had had a feeling sympathie, or lent his senses to the poore mangled wretch'.[45] Such 'inhumane outrages and barbarous excesses', Montaigne indicates, are not simply presented as objects of novelty or perverse pleasure; they are meant, if nothing else, 'to keepe the common people in awe'.[46] Most basically, the affective response to early modern judicial trauma thus often entailed a mixture of attraction and repulsion; for many viewers, the spectacle horrified even as it captivated the attention. This is, I have suggested, a basic feature of the disgusting object, which so often demands the eye's focus even as it ostensibly triggers the rest of the body to recoil.

It seems safe to say, then, that early modern viewers of *Titus* would associate theatrical killings and dismemberments with the judicial spectacles that were staged throughout London. As E. K. Chambers records, Elizabethan authorities even thought it appropriate that 'the Theatre . . . should occasionally be used for a public execution'; according to Stow, in August 1588 a foreign priest was 'hanged . . . at the Theater', while in October of that same year another priest was 'hanged . . . nigh the Theator'.[47] Francis Barker, in fact, argues that the play's extravagant spectacles of violence actually work to obscure the 'common violence of the times' – the fact that a not-insignificant number of people were hanged in the period for various crimes.[48] Whatever the case, it seems both stage and state killings, which inflicted various degrees of trauma on the human form, likely activated the competing impulses that I've associated with disgust. And disgust, in fact, is an apt framework to think about these issues more broadly, since (as Louis Noble observes) in their purgative function both state executions and stage revenge serve as a form of social 'purification'; Louis Gernet, for example, notes that in ancient Greece 'the death penalty is a means employed to eliminate a *miasma*, a "pollution"', from the public body.[49]

* * *

But it was not just the dying, mutilated criminal corpse that captivated the early modern imagination: attention was also given to the other side of the coin. As Nadia Bishai explains, the bloody contents of *Titus* are analogous to what we find in Elizabethan and Jacobean crime literature, a genre that devoted space not only to the grisly end of perpetrators but also to the misfortunes inflicted on victims – and a genre that was well stocked by the same seller of early *Titus* playbooks.[50] According to Kesselring, it was 'in the final three decades of the sixteenth century that [murder pamphlets] began to proliferate', and print accounts of notorious murders were thus growing in popularity just as *Titus* was taking the stage for the first time.[51] These documents, an ancestor of modern true-crime television programmes and podcasts, chronicle both the circumstances leading to the killing and the means by which the killer was discovered and apprehended; in this sense, they recall the investigative sequence of *Titus* 2.2, when the murder of Bassianus is discovered, and Quintus and Martius are apprehended for the crime. But I'm interested most particularly in how murder pamphlets encourage viewers to contemplate the bloody, mutilated corpses of crime victims. Despite their disturbing qualities, these bodies tell a tale, and readers are encouraged to take note.

In murder pamphlets, the victim's corpse compels attention because of its demand to be read and its capacity to inform. While space prevents me from extensively reviewing the genre, two primary methods of disclosure are nicely captured in *Sundrye Strange and Inhumaine Murthers* (1591), a pamphlet published around the time of *Titus*. This work is centred on two recent murders. In the first, a father hired a labourer to kill his children, so that he could marry a rich widow without impediment. Though both men denied their involvement in the crime, when they were brought before the children's corpses the 'woundes began to bleede afresh'.[52] What's more, the 'bodies of the children, which seemed white like vnto soaked flesh laid in water, sodainly receiued their former coulour of bloude, and had such a lively countenance flushing in theyr faces, as if they had beene liuing creatures lying asleepe'. This 'wonderful miracle' caused 'the murtherer there present not onely to confesse and acknowledge himselfe giltie of that damnable deede, but also to accuse the father of the children as principal procurer of their vntimely deaths'. The sequence, which the pamphlet author attributes to 'the wonderful works of God', demonstrates the primary way that wounded, mutilated bodies could communicate: through becoming vehicles of divine revelation. This is a common trope in murder pamphlets of the period, and the folk belief that a corpse would spill blood in the presence of its murderer (a concept called *cruentation*) played a part in legal proceedings throughout early modern Europe.[53]

The second murder described in the pamphlet, however, works somewhat differently. In this case, a woman hires two men to strangle her husband, who is subsequently said to have died from the course of disease. Though there was at first 'no suspition a long time concerning any murder performed vpon him', things change when the body is viewed by his sister: she shrewdly 'spied blood about his bosome, which he had with his nailes procured by scratching for the kercher when it was about his throate, then they moued his head, and found his neck broken, and on both his knees the skin was beaten off, by striuing with them to saue his life'.[54] After the murder is discovered, the plot quickly unravels, and the culprits are eventually executed. In this instance, the battered corpse speaks in a different manner: not through divine channels, but through ways that might be called forensic. Murder pamphlets thus offer another way in which a traumatized body is centred as an object of visual spectacle – readers may be inclined, on some level, to recoil from the gory details, but they (just like true-crime aficionados today) still find themselves wholly captivated. It seems rather likely that some in the original audience of *Titus* would have a familiarity with the genre, which, like the play invites readers to meditate on how violence (both criminal and judicial) damages the human form.

But to remain, for a moment, with something else that has affinity with the forensic: violations of the human body's corporal integrity could also prove a source of wonder in a very different context, via clinical dissection for the purpose of scientific advancement. As has been well documented, there was a 'culture of dissection' in early modern England that helped contribute to 'the emergence of a new image of the human interior', and the body's anatomical mysteries proved widely captivating across the realm.[55] Anatomies, of course, involve violating the internal boundaries of the human body, and scholars like Hillary M. Nunn explicitly link the mutilations staged in a play like *Titus* to the larger social fascination with the body's mysteries.[56] Four times a year, dissections performed by the Company of Barber-Surgeons were open to the public, and such anatomies became 'popular theatrical events even among Londoners without any professional connections to the medical realm'; in 1623, for example, Sir Simonds D'Ewes reports attending a multiple-day 'anatomye lecture with proffitt and delight, the smell excepted'.[57] We have seen how, in early modern execution rites, state violence inflicted on the condemned prisoner could compromise the boundaries of the human body – and anatomical dissections actually compounded this dynamic further, because criminal corpses were the primary supply of medical use. In 1540, an act was passed proclaiming that each year, the Company of Barber-Surgeons could 'have and take without contradiction fower personnes, condempned adjudged and put to death for felony by the due ordre of the Kinges lawe of this Realme, for anathomyes, without any further sute or labour';[58] the diarist Henry Machyn, for example, records that on 24 February 1560 there were 'hang[ed] xviij men and ij women' and 'the barbur-surgens had on of them to be a notheme [i.e. corpse for dissection] at ther hall'.[59] In this way, the criminal could be thought to perform a redemptive function in death: Donne, for example, notes that the 'Worst malefectors ... Do publike good cut in Anatomies'.[60]

And indeed, early modern subjects were so interested in the spectacle of human dissection, that there seems to have been an underground market for the practice. Surviving evidence – such as 'complaints against private persons dissecting bodies in their own houses' – indicates 'the difficulty of policing dissections and the existence of trafficking in dismembered bodies and body parts'.[61] In fact, in 1604 the Company of Barber-Surgeons railed against the unauthorized 'openinge, searinge, and imbalmeinge of the dead corpes' by tradesmen 'unskillfull in Barbery and Surgery'; this 'unseemely and unchristian lyke defaceinge, disfiguringe, and dismembringe [of] dead Corpes' constituted both a public health hazard and a general nuisance, because 'the corpes corrupteth and groweth presentlie contagious and offensive to the place and persons approachinge'.[62] Anatomical dissection is thus another cultural practice that reflects the larger ambivalent dynamics of disgust, as the body turned inside-out could both fascinate – as an object of wonder in the halls of the public anatomy theatre – and repel – as a rotting, stinking object of repugnance announcing its presence to unfortunate passers-by in some common space.

* * *

So far, I have discussed the traumatized human body as an object of visual spectacle – bodies in which natural boundaries have been crucially violated. Now I will turn to bodies that evoke a different kind of (perceived) natural violation, via the early modern discourse of monstrosity. The concept of monstrosity is invoked explicitly in *Titus* a few times, in reference to a violation of social norms or obligations; Titus, for example, deems Saturninus's rejection of Lavinia and denunciation of the Andronici to be 'monstrous . . . reproachful words' (1.1.313). Even when not mentioned, the moral sense of monstrosity is equally presented in the crimes of Demetrius, Chiron and Aaron; the latter's famous litany of misdeeds, I suspect, would trigger many Elizabethans to think in terms of monstrosity, which is equally signalled in the scene by epithets like *devil* and *beastly villain* (5.1.145; 97). But in terms of visual spectacle, the play's most obvious instance of monstrosity is the horrifying case of the mutilated Lavinia, who becomes a living monument to violated nature. With good reason, scholars have devoted considerable attention to theorizing the violence inflicted on Lavinia, who has prompted sensitive and sophisticated thinking on issues like rape and gendered trauma.[63] But while humanizing her is indeed the ethically appropriate critical move, it is also necessary to think of her potential reception as an object of theatrical spectacle – and here, I think that we cannot fully separate her post-attack condition, with missing limbs and open orifices, from the contemporary discourse of monstrosity and disgust.

In terms of disgust, we have seen how modern audiences, even when sympathetic, often cannot help but be repulsed by her sight – and monsters, perhaps unsurprisingly, are things that often are cross-culturally associated with disgust. The fact that her bodily boundaries have been so thoroughly transgressed equally informs this reading: I have suggested earlier that disgust often emerges from the violation of boundaries, and this bares on a discussion of monstrosity. Jeffrey Jerome Cohen, in his classic theorization, argues that monsters 'are disturbing hybrids whose externally incoherent bodies resist attempts to include them in any systematic structuration', and that therefore exist as a 'form suspended between forms that threatens to smash distinctions'.[64] This recalls the theorization of Mary Douglas – the famed anthropologist whose conceptualization of pollution has influenced modern understandings of disgust – who argues that notions of *holiness* are 'exemplified by completeness', requiring that 'individuals shall conform to the class to which they belong' and that 'different classes of things shall not be confused'.[65] Anomalous things like monsters, it follows, prompt horror and repugnance, a form of disgust response to our sense that boundaries are being violated. Arnold I. Davidson thus points us towards 'monsters that seem to call into question, to problematize, the boundary between humans and other animals' – like so many of the so-called monsters in the early modern world – because aberrations to the normative human form risk confounding the terms of humanity itself.[66]

Early modern theorists had much to say about such variations from the norm. Ambroise Paré, for example, differentiates between *monsters* – 'things that appear outside the course of Nature . . . such as a child who is born with one arm, another who will have two heads' – *prodigies* – 'things which happen that are completely against Nature as when a woman will give birth to a serpent, or to a dog' – and *maimed persons* – such as 'the blind, the one-eyed, the hump-backed . . . or those having spots or warts or wens, or any other thing that is against Nature'.[67] (Incidentally, Lucius in the opening scene claims that the sacrifice of Alarbus is partly 'so the shadows be not unappeased, / Nor we disturbed with prodigies on earth' [103–4].) Such deviations of nature were most famously recorded in the so-called monstrous birth pamphlets of the era, which usually framed abnormal human and non-human animals as an ominous reflection of God's displeasure (either with the unfortunate parents or with the community at large).[68] In such documents, 'the monsters themselves are texts', in the sense that 'their bodies are transparent to the crimes they punish' – and their demand to be read helps account for the complex affective response that they evoked.[69] This is because on one level, Lorraine Daston and Katharine Park observe, monsters 'were deformed and ugly, and they therefore evoked . . . repugnance and distaste'; a fact reflected, for example, in the disgust-based rhetoric of a pamphlet declaring that 'monstrous births are Moales in nature, they are Wens sticking on her cheeke to disgrace her'.[70] But on the very same page, the anonymous author also speaks of the 'wretched shape[s] . . . at which with wonder and loathing thou so often castest an eye' – and the acknowledgement that objects of loathing and disgust still captivate the viewer is crucial. Edward Fenton, translating Pierre Boaistuau's *Histoires Prodigieuses*, similarly notes that monsters inspire an affective response of both attraction and repulsion:

> amongst all the things whiche maye be viewed vnder the coape of heauen, there is nothyng to be seene, which more stirreth the spirite of man, whiche rauisheth more his senses, whiche doth more amaze hym, or ingendreth a greater terror or admiration in al creatures, than the monsters, wonders and abhominations, wherein we see the workes of Nature . . . turned arsiuersie, misseshapen and deformed.[71]

What's more, far from simply commanding attention, monsters could even serve as 'potential objects of aesthetic appreciation' – functioning both as horrifying 'signs of divine wrath' but also as 'sports of a benign nature and ornaments of a benevolent creator'.[72] Because of this, Datson and Park argue that the early modern monster prompted 'three separate complexes of interpretations and associated emotions – horror, pleasure, and repugnance'.[73]

And just as public executions compelled the early modern imagination, we know that the mysteries of nature did equally fascinate; indeed, John Earle, linking the two phenomena, grumbled that the general public 'melts [like] butter to heare.... Stories of some men of Tyburne, or a strange Monster out of Germany'.[74] Going further, Thomas Bedford lamented that 'the common sort make no further use of these Prodigies and Strange-births, than as a matter of wonder and table-talk'; this sort of engagement is unseemly, he argues, because it is not 'lawfull to delight in what may not be desired'.[75] But it was not simply that stories were swapped about such figures: they had an important early modern presence as a visual spectacle. As Mark Thornton Burnett demonstrates, the display of 'monstrous' humans and animals was a central feature of the early modern fair-ground, where spectators were coaxed into tents by 'the promise of unheard of wonder'; we find the rhetoric of such exhibitions co-opted in *Every Man in His Humor*, when Edward Knowell barks 'Here, within this place, is to be seene the true, rare, and accomplish'd monster, or miracle of nature'.[76] Marston similarly declares that 'oft haue I gazed with astonish'd eye, / At monstrous issues of ill shaped birth', and speaks of the period's 'monstrous penny-showes'.[77] And Shakespeare, of course, memorably reflects on this practice in *The Tempest*, when Trinculo fantasizes about displaying Caliban for profit: in England, he reflects, 'they will not give a doit to relieve a lame beggar, [but] they will lay out ten to see a dead Indian' (2.2.32–3). (Though surviving records are scarce, Alden T. Vaughan demonstrates that American natives both alive and dead were indeed presented for commercial display in the period.[78]) Finally, such wonders did not simply evoke the pleasure of novelty – for some, even genuine sympathy was triggered. After seeing a 'monstrous childe [displayed] to get some money with the sight of him, by reason of his strangenes', Montaigne responds by arguing that 'those which we call monsters are not so with God'; though many 'call that against nature, which commeth against custome', reason demonstrates that everything is a part of divine order, and this comfort should 'chase from vs the error, and expell the astonishment, which noveltie breedeth, and stangenes causeth in vs'.[79] While not everyone was as enlightened as Montaigne, the larger point is that the category-bending properties of early modern monsters did not simply elicit an aversion response – as is characteristic of disgusting objects more generally, they could equally seduce the attention, and even generate positive sentiments like pleasure and protectiveness.

If the ostensibly disgusting monster figure could activate such ambivalence, then it is unsurprising that these dynamics equally adhere in a related discourse that considers a less fantastic, yet still non-normative kind of body: the competing pulls of attraction and repulsion are also entwined in the literary mode that modern scholars have called the *ugly beauty* or *deformed mistress* tradition.[80] Works belonging to this genre (such as, most notably, the *contreblason*) offer 'satiric verse in praise of a deformed beloved', which celebrates qualities such as 'old age, physical defects, dark skin, [and] disproportionate body features' – they present, in other words, the ugly or deformed body as 'at once titillating and nauseating'.[81] Disgust is indeed a primary engine of this tradition: as Heather Dubrow explains, these texts 'frequently . . . render [the mistress] unappealing, even disgusting', while Baker notes that 'arguments presenting the ugly body as desirable nearly always depict it as visually disgusting, thereby enhancing the shocking impact of the speaker's apparently perverse desire'.[82] In these works, 'snot drips from the repulsive woman's nose, spots erupt on her neck: her body is transgressive, excessive, "incomplete"' – but she is still a source of ostensible desire.[83]

Scholars have pointed to many instances in the period that celebrate 'filthy Finenesse and loathsome Loveliness'.[84] One of the most notable occurs in Lyly's *Endymion*, where Sir Tophas offers a memorable mock-encomium of his love:

> O what a fine thin hayre hath *Dipsas,* what a prettie low forehead? What a tale & statelie nose? What little hollowe eyes? What great and goodly lyppes? Howe harmelesse shee is beeing toothlesse, her fingers fatte and short, adorned with long nayles like a Bytter. In howe sweete a proportion her cheekes hang downe to her brests like dugges, and her pappes to her waste like bagges.[85]

But there are plenty more examples. James Shirley begins a poem by declaring 'A Way with handsome faces, let me see / Hereafter nothing but deformity'.[86] In *A Hundreth Sundrie Flowres,* Gascoigne writes 'in prayse of a gentlewoman who though she were not very fayre, yet was she as hard fauored as might be' and 'in prayse of the brown beautie [who is] twixt faire and foule'.[87] A speaker in Barnabe Barnes's sonnet sequence strives to 'take enroulment / Of natures faultes' in his beloved; he finds 'her eyes were sharpe, and fierie: / A moule vpon her forehead, colour'd pale / Her haire disordred, browne and crisped wyerye'.[88] In *The Countess of Pembroke's Arcadia,* a mock-blazon ironically celebrates the ugly Mopsa, described as (among other things) 'like great god Saturn faire, and like faire Venus chaste'.[89] Sir John Davies writes that a woman named Gella 'hath a dull dead eye, a saddle nose / An ill shapte face . . . and rotten Teeth which she in laughing showes'.[90] And Shakespeare, of course, participates in the tradition: in *The Comedy of Errors* Dromio of Syracuse elaborately catalogues the unseemly faults of Nell (3.2.81–149), while Sonnet 130 is an iconic example with some affinity to the genre.

As modern readers have elucidated, the deformed mistress tradition is one way that Renaissance men attempted to manage the complex dynamics of beauty and desire. In one sense, Baker explains, works celebrating ugliness 'ultimately draw attention to the male creative genius that is capable of transforming even unsightly female matter into compelling art'.[91] But in another, capturing the ugly body in verse is a broader manoeuvre of social control: 'generating extreme loathing, the deformed woman nevertheless fulfills a crucial function, potentially enabling the dominant subject to expel the disruptive bodily model that she represents'.[92] For beauty is a notoriously unstable and subjective thing, as Robert Burton laments in a telling passage:

> Euery louer admires his mistris, though she be very deformed of her selfe, ill fauoured, crooked, bald, goggle-eyed, or squint-eyed, sparrow mouthed, hookenosed or haue a sharpe foxe nose, gubber-tussed, rotten teeth, beetle-browed, her breath stinke all ouer the roome . . . scabbed wrists, a tanned skinne, a rotten carkasse, crooked backe, lame, splea-footed, *as slender in the middle as a cowe in the waste,* goutie legges, her feete stinke, she breeds lice, a very monster, an aufe imperfect, her whole

complection sauours, and to thy iudgement lookes like a marde in a lanthorne, whom thou couldest not fancy for a world, but hatest, lothest, & wouldest haue spit in her face, or blow thy nose in her bosome.[93]

Baker notes the anxiety in these words: 'ensuring the revulsion which is the only justifiable response to such a monstrous spectacle, the speaker's lengthy, breathless act of description nevertheless betrays the difficulty of enforcing the correct or natural responses of desire and repulsion through which beauty and ugliness are defined.'[94] Even objects of disgust, then, risk becoming a source of attraction, and 'without the male subject's active efforts to visualise the female body as repellent, it is in danger of seducing rather than repulsing'.[95]

Furthermore, as Shannon Kelley explains, such attempts to constrain the ugly body can still activate the possibilities of non-normative desire for deformity – and in fact, some early modern lore actively eroticized the non-normative body.[96] Citing proverbs such as 'the crooked man doeth it best' and 'he knowes not the perfect pleasure of *Venus*, that hath not layne with a limping Woman', Montaigne articulates the disabled body as a site of sexual mastery; he speculates both that disabled people enjoy 'Genitall partes [that] are more full, better nourished and more vigorous', and that they 'do lesse waste they strength and consume their vertue' in other forms of exercise, and thus 'much the stronger and fuller, they come to *Venus* sportes'.[97] There is thus at least the theoretical possibility that the mutilated and disfigured Lavinia could be seen as an object of aesthetic appreciation, or even a source of erotic desire – and a director of *Titus* can lean into this presentation. In Peter Brook's 1955 Shakespeare Memorial Theatre production, Vivian Leigh portrayed the mutilated Lavinia with long streamers flowing out of her mouth and wrists. As one viewer recalled, when she first appeared on stage in this state, 'the whole audience gasped' – not because 'it was so shocking', but 'because she was so beautiful'.[98] To that end, Aebischer notes that 'again and again, what reviewers and eyewitnesses of [this] production remember is the ethereal beauty of the stage image'.[99] But Lavinia need not be portrayed as beautiful to nonetheless function as a captivating aesthetic object; Marcus's horrifying ekphrastic presentation of his bleeding niece is a case in point (2.3.11–57). Though the violated Lavinia is primed to be a source of revulsion, the dynamics of aesthetic disgust ensure that she will, for at least some viewers and readers, be hard to turn away from.

* * *

In this chapter I have considered a variety of early modern social practices and discourses in which ostensibly disgusting material can be shown to captivate the attention as a visual spectacle. But I cannot conclude without considering what is perhaps the most viscerally disgusting moment of *Titus Andronicus:* the climactic finale, in which Tamora unwillingly 'eat[s] the flesh that she herself hath bred' (5.4.60). Unsurprisingly, the role of food and cannibalism in the play has generated considerable commentary.[100] As Julia Kotzur notes, the play's obsessive interest in the theme of incorporation begins with Tamora's incorporation into the Roman body politic – 'Titus', she says, 'I am incorporate in Rome' (1.1.467) – but it reaches unimaginably horrific heights in 'the pie made with flesh', where (as Elena Bonelli puts it) the co-mingling of 'bones and blood represents a moving boundary between human and non-human, as well as a confused distinction between the internal and external parts, of the cooked bodies, which is even more abject for Tamora who re-incorporates those she once generated'.[101] Disgust, I have suggested in the Introduction, is fundamentally about the regulation of boundaries, and cannibalism is something that brings this particularly into focus. David B. Goldstein, surveying critical opinion, notes that most theorists 'agree that cannibalism is an act in which the self-other boundary is transgressed and reimagined': Daniel Cottom, for example, argues that cannibalism is 'imaginable only in and through the self-dividing articulation of cultural, psychological, and conceptual borderlines', while Maggie Kilgour suggests that 'the figure of the cannibal dramatizes the danger of drawing boundaries too absolutely'.[102] But while cannibalism itself entails a dissolution of boundaries, in the early modern period the discourse of cannibalism is equally used to shore up boundaries between the self and others, whether it be in terms doctrinal – as when a reformer argues that 'Papistes ... make *Christians* barbarous *Canibales,* and eaters of mans flesh, and drinkers of mans blood' – or racial and ethnic – as in the countless travel narratives that describe encounters with 'beastly and fearse ... *Canibales*'.[103] What is consistent, however, is that the act of consuming human flesh is presented as viscerally disgusting: Peter Martyr, for example, before describing a supposed account of mutilation and cannibalism performed by New World natives, warns, 'let euery godly man close the mouth of his stomake lest he be desturbed'.[104]

But as recent scholars have observed, the early modern English were a bit hypocritical here: because, somewhat surprisingly, the consumption of human matter was not at all unheard of in their own cultural frame. In her study of domestic practices, Wendy Wall notes that not only does it seem like 'human remains visibly circulated in the early modern world' but surviving recipe books actually suggest 'how customary it was to think of body parts in the kitchen'.[105] For instance, one seventeenth-century recipe for cowslip wine calls for 'half an ounce [of] Mans skull prepar'd', while in another, the first step of a home remedy for falling sickness orders the preparer to 'take of a mans scull, un buried, one ounce'.[106] The latter example is particularly illustrative, because it points to the practice of *medicinal cannibalism* that has long featured in the Western healing tradition.[107] As Heinrich von Staden has documented, Western medicine (particularly the Hippocratic tradition) has a robust engagement with what anthropologists call *Dreckapotheke* – 'the medical prescription of what cross-culturally has been perceived as filth' – and indeed, the idea that 'the voluntary embrace of filth can have a prophylactic power against the polluting effects of filth [is] common to the ritual practices of many cultures'.[108] Douglas notes that 'religions often sacralise the very unclean things which have been rejected with abhorrence', and thus 'dirt, which is normally destructive, sometimes becomes creative'.[109] This process is based on the boundary transgressing properties of cultural filth – because 'vulnerable margins and those attacking forces which threaten to destroy good order represent the powers inhering in the cosmos', and 'ritual which can harness these for good is harnessing power indeed'.[110] And among the kinds of cultural filth, biological products harvested from living and dead bodies played a not-insignificant role in early modern medicine.

Evidence attests to how the human body – particularly the decaying body – could be co-opted for healing purposes; John Gerard's botanical encyclopaedia, for example, recommends the medicinal properties of a particular 'kinde of Mosse . . . found vpon the skulls or bare scalps of men and women, lying long in charnell houses or other places, where the bones of men and women are kept together'.[111] But by far the most extensive usage of corpse medicine in the Renaissance concerns the complex discourse surrounding *mummy* – a concept that originated with the ancient use of bituminous materials for healing purposes, but which came to entail something very different in the early modern period. As Karl H. Dannenfeldt explains,

> by the sixteenth century Egyptian mummies, usually in broken pieces or powder, could be found in the shops of all European apothecaries as a drug for prescriptions. That the embalmed bodies of ancient Egyptians, and even the "mummified" bodies of those more recently dead, became a valued drug was due to a complicated and confusing process of transference and substitution involving originally the use of bituminous products in medicine.[112]

It was 'errors in translations and interpretations by medieval translators' that facilitated this 'change from bitumen to embalmed or desiccated bodies', and these misunderstandings had a profound effect on medicinal cannibalism in Europe. As the surgeon John Hall noted in 1565, it was common 'nowe among our Apothecaries' to feature in their shops 'the very flesh of mans body, as it weare burned to a cole: for both whole armes and whole legges, haue been here not rarly seene, being dryed as blacke as a cole'.[113] And because, unsurprisingly, it was not always convenient to get one's hands on a genuine ancient Egyptian corpse, early modern Europeans seem to have once again co-opted the bodies of executed criminals for medicinal purposes. Indeed, the famed alchemist and professor of medicine Oswald Croll suggested that 'a Tincture of Mumy' is best prepared from 'the Carcase of a red Man (b) whole (c) clear without blemish, of the age of twenty four years (d) that hath been Hanged, Broke upon a Wheel, or Thrust-through'.[114] While it is difficult to find Renaissance English authorities commenting on the use of criminal corpses for medicinal purposes, modern scholars like Noble argue that once such bodies entered 'the early modern medical corpse market', they 'often end[ed] up processed as mummy'; on the Continent, furthermore, we can point to the words of physician Antonio Brasavola, who advised that 'when an executed criminal is dissected some of his fat should be preserved for pharmacological purposes'.[115] At the very least, we do know that human flesh was proudly displayed throughout the shops of London. Pepys, for example, records 'having seen a mummy in a merchant's warehouse there, all the middle of the man or woman's body, black and hard . . . he did give me a little bit, and a bone of an arme, I suppose'. But his response to this encounter is particularly telling: 'I never saw any before, and there, it pleased me much, though an ill sight.'[116]

Pepys's *pleasure* at seeing an *ill sight* reflects the competing pulls of attraction and repulsion that I have associated with disgust in this chapter. It also reflects a larger cultural ambivalence towards medical cannibalism. As Richard Sugg records, corpse medicine was, in general, 'widely accepted by patients and practitioners', due to a number of factors, such as 'rarity, spiritual value, learned authority, and commercial normalisation'.[117] But this acceptance was often reluctant, and medical commentators frequently qualify the use of human remedies, if not object to it entirely, by suggesting the medicine's disgusting qualities. We can point to no less an authority than Galen, who prescribes for some maladies 'a drink of burned (human) bones' – but he insists that 'the patients [must be] not knowing what they drank, lest they should be nauseated'.[118] Classical precedent was not enough to justify the practice, as indicated by English doctor Thomas Moffett:

> yea in *Rome* . . . Physicians did prescribe their patients the blood of Wrestlers, causing them to suck it warm breathing and spinning out of their veins, drawing into their corrupt bodies a sound mans life, and sucking that in with both lips, which a dogg is not suffered to lick with his tongue; yea they were not ashamed to prescribe them a meat made of mans marrow and infants brains.

'What remedy call you that', Moffett wonders, 'which is more savage and abominable then the grief itself?'[119] Many agreed with Moffett; in 1538 the Italian physician Aloysius Mundella declared that the medicinal use of corpses was an 'abominable and detestable' practice, and commentators in both England and the rest of the Continent complained about the 'dead bodies [that] the Phisitians and Apothecaries doe against our willes make vs to swallow'.[120]

The French doctor Paré was explicitly disgusted by the process, which he describes as 'so horride a wickedness': patients were

> compelled both foolishly and cruelly to devoure the mangied and putride particles of the carcasses of the basest people of Egypt, or of such as are hanged, as though there were no other way to helpe or recover one bruised with a fall from a high place, than to bury man by an horrid insertion in their, that is, in mans guts.[121]

Disgust similarly features in the objections of German physician Leonhart Fuchs, who condemns pharmacies that sell 'the gory matters of cadavers received evidently from the gallows or from the torture wheel, spotted with the feces of corpses' – for 'who', he asks, 'unless he approves of cannibalism, would not loathe this remedy'?[122] And the invocation of cannibalism is especially important, because Europeans could not fully obscure the fact that their own cultural practices uncomfortably recalled those that they condemned elsewhere: as Montaigne famously observed, it was quite hypocritical to denounce cannibalism in inhabitants of the New World, when Old World 'phisitians feare not, in all kindes of compositions availefull to our health, to make vse of it'.[123]

As Noble argues, some of the 'macabre comic moments' in *Titus Andronicus* reflect cultural anxiety about corpse medicine, in the sense that 'comedy is introduced when the tragic horror onstage comes dangerously close to discomforting contemporary practices familiar to the audience'.[124] And it is certainly true, as we saw in the previous chapter, that disgusting objects have the capacity to elicit laugher, as part of the complex emotional response that they provoke. But I think Noble's comment on medical discourse may be extended more broadly, because so much of *Titus* comes dangerously close to discomforting contemporary practices – the practices that, I have argued in this chapter, contributed to the early modern culture of spectacular disgust. In Shakespeare's era, we can point to numerous instances in which objects of ostensible disgust demonstrate a considerable ability to captivate the contemporary imagination: public executions, murder pamphlets, scientific dissections, so-called monsters, deformed mistresses and medicinal cannibalism. Early modern audiences would thus be partly primed for the gruesome, disgusting violence of *Titus Andronicus*, because they lived in a culture that routinely invited viewers to gaze upon that which might otherwise cause them to look away. While there are, of course, other elements of *Titus* that engage with the discourse of disgust – I will discuss the play's use of racial disgust in Chapter 9 – I think that this basic configuration, in which revolting matter is rendered aesthetically compelling, accounts for much of the play's affective strategy.

It is vital to recognize, however, that I am not simply suggesting that early modern subjects had a different threshold of disgust – though they to some extent undoubtedly did, the fact remains that we've seen plenty of evidence that contemporaries were indeed disgusted by traumatized or monstrous bodies, even as they gazed upon them. There's no doubt, then, that *Titus* is a disgusting play, but it is still aesthetically effective, because what is disgusting also has the capacity to allure; the play participates in a culture of affective ambivalence that enshrines as visually enticing that which simultaneously might make us recoil. I have focused here on the experience of early modern audiences – but, as we saw in the last chapter, we also have our own modern culture of spectacular disgust, and it can help account for the disgusted-yet-captivated response to *Titus* that we saw in modern audiences at the start of this discussion. The fact that repulsive things demand our attention helps account for the undeniable existence of aesthetic disgust – and it is something to keep in mind as we move forward to consider the many other ways that Shakespeare engaged with the emotion.

3

Food disgust

It is a bit foolish to try to settle on the *most* disgusting moment of *Titus Andronicus* – but if we were making a list of contenders, we'd surely have to include Tamora consuming a bloody meat-pie stuffed with the piping hot flesh of her two dear sons. Food, modern researchers suggest, is the core domain of disgust, and this association seems amply supported by the stomach-turning events depicted in the final act of *Titus*.

But most people, I suspect, don't need Shakespeare to tell them that food and disgust are intimately related. To give my own example: when I was about five or six years old, I had an extremely adverse reaction to an item of food, the name of which I am now unwilling to type. The cause of this reaction was never determined – perhaps the food was spoiled, perhaps I had some sort of allergy or perhaps I was already harbouring an unrelated stomach bug – but the effect it had on my body was immediate and unmistakable: violent, uncontrollable vomiting. In that moment, this food product became forever tainted to me: the sight, smell or even thought of it is still easily able to make me vomit, some thirty years later. I must turn away when it is advertised on television; I must avoid its aisle in the grocery store; I must leave the room when someone else consumes it. Indeed, writing these sentences is causing me significant nausea, because this food's disgustingness has so thoroughly imprinted itself in my mind and body.

I described in Chapter 1 how the concept of *disgust* is connected to the matter of *distaste*, and Darwin, the first major theorist of the emotion, located food as the primary concern of the disgust response. But while food has long been recognized as the central domain of disgust, it is only in recent years that scientists have begun to fully analyse 'the influence of food disgust' on various food and eating-related phenomena, including 'eating preferences (texture-based food rejection), habits (variety seeking) and behaviours (picky eating)'.[1] Since then, however, researchers have been making up for lost time, empirically demonstrating how (as common sense suggests) disgust shapes much of our food-related behaviour. For example, those high in food neophobia ('an aversion toward novel or unfamiliar foods') tend to be more sensitive to disgust.[2] Individuals with eating disorders like anorexia nervosa also score consistently higher 'on all domains of disgust sensitivity' than control subjects.[3] One study, exploring the role of emotion in obesity, found a correlation between disgust sensitivity and lower body mass index; this lead the researchers to suggest that 'feeling disgusted by food may be a strategy to uphold restraint, whereas relatively decreased disgust could encourage overeating'.[4] Feelings of disgust have been implicated as a major contributor of food waste; some, for example, feel unease at the prospect of 'surplus' or leftover food, while others are disgusted by food that has an unusual shape.[5] Disgust similarly seems to shape how people respond to the prospect of new food technologies – most notably genetically modified foods, but also things such as 'edible nanotechnology coating film, nanotechnology food box, artificial meat/milk, [and] synthetic food additive'.[6] Unsurprisingly, vegetarians often have a disgust response to the prospect of eating meat, and disgust has been linked to one's unwillingness to eat meat more generally.[7] On a related note, there is a large body of work on how disgust fuels the aversion to insect-eating (entomophagy) that is typical in Western culture; as many have argued, this affective blockage results in the dismissal of a plentiful and nutritious food source.[8] And there has, in fact, been developed a 'Food Disgust Scale', adopted and validated in many different cultural contexts, which measures an individual's sensitivity to 'unique types of food disgust' – items include aversion to things like *animal flesh, poor hygiene, human contamination, mould, decaying fruit, fish, decaying vegetables* and *living contaminants.*[9] As the scale suggests, there are many different ways that food can disgust a person, and the experience of food disgust is one of the most immediately visceral affective experiences that it's possible to have.

Almost a century ago, Caroline Spurgeon noted that the ageing Shakespeare's plays increasingly deploy imagery that invokes the theme of 'sensitive digestion' and queasiness at various foodstuffs; this leads her to suggest that in his late thirties Shakespeare seemed to have 'suffered from some deep perturbation, shock and revulsion of nature, emotional, moral and spiritual, which translated itself into terms of physical appetite and its disgust'.[10] Whether or not we buy this biographical reading, we must acknowledge that food is a topic of considerable interest to Shakespeare – a fact reflected by the growing body of scholarship that comprises the field of Shakespearean food studies. As a larger interdisciplinary field, food studies has attracted considerable attention of late, and scholars have begun to specifically theorize the analysis of food in literature.[11] In terms of Shakespeare and the early modern period, concentrated interest in food took hold in the last two decades, anchored by monographs like Ken Albala's *Eating Right in the Renaissance* (2002), Robert Appelbaum's *Aguecheek's Beef, Belch's Hiccup, and Other Gastronomic Interjections: Literature, Culture, and Food among the Early Moderns* (2006) and, most importantly, Joan Fitzpatrick's *Food in Shakespeare* (2007).[12] Since then, there has been an explosion of research on food and Shakespeare, treating the topic both broadly and with reference to the state of food and eating in particular plays.[13] Early modern England, it has been said, had a 'cultural fixation with eating, cooking and hospitality', and such scholarship persuasively demonstrates the value of tending to food both in Shakespeare's poetic language and his dramatic design.[14] Perhaps most relevant to the study of emotion is the focus on dietetics, 'the doctrine of appropriate eating and drinking according to the mixture of the elements and humours in your body'.[15] Because the early modern understanding of humoural physiology maintained that one's corporeal (and psychological) states were intimately tied to external environmental factors, popular manuals like Sir Thomas Elyot's *The Castel of Health* (1541) and Andrew Boorde's *A Compendious Regiment or a Dietary of Health* (1547) prescribed ideal eating practices to an audience of eager readers. (Indeed, as Kimberly Anne Coles and Gitanjali Shahani note, 'it would be difficult to find a culture more invested in the adage that we are what we eat than that of Shakespeare's England.'[16]) And while there has not been a tremendous amount of work on food disgust in the early modern period, Shahani has recently shown how disgust at foreign food marked European encounters with other cultures in contemporary travel narratives – we'll see more of this in Chapter 8.

As Darwin observed, there is 'a strong association in our minds between the sight of food, however circumstanced, and the idea of eating it' – this is the reason, presumably, that I'm still made nauseous by any contact with the food that disgusted me as a child.[17] Indeed, scientists have mapped the neural activation associated with viewing images of disgusting food, demonstrating 'the brain's sensitivity to visual cues of food that are spoiled or rotten'; viewing such images has even been shown to suppress activity in the area of the brain controlling the motor functions of the tongue, suggesting that the presence of revolting food triggers 'anticipatory inhibition mechanisms, possibly preventing toxin swallowing and contamination'.[18] But while it seems clear that visual images of offending food can trigger a disgust response, I think that literary depictions of food and eating have a similarly strong hold on our mind and body, an association that Shakespeare leverages throughout his plays. By presenting poetic and dramatic images linked to the material realities of eating and digestion – especially what may be called compromised eating and digestion – the plays harness the affective power of food disgust for a number of strategic ends. I'm not, of course, suggesting that we literally gag when Hal calls Falstaff an 'obscene greasy tallow-catch' (*1 Henry IV*, 2.4.223) – though some people, as noted before, do find it a bit stomach-turning to watch Tamora eat her sons.[19] But even if we're not having constant disgust responses when reading or watching Shakespeare, characters in the plays nonetheless routinely use language that activates the concept of food disgust, and the power of this particular emotion manifests widely throughout the Shakespearean canon.

We've already touched upon food disgust in *Titus Andronicus*, and in the following chapters, we'll see how it plays a significant role in *Timon of Athens* and *Coriolanus*. In one of the only bits of previous work on food and disgust in Shakespeare, Colleen E. Kennedy shows how the pungent leek in *Henry V* becomes a marker of ethnic boundaries in the British army; Pistol's statement that he is 'qualmish at the smell of leek' antagonizes the Welsh captain Fluellen, because the leek was long recognized as a 'cultural emblem of Wales' (5.1.20).[20] But we can also point to other instances in which Shakespeare utilized food disgust to a particular dramatic, thematic or poetic end.[21] He was particularly interested, for example, in the notion that overindulging in food ultimately turns the stomach; *Twelfth Night*, of course, famously begins with the heartsick Orsino declaring, 'If music be the food of love, play on, / Give me excess of it, that surfeiting / The appetite may sicken and so die' (1.1.1–3). (A *surfeit* is defined as an 'illness attributed to excessive eating or drinking'.[22]) In *The Rape of Lucrece*, we similarly learn that 'the sweets we wish for turn to loathed sours / Even in the moment that we call them ours' (867–8), while in *A Midsummer Night's Dream*, Lysander reminds us that 'a surfeit of the sweetest things / The deepest loathing to the stomach brings' (2.2.141–2). Speaking of *Dream*, after the restoration of the play's proper love-matches, Demetrius describes his time of enchantment in terms of food disgust:

> The object and the pleasure of mine eye,
> Is only Helena. To her, my lord,
> Was I betrothed ere I see Hermia;
> But like in sickness did I loathe this food.
> But as in health, come to my natural taste,
> Now I do wish it, love it, long for it,
> And will for evermore be true to it. (4.1.169–75)

In *Troilus and Cressida*, Agamemnon grumbles that the truant virtues of the absent Achilles recall how 'fair fruit in an unwholesome dish, / Are like to rot untasted' (2.3.120–1); later in the play the jilted Troilus, describing his former lover's new devotion, cynically observes that 'the fragments, scraps, the bits and greasy relics / Of her o'ereaten faith, are bound to Diomed' (5.2.166–7). *Othello*'s Emilia, speaking of how men mistreat women, memorably notes that 'they are all but stomachs, and we all but food: / They eat us hungerly, and when they are full / They belch us' (3.4.105–7). In *Romeo and Juliet*, Mercutio's jab that the Nurse is 'a hare . . . in a lenten pie, that is something stale and hoar' unflatteringly compares her to mouldy and musty meat (2.4.130–1). And finally, Falstaff in *The Merry Wives of Windsor* partly frames his unpleasant time in the laundry basket in terms of food disgust: covered in 'stinking clothes that fretted in their own grease', he was 'more than half stewed in grease, like a Dutch dish' (3.5.108–9; 13–14).

But to conclude this chapter, I'd like to spend a bit more time on food disgust in *Antony and Cleopatra*, a play in which 'the consumption of food is a central theme'.[23] As Peter A. Parolin notes, when Shakespeare considered this subject, 'he inherited a powerful tradition in which his characters were evaluated in relation to their attitudes toward food' – and he in fact 'exploits this tradition, using attitudes toward food not only to define characters but also to structure the play's political conflict and to suggest competing ideas about what constitutes value'.[24] For our purposes, it is particularly notable that the excessive eating habits of the titular characters are regularly presented as both viscerally and morally disgusting: given what we saw above about surfeiting, the limitless consumption of Antony and Cleopatra always risks tempting the activation of physical revulsion. Furthermore, in the early modern period such excessiveness was thought to be self-perpetuating, and thus also took on the quality of a dangerous moral stain: Matt Williamson records how 'numerous early modern texts claimed that gluttony generated appetite', and the Church of England's 'Homilee Agaynst Gluttony and Drunkennesse' solemnly warned that 'he [who] eateth and drynketh vnmeasurably, kyndeleth ofte tymes suche an vnnaturall heate in his bodye, that his appetite is prouoked thereby to desire more then it should'.[25] Antony's appetite in Egypt was thus understood to be disgustingly excessive by moralists like Elyot, who condemned how he 'lyued in moste prodigall riotte, and thynkyng all thynge in the see, the lande, and the ayre to be made for satisfienge his glotony, deuoured al fleshe and fishe that moughte be any where founden'.[26]

Shakespeare insistently associates Antony's time in Egypt with excessive eating – a task accomplished, as Robert Lipscomb observes, by the 'many references to the trappings of Egypt . . . couched in terms of banqueting and gluttony'.[27] Characters routinely remark on Antony's 'Egyptian Bacchanals' (2.7.103), in which he is imagined to be 'in a field of feasts' (2.1.23) where 'he fishes, drinks, and wastes / The lamps of night in revel' (1.4.4–5). It seems that 'Egyptian cookery' had a special allure – it is said that 'Julius Caesar / Grew fat with feasting there' (2.7.63–5) – and it is believed that Antony indulged heartily, so much so that Octavius Caesar predicts that he will suffer from 'full surfeits' (1.4.27). In one notable occasion, Enobarbus recalls a breakfast in which 'Eight wild boars roasted . . . but twelve persons there' – and this, he boasts, 'was but as a fly by an eagle', compared to the 'much more monstrous matter of feast, which worthily deserved noting' (2.2.189–94). And, as Pompa Banerjee reminds us, Cleopatra herself is another kind of flesh that Antony consumes: throughout the play, the queen is regularly described in terms of food, as when she is called an 'Egyptian dish' (2.6.126), 'a morsel for a monarch' (1.5.32) or a 'morsel cold upon / Dead Caesar's trencher' (3.13.121–2).[28] Unsurprisingly, forms of excessive bodily pleasure become entwined in Egypt, as appetites for food and appetites for sex grow in tandem; as Lipscomb points out, food and drink are explicitly sexualized in the play, as when Caesar describes Antony's Egyptian *wassails* as *lascivious* (1.4.57).[29] This is partly because, consistent with what we just saw about early modern physiological understanding, both Egyptian food and the Egyptian queen only increase the appetite of those who consume them: of Antony's eating, it is said that 'Epicurean cooks' should 'Sharpen with cloyless sauce his appetite' (2.1.24–5), while 'Other women cloy / The appetites they feed', but Cleopatra 'makes hungry / Where most she satisfies' (2.2.247–9).

This idea of *cloying* – 'To overload with food, so as to cause loathing', or 'to disgust, weary (with excess of anything)' – is central to the discourse of disgust in *Antony and Cleopatra,* and is central to how other Romans understand Antony's appetite.[30] He *should,* by rights, be sickened by the lavish consumption of his Egyptian life, and the fact that he does not becomes construed as a moral flaw, a source of disgust in his observers. When describing his behaviour, Caesar claims that Antony is 'not more manlike / Than Cleopatra, nor the Queen of Ptolemy / More womanly than he'; in this analysis, Antony's manly Roman virtue has become degraded by his bodily excesses (1.4.5–7). Caesar, of course, is excessively sober, and has been said to possess a 'grim vision of political gain through self-denial'; when the Triumvirate are imbibing together at the beginning of the play, he disapprovingly characterizes drinking as the 'brain . . . grow[ing] fouler', and grumbles that he'd 'rather fast from all, four days, / Than drink so much in one' (2.7.98–9; 101–2).[31] But while Caesar's asceticism is perhaps unappealing, it still sheds vital insight into how Antony's behaviour is construed, especially when his habits in Egypt are contrasted with a vision of his former self. When lamenting the change in Antony's character, Caesar recalls a (to him) inspiring anecdote from his countryman's military past:

> When thou once
> Was beaten from Modena, where thou slew'st

> Hirtius and Pansa, consuls, at thy heel
> Did famine follow, whom thou fought'st against,
> Though daintily brought up, with patience more
> Than savages could suffer. Thou didst drink
> The stale of horses and the gilded puddle
> Which beasts would cough at. Thy palate then did deign
> The roughest berry on the rudest hedge.
> Yea, like the stag when snow the pasture sheets,
> The barks of trees thou browsed. On the Alps,
> It is reported, thou didst eat strange flesh
> Which some did die to look on. And all this –
> It wounds thine honour that I speak it now –
> Was borne so like a soldier that thy cheek
> So much as lanked not. (1.4.56–72)

In this recollection, Antony's virtue is explicitly construed as a function of his palate: he is praised here for sustaining himself on that which hardly warrants the name of food. And it is vital, of course, that what he eats is not only unpalatable but also viscerally disgusting. Shakespeare, in fact, amplifies his source to make the passage more repulsive; whereas Plutarch simply notes that Antony came 'so easily to drinke puddle water', Shakespeare adds the detail about him also quenching his thirst with horse urine.[32] Another alteration makes this consumption a unique measure of Antony's character: in Plutarch, all of the Roman soldiers are said to 'eate . . . such beasts, as neuer man tasted of their flesh before', while Shakespeare's Antony horrifies and disgusts his comrades by uniquely embracing 'strange flesh'.[33] (Indeed, the OED suggests specifically that *strange flesh* means not only 'usual' but also 'loathsome food'.[34]) What's more, not only does Antony consume disgusting food, but he apparently thrived on it: as Caesar recalls, he ate so well that not even his face grew thinner. Antony's eating habits in the field stand in obvious contrast to his consumption in Egypt, and the discrepancy between the two is offered as a central marker of the extent to which he is said to be corrupted by luxury.

Antony and Cleopatra, then, offers a useful reminder of the flexibility of disgust as a thematic category, here in the realm of food. Antony's enthusiasm for disgusting food is taken as a sign of moral excellency; his enthusiasm for the presumably tasty food of Egypt is a sign of his moral degeneration. What's more, even the visceral elicitors of disgust are contextually flexible, as overconsumption of decedent Egyptian foodstuffs should, according to common logic, invoke in Antony the physical repulsion that drinking horse urine and eating strange flesh did not. Food, most critics agree, is central to *Antony and Cleopatra* – but it is not simply about food, it is also about when food does or does not induce disgust. Disgust is thus crucial for connecting the theme of food to the play's larger moral exploration – and indeed, we'll see this connection between food and morality further explored in the next chapter.

4

Timon of Athens

The cycles of disgust

After beginning my discussion with Shakespeare's most explicitly disgusting play, this chapter considers the workings of disgust in one of his most puzzling: *Timon of Athens,* the collaborative effort with Thomas Middleton written sometime in the first decade of the seventeenth century.[1] Anthony B. Dawson and Gretchen E. Minton, the most recent Arden editors of *Timon*, introduce the play by reflecting on its significant weirdness: it is disjointed, inconsistent and at times feels incomplete. (Indeed, acknowledging the strangeness of *Timon* is a frequent trope deployed by scholars writing about it.) This chapter will not solve the problems of this play, but it will try to show how the lexicon of disgust underwrites many of *Timon*'s key poetic and thematic investments, as well as how thinking broadly about the dynamics of revulsion can help reveal some structural consistencies among several of the play's jagged elements.

Having read this far, you are now familiar with the sorts of things that circulate in the universe of disgust. The emotion's relevance to *Timon*, I hope, should thus become rather apparent once we consider the satiric tragedy's major points of thematic content: if nothing else, *Timon of Athens* is a play that concerns itself with food, disease and corrupted sexuality. The first sequence of *Timon* revolves around an extravagant, decadent banquet, and the transition to the play's second half is occasioned by a ritual mockery of that banquet; these dramatic set-pieces are reinforced by dialogue that consistently invokes images of compromised eating and consumption, including cannibalism. Once Timon flees to the wilderness, the rhetoric of disease becomes a key component of his misanthropic invective; he fantasizes particularly about the city-shaking potential of the plague, an entity powerful enough to depopulate his hated Athens. And in this infamously male play – in which the only women who appear are unnamed dancers and two named prostitutes – sexuality is presented as an entirely debased, transactional exchange; complimenting the broader interest in the plague, venereal disease is positioned specifically by Timon as a tool apt to poison his fellow countrymen, whose corrupt behaviour is seen as worthy of physical rot.

But *Timon*'s engagement with disgust is not simply restricted to Shakespeare and Middleton's poetic investment in images of particular elicitors. Rather, I think there is a larger sense in which the basic functioning of disgust is recalled by the dramatic trajectory of the play's central characters. Disgust, we have seen earlier, is fundamentally an emotion of regulation, which governs the integrity of literal and symbolic bodies through the process of incorporation and expulsion. Accordingly, I will argue in this chapter that *Timon*'s three central characters – Alcibiades, Apemantus and Timon himself – enact three related stories of expulsion from the social body of Athens. In this, I build on the compelling work of Jodie Austin, who has recently argued (in an article on notions of the plague in *Timon*) that the play 'concerns itself with modes of civic purgation'.[2] But while Austin focuses specifically on 'a conception of pestilence as a nihilistic yet potentially necessary force for purging the sickly polis', I focus more broadly on the play's dramatics of expulsion, which I see as exacting a social function analogous to the human disgust system.[3] *Timon of Athens,* Philip Brockbank observes, is a play that revolves around 'Timon's indictments of the social and natural orders' – and disgust, it should be recalled, is a mechanism that regulates both of those concepts.[4] Accordingly, the main characters of *Timon* variously see themselves as purging the sickness from the corrupted body of Athens, and they do so as men who have themselves been (voluntarily or involuntarily) expelled from the city's social borders. *Timon* is thus fundamentally a play about the policing of boundaries, a thematic investment that links it to the dynamics of disgust.

* * *

As we explored in the last chapter, food is the originary domain of disgust – and *Timon*, to be sure, has a concentrated investment in the social politics of eating. Joan Fitzpatrick has described *Timon's* interest in moments of 'profane feeding', which provide metaphors 'used to denounce the greed and hypocrisy of humanity'.[5] The visceral act of eating is transformed into a site of moral offence, as images of debased consumption reflect social behaviours that are understood as revolting. The opening of the play revolves around an exquisite banquet, in which Timon literally (and, as we shall see, symbolically) feeds the sycophants and parasites who attach to him; this feeding sets up an expectation of reciprocal goodwill, which is not met by Timon's false friends in his time of crisis. After informing his master of his dire finances, Flavius is particularly incensed by these 'riotous feeders' – wondering 'how many prodigal bits have slaves and peasants / This night englutted' (2.2.159; 165–6) – and not much later, a stranger who notes the ingratitude of Timon's flatterers similarly asks, 'Who can call him his friend / That dips in the same dish?' (3.2.68–9). Soon after, Flavius offers an even longer indictment of his master's creditors, denouncing them to their petitioning servants:

> Why then preferred you not your sums and bills
> When your false masters ate of my lord's meat?
> Then they could smile and fawn upon his debts,
> And take down th'interest into their gluttonous maws.
> (3.4.47–50)

Taken together, such comments remind us that in the tarnished world of Athens, breaking bread together is no longer an assurance of goodwill and honourable treatment: the social implications of eating have been poisoned, which calls into question the very process of eating itself. We see this most precisely in Flaminius's harangue, where Timon's sycophants are explicitly imagined in terms of vomit and disease:

> This slave
> Unto this hour has my lord's meat in him:
> Why should it thrive and turn to nutriment,
> When he is turned to poison?

> O, may diseases only work upon't,
> And, when he's sick to death, let not that part of nature
> Which my lord paid for be of any power
> To expel sickness, but prolong his hour! (3.1.57–64)

Here, Timon's servant actually prays for a *failure* of the disgust system – he wants the offending party to be tortured by the spoiled meat that cannot be rejected from the body. By evoking visceral and moral offence, sentiments like these reinforce a central theme of the play: in an ideal world, the physical sharing of food would imply the cementing of social bonds, but this is a principle that is continually corrupted in *Timon*.

But 'profane feeding' is not only the domain of these false friends, because Timon himself also participates in this cycle. As Daniel W. Ross notes, Timon equally engages in debased eating, 'digesting [and] thriving on the meaningless flattery which the Athenians gladly gorge him with'.[6] The irony of this exchange is obliquely suggested by Apemantus, who exposes the pointlessness of flattery in a telling image:

> We make ourselves fools to disport ourselves,
> And spend our flatteries to drink those men
> Upon whose age we void it up again
> With poisonous spite and envy. (1.2.137–40)

In this imagining, the alcohol with which we chase down our flatteries is transformed into the vomit of malice and detraction – an expulsion of our presumably more authentic feelings, in another version of corrupted consumption. As Austin points out, this recalls a contemporary notion that flatterers and false friends can serve as a source of indigestion: *The Triall of True Friendship* (1596) warns that 'if we haue once entertained a knaue we shal not easily be rid of him, but presently hee becomes like fulsome meate which wee cannot keepe in our stomackes, without hurting vs, nor vomit it vp alone as it went in, but mingled with other meate, which would haue nourished and cherished vs'.[7] We may thus see Timon as sickened by the flattery he so desperately consumes, especially when he realizes the moral offence occasioned by its emptiness. Furthermore, even Apemantus's cynic detachment does not insulate him fully from the motif of profane eating: though he dramatically denies himself the culinary luxuries of Timon's table, there is still a sense (as Ross observes) that he feeds 'on the banquet as his object of scorn'.[8] Indeed, in this act of self-interested indulgence, Apemantus remains implicated in consumption, his cynicism itself 'accommodating his distaste for men's faults'.[9]

Athens, then, is a place in which the process of eating is often morally tainted, a feature which recalls the key domains of disgust. But, as many have shown, it is specifically the spectre of cannibalism that characterizes images of compromised eating in *Timon*, an association that more explicitly links it to the discourse of disgust. We have explored literal cannibalism in our earlier discussion of *Titus*; in *Timon*, metaphors of eating human flesh further epitomize the play's thematic concern with debased consumption, which represents 'not only the predominant image pattern of the play, but the clearest indication of the radical bitterness which permeates *Timon* as well'.[10] Images of cannibalism appear almost immediately; when Timon asks Apemantus to join his banquet in the play's first scene, the philosopher glibly replies that he 'eat[s] not Lords' (208), while shortly after the soldier Alcibiades draws a cannibalistic connection between sharing a meal with friends and killing enemies in the field:

> TIMON You had rather be at a breakfast of enemies than a dinner of friends.
> ALCIBIADES So they were bleeding new, my lord, there's no meat like 'em. (1.2.76–9)

But it is Timon himself, of course, who is most readily consumed by his would-be friends, who eagerly dine on his abundant generosity. Alcibiades introduces this theme when he first greets Timon, exclaiming that he 'feed[s] / Most hungrily on your sight' (1.1.258–9); after Timon's fall, an on-looker notes that he 'never tasted Timon in my life', unlike the parasites who sustained themselves on his goodwill (3.2.80). Apemantus expresses this sentiment most directly, explicitly warning Timon of the danger posed by his flatterers:

> I scorn thy meat, 'twould choke me 'fore I should e'er flatter thee.
> O you gods, what a number of men eats Timon and he sees 'em

not! It grieves me to see so many dip their meat in one man's blood, and all the madness is, he cheers them up too. (1.2.38–42)

It is hard to be more direct than that – though Timon doesn't heed this warning, and it is not until his disgrace that he comes to understand that he is being devoured by his supposed friends. This realization begins before he leaves Athens, as he offers his flesh and blood up for his creditor's consumption; 'cut my heart in sums', he begs, 'Tell out my blood . . . Five thousand drops pays that' (3.4.90; 92; 94). It is when he embraces a life of misanthropy, however, that he finally appreciates the cannibalistic way that humans prey on humans, a way of relating that he recommends to the hungry thieves he meets in the forest: rather than feasting on 'beasts themselves, the birds and fishes', Timon commands that they 'must eat men' (4.3.420–1). Eating men becomes synonymous with thievery, an association that retroactively informs the exchange dynamics of Timon's previous relationships, and which shows his belated recognition of Apemantus's prescient warning. This realization about eating, in fact, is partly reflected in the hermit Timon's new rustic diet; as Keri Sanburn Behre observes, by abjuring 'any food but water and roots dug from the earth', Timon 'ensur[es] that there is less of his formerly well-fed body for the citizens of Athens to cannibalize'.[11] But while Timon gains insight into how his former self was consumed by others, his final state of being is largely one of self-consumption – he is 'in effect himself eaten up with misanthropy', his 'previous magnanimity and desire to feed replaced by the desire to poison others'.[12]

Images of compromised or corrupted eating thus pervade *Timon of Athens*, particularly in the first half of the play. In the second half, however, the thematic lexicon somewhat shifts, and begins drawing primary inspiration from a different disgust elicitor: that of disease. We see this begin in the mock-banquet of 3.7, the turning point of the play. After serving his guests the meal of stones – another instance of profane feeding – Timon begins his attack by reconceiving their flatteries as an object of disgusting defilement, a form of 'reeking villainy' that he 'washes . . . off' with the banquet's water (3.7.92; 91). But he immediately after hurls the rhetoric of illness at his guests, praying that 'of man and beast the infinite malady / Crust you quite o'er' (97–8). As Dawson and Minton note, these lines inaugurate 'Timon's obsession with disease', which only intensifies as the play continues. Maria Teresa Micaela Prendergast has elaborately explored how early modern invective was grounded in the 'nasty vocabulary of disease and excrement', and as Timon's speech becomes increasingly consumed by railing, images of disease and illness become commonplace.[13] When he next appears on stage, disease features prominently in his long curse of Athens:

> Plagues incident to men,
> Your potent and infectious fevers heap
> On Athens, ripe for stroke. Thou cold sciatica,
> Cripple our senators that their limbs may halt
> As lamely as their manners . . .
> . . .Itches, blains,
> Sow all th'Athenian bosoms, and their crop
> Be general leprosy; breath, infect breath,
> That their society, as their friendship, may
> Be merely poison. (4.1.21–5; 28–32)

Soon after, Timon begs the earth itself to deliver pestilence to Athens: 'O blessed breeding sun, draw from the earth / Rotten humidity, below thy sister's orb / Infect the air!' (4.3.1–3). It is in this speech that Timon begins digging in the soil – ostensibly to find food, but also, it seems likely, to aerate the poisonous agent he just summoned.[14] What he finds, of course, is gold – which he now sees as also tied to disease. Gold, he decides, 'embalms and spices / To th' April day again' she 'whom the spittle-house and ulcerous sores / Would cast the gorge at': in other words, the right price will make marriageable even the woman who is disgusting enough to make hospital wards and open wounds vomit (41–2; 40–1). This incredible image suggests the extent to which, in Timon's new outlook, thirst for wealth can override even our most natural responses to visceral horror – an indication of just how much his former perspective has changed.

In the early stages of his misanthropy, the diseases that Timon invokes are mostly generalized. But when he encounters Alcibiades and the prostitutes Timandra and Phrynia, his rhetoric shifts to become overwhelmingly focused on the toxic potential of venereal disease. As we'll see in Chapter 11, syphilis was a favourite theme of Shakespeare (particularly in his later plays), but *Timon* presents what is perhaps his most memorable concentration of poxy imagery.

While Timon still speaks of disease generally – bidding Alcibiades to be 'as a planetary plague when Jove / Will o'er some high-viced city hang his poison / In the sick air' (108–10) – he quickly fixates on the notion of sexual infection, telling the soldier that 'this fell whore of thine / Hath in her more destruction than thy sword' (62–3). As their conversation progresses, Timon becomes much more explicit, as he further imagines how a willing prostitute might serve as an excellent vector of disease:

> Be a whore still, they love thee not that use thee;
> Give them diseases, leaving with thee their lust.
> Make use of thy salt hours: season the slaves
> For tubs and baths, bring down rose-cheeked youth
> To the tub-fast and the diet. (83–7)

Timon repeats this construction not long after, his rhetoric continuing to intensify:

>   Be whores still,
> And he whose pious breath seeks to convert you,
> Be strong in whore, allure him, burn him up;
> Let your close fire predominate his smoke
> And be no turncoats. Yet may your pain-sick months
> Be quite contrary. And thatch your poor thin roofs
> With burdens of the dead – some that were hanged –
> No matter, wear them, betray with them. Whore still,
> Paint till a horse may mire upon your face.
> A pox of wrinkles! (139–48)

And it is his final salvo that is most elaborate, a passage worth quoting at length:

>   Consumptions sow
> In hollow bones of man, strike their sharp shins
> And mar men's spurring. Crack the lawyer's voice
> That he may never more false title plead
> Nor sound his quillets shrilly. Hoar the flamen
> That scolds against the quality of flesh
> And not believes himself. Down with the nose,
> Down with it flat, take the bridge quite away

Of him that, his particular to foresee,
Smells from the general weal. Make curled-pate ruffians bald
And let the unscarred braggarts of the war
Derive some pain from you. Plague all,
That your activity may defeat and quell
The source of all erection. (150–63)

Timon feverishly envisions the suffering of those inflicted with syphilis – not just the hollowing of the bones, but especially the facial deformities that make them physically grotesque. But it is his final curse, the command to render the world impotent, that is most revealing. Misjudging the rhythms of social intercourse is what brought Timon to his ruin – so he fantasizes about corrupting the barest form of intercourse there is. This is appropriate enough for a misanthrope, because the realization of this vision is a social order that is no longer populating humans to be hated: Timon would be finally alone, in a world where sex brings not life, but only death. Enlisting the prostitutes to this end is also appropriate, in the sense that (as Ross notes) Timon formerly was 'the whore of Athens, making himself available to anyone for the price of "friendship"'.[15] Timon thus turns to the rhetoric of venereal disease to get his revenge on his countrymen – and Timandra and Phrynia, propped by his newfound gold, are happy to comply.

In *Timon*, disease 'serves as a natural analogy for societal deterioration', and the play 'presents a radical reimagining of the epidemic as a necessarily violent form of civic restoration'.[16] This is the force of his final statement on earth, when he declares 'what is amiss, plague and infection mend' (5.2.106). Whether disease comes from divine intervention, natural perturbations or the transactions of a prostitute, there is no doubt that Timon seeks to inflict rot and trauma on the physical body, as a way of ironically mending the social body from which he feels rejected. Timon, in this sense, sees himself as agent of purgation – though he is perhaps better thought of as a necropurgative, in the sense that (for him) the only way to cleanse this social body is to empty it of all life. Though his exile is voluntary, he understands himself as functionally expelled from Athenian society; in seeking revenge, he thus fantasizes about emptying the city of its citizens, levelling the ground to start a new. The many instances of profane eating prepare us for this process of purgation, while the emphasis on sickness and disease realizes it. Both instances are underwritten by the thematics of disgust.

The story of Timon, then, is a story of expulsion, purgation and correction. I will suggest in the remainder of this chapter that this same basic dynamic equally governs (with some variation) the situations of Alcibiades and Apemantus. In each case, we see a series of social dynamics that reflect the actions of the human disgust system: offending matter is rejected from the public body, but that matter reimagines itself as a purgative that will, however perversely, ultimately offer a healing corrective. All three characters are involved in this process of social regulation, a thematic arc that is underpinned by the play's considerable investment in the visceral images of disgust.

* * *

Though he would see it differently, Timon's exile is fundamentally self-imposed: he chooses to reject the social order that he feels rejected him. The case of Alcibiades, however, is quite different, as he is formally banished from the gates of Athens. Critics have long puzzled over the Alcibiades narrative, which feels inadequately integrated into the main plot. But when we frame it in terms of a story about social purgation and social correction, I think there are ways to see its thematic linkage to other aspects of the play, via its alliance with disgust.

There seems little doubt that Alcibiades's banishment – for the apparent crime of advocating on behalf of a friend and fellow soldier – is meant to be seen as unjust. Much like the case of Timon, it is an example of severe civic ingratitude: Alcibiades has 'kept back their foes / While they have told their money and let out / Their coin upon large interests' (3.6.105–7). Anticipating what we will see in *Coriolanus*, the exiled soldier's service has only been repaid with 'captains' wounds', an indictment of the Senate's callousness and corruption (110). But the specific *Athenian* context of Alcibiades's banishment must be considered, for his exile is informed by early modern understandings of Athens as a corrupt city. Decades ago, Robert S. Miola established the importance of *Timon*'s Athenian locale; the play, he convincingly argues, 'exhibits many of the vices that Shakespeare's contemporaries, steeped in Athenian history and legend from earliest school days, associated with Athens'.[17] Unlike

A Midsummer Night's Dream, which presents a vision of 'the romanticized city under the earlier rule of Theseus', *Timon* depicts what Plutarch calls the 'foolish appetites and corrupt humors' of the people who inhabited fifth-century Athens.[18] The 'canckred natures of the *Atheniens'* was proverbial among classical authorities, and popular early modern texts like Erasmus's *Apothegms* followed suit in recording 'the moste corrupte maners of the *Atheniens*'.[19]

Unsurprisingly, many of the vices embraced by the characters of *Timon* are condemned in this contemporary discourse. According to a translation of Claudius Aelianus – which provided ample disapproving commentary on the city – Athens was a place known for 'delicate Dinners, sumptuous Suppers, and prodigall banqueting'.[20] Indeed, gustatory excess was a subject of the city's great orators: Isocrates advised to 'refraine thy self from banketing and feasting', while Demosthenes lamented that his fellow Athenians 'bestowe [their] money vpon feastes & games'.[21] But Athenian indulgence wasn't only about culinary exploits – Aelianus equally associates the city with 'lauishing of substaunce, vnthrifty & wastfull spending, voluptousnes of life, & palpable sensualitie'.[22] Even more relevant to the moral heart of *Timon* is Athens's reputation as home to 'Sycophants, false accusers, carrytales, and yll disposed persons', as well as 'Pickthanks, Clawbackes, and Flatterers, of whom *Athens* nourished a great number, for the Citie was naturally addicted to harbour and lodge such Helhounds'.[23] And, most suggestively of all for our current discussion, at times the corruption of the Athenians was figured specifically in terms of disgust elicitors: contrasting the virtuous Socrates to his degenerate countrymen, Aelianus suggests that there was 'a vniuersall infection [by which] the *Athenians* were disseased one by another lyke scabby and rotten sheepe', while in Lyly's *Campaspe* (1584), Diogenes denounces the 'wicked and beewtiched Atheneans, whose bodies make the earth to groane, and whose breathes infect the aire with stench'.[24]

For both classical and early modern commentators, Athenian decadence and corruption was intimately connected to the way in which the city was governed: that is, its infamous democracy. As Cesare Cuttica and Markku Peltonen have recently observed, 'most early modern authors who discussed democracy emphasised its negative character,' and the current 'historiographical consensus asserts that in the early modern period democracy was reputed to be the worst form of government'.[25] Much of this owes to the influence of Aristotle, whose views were known through translations and commentaries like Louis Le Roy's French edition of the *Politics*, published in English in 1598.[26] In this text, readers would have found 'a Democraty or popular state' described as 'that where there is nothing but liberty and disorder in the people, [who are] exceeded and ouerflowed in all liberty without feare of Magistrates or obseruance of lawes'.[27] Because 'the people, of their owne Nature . . . are insolent and excessiue in all liberty and licence', the fundamental premise of democracy simply did not make sense to many early modern thinkers.[28] 'Who is he', an anonymous editor asks, 'that perceiueth not at first sight, that among men there are some, who haue lesse iudgement then brute beasts'; those 'that seeke after equality', it follows, 'would haue authoritie giuen to furious, ignorant, and insensible Men, as well as to the wise, and best vnderstanding'.[29] Democracy, then, was inherently suspect, and ancient Athens was history's most famous democracy. This viewpoint is evident in the words of later writers like Marchamont Nedham, who notes that when Athens 'erected a pure *Democracy, or Government by the people*', they were 'so insolent, that no Integrity, no good desert was able to preserve the estate of any such as had born any great Office, longer then by flattering the rascall Multitude'.[30] Aristotle's *Politics* similarly maintained that 'the Athenian people was so disordered and let loose to all vnbridled libertie, that they were almost past all shame and obedience to their lawes or Magistrates and consequently depriued of all mutuall amitie and familiaritie, which men liuing vnder one state should haue'.[31] Accordingly, Athenian democracy was notorious for the shameful way it treated its most virtuous citizens, as catalogued by *The Treasurie of Auncient and Moderne Times* (1613): '*Athens* expulsed iust *Aristides: Themistocles* died in exile; *Miltiades* in Prison; *Socrates* was put to death; and *Phocion*, the most intire and vertuous man of his age . . . was condemned to death, with forty other famous men, onely because they were his friends.'[32]

The mention here of Aristides's expulsion is particularly important, because one specific element of Athenian democracy has a special relevance for *Timon*, given the saga of Alcibiades: the 'straunge maner of exile vsed in Athens', where 'the most honourable and worthiest personages were oftentymes banished, without any offence, or faulte at all committed'.[33] Peltonen notes that "for Aristotle, *ostrakismos* had been a central element in democracy', and early modern theorists found the practice of banishment amply discussed by classical authorities.[34] For most, this custom exemplified the unruly excesses of Athenian democracy, in the sense that it was motivated not by sound political principles, but by personal animus:

> This kinde of banishment called Ostracisme, or Exostracisme, was not a punishment ordained for anie crime or offence, but as some say, to giue vnto it an honest vizard, it was inuented onely for an abating and weakening of too great authority, and power too excessiue for a popular state: but in verie deede, it was no other thing bit a deuise to content and asswage gentlie and fauourablie the enuy which the people conceiued against some particular person: which enuie did not disgorge it self in anie vnrecouerable euill against him whose greatnesse displeased them.[35]

Plutarch similarly describes this 'banishment by *Ostracismon*', noting that the 'manner & custome of this kynde of banishment was for a time to banish out of their cittie such a one, as seemed to haue great authoritie and credit in the cittie: and that was, rather to satisfie their enuie, then for to remedy their feare'.[36] For many early modern thinkers, the banishment of Alcibiades in *Timon* would thus be understood as the output of a regulatory system that was fundamentally broken – one that reflected the shifting whims of the multitude.

In regulating both the literal boundaries of the city and the behaviours permitted within them, the form of banishment wielded by the Athenian democracy can be seen as a kind of disgust system – though one that many would have understood as fatally flawed. The action of this system results in Alcibiades being, in essence, excreted from the city as socially undesirable – and this abject status aligns him with the rest of the characters who find themselves outside the walls of Athens. When thinking of this band of exiles, it is valuable to consider how an early modern audience would have understood the kinds of people who find themselves displaced from the city in *Timon*: prostitutes, thieves and seditious private soldiers. Adam Hansen importantly draws our attention to this set of characters, which he deems the 'others' of the play – those 'vagrants and vagabonds' that exist in the social margins of Athens, and that recall similar categories of people that existed in the margins of early modern London.[37] Contemporary social discourse differentiated between those 'impotent persons not able to releeue themselues with their labor' and the 'idle poor', which included vagrants like 'the Theefe, the Rogue, the Strumpet, the sturdy Beggar, the Filcher, the Couzener, Cut-purse, and such like'; it is members of this second category, comprising what modern scholars sometimes call London's 'underworld', who populate the wilderness in *Timon of Athens*.[38]

These characters emerge from the robust discourse of early modern vagrancy – a discourse that captivated many of Shakespeare's contemporaries, evidenced not only by the proliferation of 'rogue' and 'cony-catching' literature in the period but also by the voluminous legislation that was generated in response to it. The data is remarkable: according to the research of J. Thomas Kelly, England passed 14 statutes and released over 200 royal proclamations concerning vagrancy during Shakespeare's life alone.[39] As modern historians of poverty have persuasively argued, Renaissance lawmakers actually policed the problem with a furore that far exceeded its actual status as a social issue; Linda Woodbridge notes that 'it seems clear from hindsight that early modern opinion-setters exaggerated . . . the threat that vagrancy and beggars posed', and William C. Carroll agrees that 'Tudor authorities feared vagrants far out of proportion to their actual menace'.[40] But whatever the reality, there is no doubt that early modern England (and Europe more generally) was pre-eminently concerned with this feature of urban life, which 'leading reformers, political figures, and eminent literary men of the time' considered to be 'the chief evil of their age'.[41]

And those on the edges of early modern society – vagrants, rogues, prostitutes, criminals and other members of the London underworld – were often portrayed in terms of disgust elicitors, indicating their exclusion from the proper boundaries of the social body. There is ample evidence in contemporary accounts. The Reverend Robert Sanderson, for example, sees England's '*Rogues* and vagrant towns-end *Beggars*' as the 'very scabs, and filth and vermine of the *Common-wealth*'; Richard Johnson calls society's undesirables the 'fouler matter' and 'wounds of a Common-wealth', while Samuel Rid deems them 'pestiferous carbuncles in the commonwealth'.[42] It is telling how such expressions consistently rely on the notion of an embodied English commonwealth: the country is envisioned as a physical body, and people dwelling in the urban margins are envisioned as the signs of degradation that make that physical body disgusting. Robert Greene goes further, dismissing them as the waste of the social body: rogues and vagrants are both 'base excrements of dishonesty' and the 'excremental reuersion of sin'.[43] Because a society's undesirables have always been 'rhetorically associated with filth and excrement', Woodbridge notes that in early modern England 'cleansing a city of filthy vagrants' entailed 'pushing others ... outside of respectable society, either literally (through roundups and expulsions) or verbally (through jests or excremental invective)' – accordingly, vagrants became 'public enemies', in the sense that 'they were naturally dirty or endowed with filth by the imaginings of the respectable'.[44] Indeed, at times the purgation of early modern London's social body was literalized as an actual (disgust-like) expulsion from the city; in the year of Shakespeare's birth, for example, Queen Mary did 'charge and command all . . . vagabonds and other loitering, idle persons, as well Englishmen as strangers of whatever nation, being masterless and having none entertainment . . . to depart from the said cities of London and Westminster and the suburbs and places adjoining'.[45] Because of this, it follows that the thieves and prostitutes who Alcibiades joins beyond Athens's walls reflect a much larger mechanism of social control in early modern England, a form of social control that recalls the regulatory function of disgust.

It is also important to remember, however, that there is another category of persons who join this outsider community: Alcibiades's displaced soldiers. Claire S. Schen notes the 'liminal status of war veterans' in the early modern period, who were 'servants of the state yet potentially unruly and dangerous men'; as Linda Bradley Salamon explains, 'former soldiers who returned from battles foreign or civil were construed as a transgressive presence on the margins of public life: tramping the roadways, sleeping rough, foraging for their daily needs by any available means, indulging in petty vice'.[46] Accordingly, veterans and vagabonds were often aligned in the period, and it was hard to determine the boundaries between them. Contemporary writings on the subject affirmed that one type of rogue 'goeth wyth a weapon to seeke seruice, saying he hath bene a Seruitor in the wars, and beggeth for his reliefe' – but 'his chiefest trade is to robbe poore wayfaring men and market women'.[47] This thinking is reflected in a royal proclamation from 1591, which warns that among the 'sundry sorts of base people' are those 'coloring their wandering by the name of soldiers returned from the war'.[48] (Indeed, when the thieves meet Timon in the forest, they first declare that they are 'soldiers, not thieves' [4.3.409].) Furthermore, the linkage between veterans and social pariahs also worked in the other direction, as some early modern commentators believed that foreign military service was the best way to expel undesirables from society. 'There is a certain waste of the people for whome there is no vse, but warre,' claims a famous passage in Nashe's *Pierce Penilesse* – and because the state 'cannot exhale all these corrupt excrements', it is better that they have 'haue . . . seruice abroad' so they do not 'make mutinies at home'.[49] This sentiment is echoed in a pamphlet by the soldier Barnabe Rich, again in the explicit language of disgust: here, a constable speaking of 'Rogues, Wagabonds, and other like excrements of the Commonwealth' thinks it 'a happie riddance to purge the Countrey of that infection . . . by sending them to warrs'.[50] (We will return to this idea later in our discussion of *Coriolanus*.) Many in Shakespeare and Middleton's original audience, then, would see Alcibiades's soldiers – veterans of foreign wars who now populate a seditious private army – as naturally aligned with the other marginal figures who visit Timon in the wilderness. *Timon of Athens*, Hansen argues, thus 'insist[s] upon connections between dislocated veterans, vagabond and vagrants, and the authorities and locations that deny them their humanity and a place in the city'.[51]

The displaced Alcibiades finds himself exiled with the other excrements of society – and indeed, it seems that he is the de facto leader of this new pseudo-community. As Hansen observes, these allegedly 'useless, superfluous dregs of society' are, in fact, a 'growth, however hybrid or excrescent, from that society' – and though expelled, they demand not to be forgotten.[52] This is because, in leading his troops back against Athens, Alcibiades reverses the symbolic trajectory of his banishment, rejecting his identity as purged and instead becoming the purgative – one whose sword will cleanse Athens of its corrupted matter. As noted earlier, Timon sees Alcibiades as a corrective force, one in whose brutal regime he might take pleasure; 'let not thy sword skip one', he declares, 'pity not honoured age for his white beard', nor let 'the virgin's cheek / Make soft thy trenchant sword' (4.3.110–11; 114–15). Ironically enough, it is the destructive presence of Alcibiades that occasions a potential reconciliation of Timon and Athens, as the senators offer him 'absolute power' to aid in the city's defence – but he, of course, will have none of it (5.2.47), and the city finds itself without a protector. This leaves Alcibiades in total control, as Athens has no recourse but to beg for mercy. In a telling moment, a senator acknowledges the city's corruption, but hopes that their invader will be surgical in its removal:

> Then, dear countryman,
> Bring in thy ranks but leave without thy rage;
> Spare thy Athenian cradle and those kin
> Which in the bluster of thy wrath must fall
> With those that have offended; like a shepherd,
> Approach the fold and cull th'infected forth,
> But kill not all together. (5.5.38–44)

Timon would have scoffed at this proposition, seeing all of Athens as terminally infected. But Alcibiades is more measured, and declares that only 'those enemies of Timon's and mine own / Whom you yourselves shall set out for reproof / Fall, and no more' (56–8). Alcibiades is thus reintegrated into Athens, purging its worse corruption in the process. This is indicated finally in the play's last lines, as he declares 'make war breed peace, make peace stint war, make each / Prescribe to other, as each other's leech' (81–2). *Timon* concludes with an image of medical purgation, as war and peace mutually work to correct the many faults of Athenian social order.

The Alcibiades narrative tells how a citizen expelled from Athens marshals an army of social excrements and becomes the figure who cleanses the same city of its rampant infection. Timon, we have seen, extensively deploys the rhetoric of disgust in his corrective prophecies and excremental invective; Alcibiades's actions literalize the disgust system, by being first ejected from the social body as a dangerous substance, and then being reintegrated into it as a healing purgative. To conclude this chapter, I will consider the case of the philosopher Apemantus, a figure who, like Timon and Alcibiades, relates to themes of exile and social correction. In this sense, Apemantus similarly engages the discourse of disgust – though once again, it depends on situating him in his early modern context.

* * *

An early modern playwright would have encountered the figure of Apemantus in Plutarch's account of Timon; in this source, it is noted that '*Timon* sometimes would haue *Apemantus* in his companie, bicause he was much like to his nature & condicions, and also followed him in maner of life'.[53] But Shakespeare and Middleton greatly expand his significance in their play, by presenting Apemantus as an archetypal Cynic philosopher. This is indicated not only by his attitudes and his behaviours but also by verbal shorthand; drawing upon a long-standing association, Apemantus is routinely referred to as a *dog* throughout the play, recalling contemporary remarks on the 'Cynick dogge' or 'dogged Cynick'.[54] The most famous Cynic philosopher, of course, was the 'dogged *Diogenes*', and scholars of *Timon* have valuably shown how fabled lore about Diogenes informs the characterization of Apemantus.[55] Though Diogenes left no writings of his own, he was well known in the early modern period through the anecdotes preserved by other classical authors, which found their way into a variety of sixteenth- and early-seventeenth-century English texts that centre the philosopher.[56] It seems that early modern authors 'were fascinated by the legendary figure of Diogenes', presenting him 'variously by a "low view" of him as a scurrilous wit, a jester, an ill-tempered brute, or by a "high view" that perceived him as a serious philosopher whose eccentric behavior exemplified his admirable moral stance'.[57] As a biting satirist whose bare, humble lifestyle exposed the pretensions of his fellow Athenians, Diogenes provided a model for the churlish philosopher Apemantus, who both resembles and qualifies the titular character's final state of misanthropy. As we will see more herein, there was in fact early modern precedent for seeing Diogenes and Timon in relation to one another – as in the pamphlet that writes of men who are 'a *Timon* by nature, or a *Diogenes* by disposition' – and it seems clear that both Diogenes and the discourse of Cynicism left their mark on the thematics and characterization of *Timon*.[58]

But while modern scholars have explored this intellectual context of *Timon*, they have not emphasized a particular aspect of Cynic philosophy that bares heavily on our discussion of the play: the legendary shamelessness of Diogenes and his disciples. As Derek Krueger explains, the 'portrayal of Diogenes that emerges from ancient texts reveals that shamelessness (*anaideia*) was an integral component of Cynic lore'; it thus became common understanding that 'the Sect of the Cynicks . . . were shameless of their shame', and Diogenes himself allegedly proclaimed that 'he was no meete or apte disciple for philosophie, that could not contemne and shake of folishe shame'.[59] For our current purposes, the most important fact is that the historical tradition emphasizing this shamelessness is distinctly explicit: ancient texts readily record how Diogenes 'performed inevitable activities, such as farting, urinating, ejaculating, and defecating, normally carried out in the privacy of the home, in full view'.[60] Early modern culture, Paster has influentially shown, 'increasingly sought to regulate and regularize a subject's experience of his/her own body and relations with the bodies of others'; such 'changes in the canons of bodily propriety' greatly impacted the social significance of affects like embarrassment and shame, which functioned in a regulatory and disciplinary capacity.[61] It is notable, then, that Diogenes was known as 'a Philosopher, and (as it wer) a preacher of nature', and was frequently said to have affirmed that he 'obeyed nature onely' and knew 'no other law then the law of nature'.[62] Nature is the key here, because the Cynic celebration of shocking and shameful behaviour was 'cover[ed] with a pretext of Nature', via their assertion 'that all natural actions may be done in the face of the Sun'.[63] Diogenes reached this conclusion with some simple logic, recorded by Erasmus in his collection of anecdotes about the philosopher:

> Whatsoeuer thing wer not of it selfe vnhonest, he affirmed not to be vnhonest in open presence, or in the face of all the worlde neither. Whereupon he made a reason or argument in this maner & forme. If to dyne be not a naughtie or euil thing, then to dyne abrode in the open streate is not euill neither, but to dyne is no pointe of naughtinesse, Ergo, to dyne in the mids of the street is no euill thing neither.[64]

For Diogenes, 'to ease the body by going to stoole, or to make water, or one to compaignie with his wyfe, or a body to turne himself naked out of al his clothes . . . in the open strete is no point of naughtinesse neither', because such natural processes weren't shameful in their own right. Unsurprisingly, this argument was frequently unconvincing – indeed, Erasmus's English translator Nicolas Udall firmly rejects it, noting that 'vertuous and weldisposed persones loue honestee & shamefastnesse eueryhwere'. And while this did not, as we saw earlier, stop a segment of Renaissance thinkers from embracing Cynic thought, the larger point concerns the cultural representation of Diogenes in the period: by invoking the lineage of the infamous philosopher in *Timon*, Shakespeare and Middleton invite into their play the spectre of a man known to disgustingly destabilize social conventions through a willingness 'to openly commit filthinesse even in the streets'.[65]

And early modern commentary on Diogenes and Cynicism didn't simply speak abstractly about this filthiness: the anecdotes that were circulated were quite explicit. In the first place, Diogenes was said to be 'a verie slouen, and one that cared for no clenlinesse'; in one repeated story, he gleefully trampled 'his beastly and durty feet' on Plato's carpets, exclaiming that he 'tread upon *Platoes* pride'.[66] But commentators mostly emphasized his willingness to perform bodily functions openly among his fellow Athenians – because, in terms of communal spaces, 'the thing that was publike, he enterpreted to be made and ordeined for him also particularely'.[67] On one occasion, for example, the philosopher was invited as a guest to a sumptuous house: 'Diogenes, seeking where to spit, and finding all corners so neate and cleane, and the man so homely and vnhandsome, he spit on the good man himselfe, saying that he was the fowlest, and therfore the meetest place in the house to receaue such excrements.'[68] Another dinner party provides an even more outrageous anecdote:

> As it fortuned Diogenes to be present . . . at a dyner, the companie calling him doggue, cast bones to him in derision, in consideration that thesame is a thing customably vsed to be doen to doggues. But he, in departing from the company, pissed vppon euery of the geastes that sate at the table, behind at their backes, signifiyng the same also to be one other propertee belonging to doggues.[69]

It's no wonder that the association of Diogenes and dogs endured long after his death. What's more, another classical legend (recorded by Dio Chrysostom) recalls how Diogenes, after giving a well-received public oration, 'ceased speaking and, squatting on the ground, performed an indecent act, whereat the crowd straightway scorned him and called him crazy'.[70] Public defecation may have been a tad too scurrilous for early modern English writers, as I've yet to find one that explicitly recounts this particular act – but, as we saw above, Udall on multiple occasions notes that Diogenes's philosophical convictions were such that he 'might haue defended hymselfe if he did his easemente . . . in the open streate', a hypothetical suggestion that perhaps implies (to savvy readers) that Diogenes was alleged to have done precisely that.[71]

Finally, openness towards sexual behaviour – another aspect of natural biological functioning – was equally part of Cynic lore. Diogenes apparently had no qualms about sleeping with prostitutes in public view; 'Diogenes the Cynick', it was said, 'had no more shame in this action, then to say he was planting a man, as if he would say, that it should bee as lawfull to plant publikely Men, as Trees.'[72] But it was his tendency to masturbate in public that was particularly recounted in the early modern period: in the most famous story, Diogenes, after 'abusing himselfe, by forcing his nature to passe from him in the open street', said to onlookers, 'Oh, that I could chase hunger as well from my belly.'[73] Montaigne equally speaks of '*Diogenes,* in sight of all, exercising his Maisterbation', Marston jokes about 'Cynick friction' and a contemporary French dictionary translates the euphemism 'faire le sucré' as 'to frig; to wriggle; to commit Diogenes his sinne'.[74] There are few bodily functions, then, that Diogenes does not anecdotally perform under the open sky, and this aspect of his character and philosophy was carried through to the early modern period. To be sure, Hugh Roberts notes that 'there is a sense . . . in which the scandalous antics of the Cynics could never be [truly] commonplace, since they pose too great a threat to civilized values' – but, as these paragraphs indicate, the early modern discourse of cynicism was well aware of Diogenes's rather revolting inclinations.[75]

It would have been impossible, I think, for Shakespeare and Middleton to be unaware of these associations between cynicism and filthy shamelessness, which would have been equally apparent to many in their original audience. And it should be clear to us how this linkage activates the thematics of disgust, in the sense that cynic shamelessness leveraged bodily revulsion into a form of social critique. Roberts elaborates:

> Shamelessness is one of Diogenes' most devastating heuristic strategies for shocking his contemporaries into re-evaluating social norms. By making his body the centre of attention, Diogenes constantly reminds his audience of the physical constraints of their existence. . . . Since all people are embodied, jokes or obscenity

that derive from the body are sure-fire subversive techniques. Diogenes' authority or license comes from his performative use of his body, which simultaneously demonstrates his exemption from civilized values and his commitment to nature. The danger of Diogenes' performance derives from the inevitable association of bodily control with social control. The Cynics blur the boundaries of the body by focusing their audience's attention on the fluids and gases that pass from and between bodies.[76]

By forcing their fellow citizens to experience the disgusting features of their natural body, Cynics thus challenged the very foundation of social convention itself. In this sense, they stood in opposition to the human disgust system, by emphasizing freedom, rather than control – but they leverage their onlookers' disgust to achieve their philosophical aims.

Timon of Athens doesn't emphasize the vulgar extremities of Cynic shamelessness, which would be tonally incongruous with the rest of the play. But there is little doubt that many in Shakespeare and Middleton's audience would associate Apemantus's cynicism with the breaking of social taboos that govern bodily comportment, as this was a key component of the widely circulated lore about Diogenes. I thus suggest that the shock and revulsion occasioned by the exposed Cynic body is a latent component of *Timon*'s engagement with the discourse of disgust, reinforcing the play's more direct exploration of the theme. What we do get explicitly, however, is plenty that establishes Apemantus as a man apart from the mainstream of Athenian civic life – and in this sense, he is both foreign matter in the urban centre of the playworld and, through his savage indictment of his fellow citizens, an agent of social purgation.

I have said earlier that the lifestyle of Apemantus both anticipates and qualifies Timon's ultimate misanthropy, and it's worth pausing for a moment to consider the difference between the two: though they both voluntarily separate themselves from Athenian corruption, Timon's self-exile is absolute, uncompromising and physically literal, while Apemantus detaches himself philosophically from the customs and corruptions of his countrymen, but is more than willing to remain in the city as a social irritant. Detachment is indeed a key word, because the extremity of Timon's hatred for mankind reveals an intense emotional investment that is markedly different from the cooler, more distanced barbs of cynic critique. Montaigne, in fact, says exactly this when contrasting the outlooks of Timon and Diogenes:

> *Diogenes,* who did nothing but triflle, toy, and dally with himselfe, in rumbling and rowling of his tub... was a more sharpe, a more bitter, and a more stinging judge [than] *Timon,* surnamed the hater of all mankinde. For looke what a man hateth, the same thing he takes to hart. *Timon* wisht all evill might light on-vs; He was passionate in desiring our ruine. He shunned and loathed our conversation as dangerous and wicked; and of a depraved nature: Whereas the other so little regarde vs, that wee could neither trouble nor alter him by our contagion.[77]

The word *contagion* here is crucial: Diogenes (and thus Apemantus) did see Athenians as morally sick, but he was not endangered by their sickness – instead, he was the amused physician, the administrator of a necessary social purgative. Despite their superficial similarity, this is in strong contrast to Timon, who is consumed by malice and rancour. While the sting of Apemantus is corrective, the sting of Timon is poisonous – not only to his would-be targets but also to himself. Indeed, the difference between them is the key theme of their encounter in the forest, as Apemantus had heard 'men report / Thou dost affect my manners' (4.3.197–8).[78] He warns Timon to 'not assume my likeness' nor 'shame . . . these woods / By putting on the cunning of a carper' – because the newly minted misanthrope, he suggests, had not come to hate man honourably (217; 207–8). 'If', the philosopher declares, 'thou didst put this sour cold habit on / To castigate thy pride, 'twere well; but thou / Dost it enforcedly'; for Apemantus, there is a clear distinction between adopting disdain as a considered principle of conviction and having it thrust upon him by ruined fortune (238–40). Timon impotently attempts to reverse this attack, by claiming that Apemantus was never given cause for his cynicism – but the difference between his own fierce choler and his rival's 'icy precepts' only becomes more pointed (257).

But the key to understanding Apemantus comes not in his final interactions with Timon, but rather in his behaviour during the play's first half, when peddling his philosophical wares within Athens. It is 'only in the city', notes Peter Sloterdijk, that 'the figure of the cynic [can] crystallize in its full sharpness', because cynicism draws its power from being in proximity to the objects of its critique.[79] The whole point, of course, is that cynics like Diogenes and Apemantus claim exemption from the social order in which they willingly embed themselves; though Apemantus is critiqued by Athenians for being 'opposite to humanity', this characterization accurately reflects his own sense of himself as one who has not been corrupted by the conventions of social intercourse (1.1.280). Apemantus makes clear that he sees all the inhabitants of Athens as compromised – hence his claims that it has 'become a forest of beasts' (4.3.347), and that he can 'knock out an honest Athenian's brains' without fear of legal repercussion (1.1.195). He thus positions himself as an outsider, but (as his behaviour makes clear) as one that is not *too* outside. This manifests most obviously in his decision not to turn down the invitation to Timon's banquet, but to attend it with an ironic detachment that undermines and indicts the sincere guests – appropriately enough, since the sincere guests only attend for the purpose of flattery. Sequestered at a table of his own, he skewers the event by opining his own view of degraded humanity in his famous mock grace:

> Immortal gods, I crave no pelf,
> I pray for no man but myself;
> Grant I may never prove so fond
> To trust man on his oath or bond,
> Or a harlot for her weeping,
> Or a dog that seems a-sleeping,
> Or a keeper with my freedom,
> Or my friends if I should need 'em,
> Amen. So fall to't.
> Rich men sin and I eat root. (1.2.61–71)

Apemantus here deflates everything on which Timon's banquet is premised: wealth, decadent food, and the ostensible security provided by the bonds of social trust. It is no surprise, then, that the philosopher can be described as one who 'only delights in making himself loathed'; his entire identity is bound in being a foreign pathogen in the social body, the social body that he is tasked with purging.[80] It thus makes perfect sense when Apemantus, being welcomed at Timon's house, indicates that 'you shall not make me welcome - / I come to have thee thrust me out of doors' – he comes to the party specifically for the purpose of being such a disruption that he is expelled from it (1.2.24–5).

Disgust, I have argued in previous chapters, is a regulatory system designed to cleanse both the physical and social body. In *Timon of Athens*, the three central characters each enact this process, both as figures who are expelled from the social order (either voluntarily or involuntarily) and as figures who come to understand themselves as social purgatives. Indeed, these dual identities reflect the very nature of medical purgation, in the sense that the curing remedy is, by the violence it induces, equally ejected alongside the offending matter that it relieves. It is thus no surprise that *Timon* is overladen with images of disgust – cannibalism, vomit, plague, syphilis – and these striking poetic features are in line with the play's larger structural themes, which I see is intimately bound to the dynamics of revulsion. I readily acknowledge, with so many other critics, that the major strands of *Timon* align somewhat roughly with one another – but when we see the play's components in terms of disgust, it may be possible to reveal an affective unity that would otherwise go unnoticed.

5

Disease disgust

In his time of rage, we have just seen, Timon of Athens vents his misanthropy with the language of sickness: revolting images of both syphilis and plague increasingly shape the utter disgust that he feels for his fellow humans. This is quite apt, because as noted in Chapter 1, there is a consensus among scientists – even scientists who view the emotion quite differently – that the human disgust system, in both origin and its subsequent evolutions, is tied to pathogen avoidance behaviours. Tybur's evolutionary adaptationist model, it will be recalled, attributes almost all disgust responses to pathogen avoidance, and it is hard to ignore how many prototypical disgust elicitors – spoiled foods, bodily fluids, animals, bad hygiene, corpses, sexual acts, contact with strangers – are potential vectors of dangerous pathogen transmission. As a (or perhaps *the*) primary mechanism of disease avoidance, disgust is thus understood as quite essential to the survival of the human species: it has been called 'arguably the most important' element in the entire 'repertoire of behaviors that function to minimize contact with pathogens'.[1]

Infectious disease, we saw earlier, is likely the greatest cause of death in human history, so it is not surprising that evolutionary pressures have developed behavioural systems to help contend with the fact that our species, throughout its existence, has faced the constant threat of dangerous pathogens.[2] Because of the need to avoid such noxious substances, some scientists theorize that we have evolved a *behavioural immune system* (BIS), a mechanism that 'serves as an organism's first crude line of defence against potentially harmful parasites and pathogens'.[3] The human BIS is 'triggered by the perception of specific kinds of stimuli' that might suggest the presence of dangerous pathogens (such as 'infected food, objects, or people'); when such stimuli are detected, 'there ensues the automatic activation of the specific emotions and cognitions (e.g. disgust; automatic inferences about disease-connoting traits) that facilitate functional behavior reactions (e.g., avoidance, social exclusion)'.[4] As Mark Schaller and Justin H. Park note, 'sensory cues that most clearly connote proximity to infectious pathogens are especially likely to arouse disgust,' while disgust is also 'evoked by behaviors that violate normative expectations in behavioral domains that are functionally associated with disease transmission (e.g. food preparation, personal hygiene, sexual interaction)'.[5] Accordingly, theorists suggest that 'the emotional experience of disgust is the affective signature of the behavioral immune system' – and, in fact, it is further said that 'pathogen disgust and the behavioral immune system are indeed functionally and computationally the same'.[6]

What's more, the BIS theory helps account for the extraordinary range of things that elicit disgust – including why we're so often disgusted by objects that pose no actual danger. Because 'the cost of mistakenly responding to a potential threat is less than the cost of ignoring it', threat detection systems like the BIS inevitably produce many false positives and are necessarily 'hypervigilant'.[7] Scientists explain why 'evolved systems that regulate protective responses often give rise to false alarms and apparently excessive responses' via the so-called Smoke Detector Principle, which notes that 'false alarms from the body's protective systems are like smoke detector alarms – frequent minor annoyances that are necessary to avoid possible catastrophes'.[8] Just as false alarms are much preferable to the smoke detector failing to recognize a genuine fire, systems like the BIS promote 'protective responses whose costs tend to be small relative to possible catastrophic costs if no response is expressed when a danger is present'; thus, in actuality, 'false alarms or excessive responses are expected from optimal regulation systems.' In terms of pathogen-detection mechanisms, Park and colleagues explain, 'the following errors are possible':

> perceiving a [disgust elicitor] to be a pathogen carrier (false positive) and perceiving a pathogen carrier to be healthy (false negative). The costs associated with these two errors are asymmetrical. In this domain, false negatives impose substantially greater fitness costs than false positives; consequently, the

inferential mechanisms are likely to be biased toward minimizing false negatives.[9]

There is good reason, then, that the disgust system can activate such an oversized response – including ones, like my own traumatic experience with that unmentionable item of food, that can fundamentally alter subsequent behaviour. The hair-trigger reactivity of the disgust system is thus an evolutionary safeguard designed to keep us alive – but, as we'll see in chapters to come, this hypervigilance often has extremely harmful consequences in other domains, especially when it comes to social interactions. But these disgust mechanisms, however flawed, are what we have, and so much of their activity revolves around the working of disease.

Given the centrality of disease to human life, it's unsurprising that a playwright like Shakespeare showed considerable interest in its literary potential. A full-length book could hardly begin to account for Shakespeare's complete engagement with the rhetoric and thematics of disease, so the idea of doing it in a couple of pages is ludicrous. Still, it's possible to outline a few areas of concern. Decades ago, David M. Bergeron offered an account of broad tendencies in the plays:

> One of the imagery and thematic threads that run throughout Shakespeare's drama is sickness; in the tragedies illness is not susceptible to cure, while typically in the comedies a healing agent or device makes all whole. The concrete, physical examples of sickness are subsumed in the larger, metaphorical pattern which allows the dramatist to construct the play-world either with spiritual desease [*sic*] and corruption (tragedy) or with graceful healing and reconciliation (comedy). The remedies offered in tragedy are ineffective, while in comedy they are efficacious.[10]

More recently, there has been no shortage of scholarship on Shakespeare's engagement with early modern medical discourse, with particular emphasis on how it is used 'to manage and discipline the body-politic'.[11] But in terms of our current focus, disease is a concept that activates notions of both physical and moral corruption, and thus belongs squarely to the realm of disgust – as William Spates puts it, in early modern English thought there was 'a complex network of associations that linked disease, excretion, decay, death, and sin'.[12]

We've already explored *Timon*'s investment in the rhetoric of illness; in coming chapters, we'll see how disease imagery is prominently linked to disgust in *Coriolanus* and *Hamlet*. (It has a lesser, but notable presence in *Titus* and *Othello*.[13]) But there's much more that can be said about the topic, even in a short space. Contagion features heavily in the affective discourse of the time, via the commonly held belief that (as *Caesar's* Antony puts it) 'passion . . . is catching' (3.1.282); recent scholarship has revealed the vital linkage between theatricality and notions of contagion, in the sense that 'the playhouse [is] a location for representing and playing out various kinds of contagious operations'.[14] Darryl Chalk, in fact, reminds us that antitheatrical discourse in the period often thought of theatre in terms of noxious infection: John Rainolds, for example, in *Th' Overthrow of Stage-Playes* (1599), sets forth how 'the maners of all spectators commonlie are hazarded by the contagion of theatricall sights', and describes how the 'venome and poyson' of acting 'goeth about to spred it selfe abroad through more partes of your body . . . by meanes that you likewise instill the same humour . . . into the rest of all your players, their teachers and instructors, and in conclusion your whole house'.[15] (Julia D. Staykova, in fact, locates 'the language of disease at the rhetorical centre of the antitheatrical controversy'.[16]) This rhetoric recalls what we've seen in Timon's use of plague-based invective, and scholars have also more generally considered how the lived realities of early modern plague time manifest in Shakespeare's work; most notably for our present discussion, Shakespeare features throughout Nat Wayne Hardy's unpublished dissertation, which explores 'the satirical anatomy of pestilence and the satiric disgust of plague in early modern London'.[17] The plague obviously makes its mark in Shakespeare – locally, as when Lear denounces Goneril as 'a boil . . . a plague-sore, or embossed carbuncle / In my corrupted blood' (2.2.418–19), or more broadly as in *Romeo and Juliet*, where the plague serves a catastrophic role in the plot – assuring the tragic misunderstanding that dooms the lovers – and where a broader investment in the language of sickness comes to 'epitomize a world infected and in need of healing'.[18]

But it's not just about the plague. Syphilis, we saw in *Timon*, is a particular concern of Shakespeare; we'll explore this in more detail in Chapter 11 on sex disgust. On a related, but very different note, Ian Frederick Moulton has revealed how lovesickness was thought to be 'a serious medical condition' in early modern England; the disease is 'epidemic in Shakespeare, from Venus longing for Adonis to Roderigo suicidal over Desdemona, from the idiosyncratic Beatrice and Benedick of *Much Ado About Nothing* to the fungible young lovers of *A Midsummer Night's Dream*'.[19] In Sonnet 147, Shakespeare addresses it directly, in a manner that recalls the dynamics we saw earlier about the repulsive surfeiting of food:

> My love is as a fever, longing still
> For that which longer nurseth the disease,
> Feeding on that which doth preserve the ill,
> Th'uncertain sickly appetite to please. (1–4)

Furthermore, Alanna Skuse shows how the *Sonnets* engage the themes of disease and disgust more broadly through the image of the *canker*, as in Sonnets 35, 54, 70 and 95.[20] And more examples of the connection easily spring to mind. Appropriate enough for a play concerned with both physical and moral foulness, *Macbeth* has also been read in terms of corrupting disease; most pointedly, Bryan Adams Hampton analyses the tragedy by thinking about purgation, noting that Macbeth is 'a king whose own unstable body – beheaded and obfuscated at the end of the play – functions as a synecdoche for the filth-ridden "kitchen" of the Scottish body politic'.[21] In *Troilus and Cressida*, a play thoroughly concerned with all things disgusting, we encounter endless description of the ailing body; in one notable passage, Thersites rails about 'the rotten diseases of the south, guts-griping, ruptures, catarrhs, loads o' gravel i'th' back, lethargies, cold palsies, raw eyes, dirt-rotten livers, wheezing lungs, bladders full of imposthume, sciaticas, limekilns i'th' palm, incurable bone-ache and the rivelled fee-simple of the tetter' (5.1.17–22). Finally, because *All's Well That Ends Well* is a play full of 'anal and scatological references', some scholars have convincingly argued that the King of France's fistula, undifferentiated in the text, is most likely an intimate and disgusting *anal* fistula – that is, 'a burrowing abscess near the anus, requiring for its cure a series of probings and cuttings and cleansings that even the most skilled physicians of the early modern period could not perform without danger'.[22] Given that the play's 'bawdy jokes about the wound suggest a potentially embarrassing area' – and that Shakespeare's deliberate anal emphasis 'differs from all previous versions of the story' – it has recently been argued that the 'anal fistula [is] a constitutive, even essential, feature of the play's structure and generic identity'.[23]

But while we could develop such analysis of many plays, I find disease disgust to be a particularly useful lens for thinking about *Henry IV, Part Two* – a play in which, by Jennifer Richards's calculation, Shakespeare deploys 'more references to the words "sick," "disease," and "health" ... than in any other in his canon'.[24] As the play marches towards its climax, the archbishop of York declares that 'we are all diseased', and this assessment is borne out by the play's aggressive interest in how disease functions as a literal and symbolic measure of corruption (4.1.54). Illness, of course, has already shaped this sequel's opening dramatic context, because in the preceding events of *Henry IV, Part 1* the rebels' defeat at Shrewsbury was in part decided by Northumberland's abandonment, allegedly on account of illness.[25] On hearing the news, his allies express what can only be thought of as a suspicious disbelief; Hotspur wonders 'how has he the leisure to be sick / In such a jostling time' (4.1.17–18), while Worcester sceptically wishes that 'the state of time had first been whole / Ere he by sickness had been visited' (25–6). This sickness, which 'doth infect / The very lifeblood of [the] enterprise' (28), not only entails a loss of troops but also threatens to poison the rebel cause more broadly in the public mind: as Worcester notes,

> it will be thought
> By some that know not why he is away
> That wisdom, loyalty and mere dislike
> Of our proceedings kept the Earl from hence. (61–4)

The rebels, then, float between portraying Northumberland as both physically and morally compromised – an assessment that seems authorially confirmed in *Part 2*'s Induction, which designates him as 'crafty-sick' (37). After hearing of his allies' defeat and his son's demise, Northumberland must awkwardly account for the illness that kept him from battle – and, more importantly, account for his miraculous recovery – in a speech that contorts medical discourse to announce his new resolve to fight:

> In poison there is physic; and these news,
> Having been well, that would have made me sick,
> Being sick, have in some measure made me well.
> And as the wretch whose fever-weakened joints
> Like strengthless hinges buckle under life,
> Impatient of his fit, breaks like a fire
> Out of his keeper's arms, even so my limbs,
> Weakened with grief, being now enraged with grief,
> Are thrice themselves. (1.1.137–45)

This suspect pronouncement, which anchors the opening scene, prepares us for a play incessantly concerned with how bodies (human and stately) fail both physically and morally, as well as with the language that we use to frame such ailments.

This is because Northumberland is not the only sick character. Scene Two begins with Falstaff, fresh from getting his urine checked – he's told that while 'the water itself was a good healthy water', the person who supplied it 'might have more diseases than he knew for' (3–5). Falstaff, who ironically enough claims to be a reader of Galen (115), finds his diseased, ageing body on constant display; in one memorable moment, the Lord Chief Justice notes that he has 'a moist eye, a dry hand, a yellow cheek, a white beard, a decreasing leg, an increasing belly' (177–9). And while both Elizabethan and modern audiences might take a carnivalesque pleasure in Falstaff's grotesque excesses, at least one strand of the play's moral argument asks us to consider a more sober response to his antics. The connection between his physical health and moral character is made explicit at the end of the scene, in which he manages to reframe the painful effects of gout and/or syphilis:

> A pox of this gout, or a gout of this pox, for the one or the other plays the rogue with my great toe. 'Tis no matter if I do halt: I have the wars for my colour, and my pension shall seem the more reasonable. A good wit will make use of anything. I will turn diseases to commodity. (239–44)

Given what we saw in the last chapter about the genuine early modern social problem of disabled veterans, it is hard to think that we're intended to unreservedly endorse Falstaff's plan to leverage his personal vices into a more lucrative military pension. Whatever the case, from the perspective of the newly crowned King Henry V, the 'surfeit-swelled' Falstaff is ultimately deemed a corrupt humour that must be purged for the wellbeing of the state; banishment, we've seen (and will see further), is an analogous mechanism to the human disgust system, in the sense that unhealthy matter is expelled from the social body as a regulatory defence (5.5.49). It's telling that Hal links Falstaff's moral faults with his physical ones ('Make less thy body hence, and more thy grace' [51]), as his diseased, failing body is presented as an index of his deeper corruption.

Other minor characters are similarly in bad health; Mowbray, for example, finds himself 'on the sudden something ill' (4.1.308), while Bullcalf describes himself as a 'diseased man' (3.2.178). But it is the illness of King Henry IV that features most heavily in the play, as his struggles with 'this same whoreson apoplexy' cast an ominous pall over the end of his reign (1.2.105). As Pauline Ellen Reid explains, Henry's progressive degeneration is of a 'uniquely disruptive nature ... to the body politic', and it's easy to see how this malady is a reflection of the corruption of his rule more generally.[26] According to Falstaff, Henry's illness 'hath it original from much grief, from study, and perturbation of the brain' (113–14) – an appropriate condition to befall a man who has been plagued by guilt since his violent usurpation of his predecessor. Guilt seems at least in part behind his famous insomnia, which exacerbates the disease; alone at night, he pleads for sleep to 'steep [his] senses in forgetfulness' (3.1.8). Not long after, he reflects explicitly on his ill-gotten crown, remembering King Richard's prescient words:

> You, cousin Neville, as I may remember –
> When Richard, with his eye brimful of tears,
> Then checked and rated by Northumberland,
> Did speak these words, now proved a prophecy?
> 'Northumberland, thou ladder by the which
> My cousin Bolingbroke ascends my throne' –
> Though then, God knows, I had no such intent,
> But that necessity so bowed the state
> That I and greatness were compelled to kiss –
> 'The time shall come', thus did he follow it,
> 'The time will come that foul sin, gathering head,
> Shall break into corruption' – so went on,

Foretelling this same time's condition
And the division of our amity. (66–79)

The word *corruption* here is vital – because though Henry may disingenuously affirm that he 'had no such intent', his bloody path to the throne has left him destined to suffer a rotting of his bodies natural and politic. Both are fundamentally compromised, which is why, several scenes later, his physical condition shockingly degenerates even in the face of good political fortune:

And wherefore should these good news make me sick?
Will Fortune never come with both hands full,
But wet her fair words still in foulest terms?
She either gives a stomach and no food –
Such are the poor, in health; or else a feast
And takes away the stomach – such are the rich,
That have abundance and enjoy it not.
I should rejoice now at this happy news,
And now my sight fails and my brain is giddy.
O me, come near me, now I am much ill. [*Swoons*]
   (4.3.102–11)

The consequence of the disease's progression leads to an even greater indignity: his crown usurped by his own son, who mistakes his father's symptoms for death. 'This part of his conjoins with my disease / And helps to end me,' Henry laments in the aftermath, beginning a sequence in which the final moments of his life become flooded with disappointment and anguish (195–6). When addressing Hal for the last time, King Henry can only prophesize the depravity of his son's future reign, and what it will mean for his 'poor kingdom, sick with civil blows' (264); in a telling metaphor, he imagines that England's boroughs will 'purge' themselves by sending their 'scum' to the new royal court (254). And though he and his son are finally reconciled, it is only accomplished by affirming that Hal's reign will enjoy a legitimacy that his own never did – the 'soil [i.e. taint] of the achievement', he reflects, 'goes / With me into the earth' (319–20). This is an appropriate ending for Henry, whose body and soul are indeed both soiled; his failing body reflects the larger stain of corruption that indelibly tainted his royal career.

Finally, besides staging a host of ill bodies, *Henry IV, Part 2* consistently presents an image of England itself as direly sick. Spates argues that the play contains 'Shakespeare's most involved analogies of macrocosmic disorder as sickness', and characters on both sides of the rebellion meditate on the nation's maladies.[27] King Henry does so in the explicit language of disgust: 'you perceive the body of our kingdom,' he says to Warwick, 'how foul it is, what rank diseases grow, / And with what danger, near the heart of it' (3.1.38–40). We've explored already how *foul* is a key word in the Shakespearean lexicon of disgust – and, as we will further see in chapters to come, *rank* was equally associated with revulsion in early modern English, as in comments on the 'stinke and ranke smell of the arme-pits', or a 'smell as rank as a Carkass'.[28] The archbishop, as noted earlier, claims that the country is collectively diseased, but the rest of his assessment is worth quoting:

> And with our surfeiting and wanton hours
> Have brought ourselves into a burning fever,
> And we must bleed for it; of which disease
> Our late King Richard, being infected, died.
> But, my most noble Lord of Westmorland,
> I take not on me here as a physician,
> Nor do I as an enemy to peace
> Troop in the throngs of military men,
> But rather show a while like fearful war
> To diet rank minds sick of happiness
> And purge th'obstructions which begin to stop
> Our very veins of life. (4.1.55–66)

Once again, the diseased body politic is construed in the language of disgust; here, the state is imagined in terms of *surfeiting*, *infection*, *rankness* and *purgation*. But the play's most explicit and interesting engagement with disgust rhetoric occurs in the archbishop's earlier speech, during his first moments on the stage:

> The commonwealth is sick of their own choice;
> Their over-greedy love hath surfeited.
> An habitation giddy and unsure
> Hath he that buildeth on the vulgar heart.
> O thou fond many, with what loud applause

> Didst thou beat heaven with blessing Bolingbroke
> Before he was what thou wouldst have him be?
> And being now trimmed in thine own desires,
> Thou, beastly feeder, art so full of him
> That thou provok'st thyself to cast him up.
> So, so, thou common dog, didst thou disgorge
> Thy glutton bosom of the royal Richard,
> And now thou wouldst eat thy dead vomit up
> And howl'st to find it. (1.3.87–100)

In this striking image, the people have englutted themselves on Henry and Richard to the point of sickness, but like a dog return to further consume the gross matter they have expelled. In passages like this, Shakespeare demonstrates how various categories of disgust elicitors are conceptually entwined; here, we may draw association with matters of food, cannibalism, disease, animality and moral offence. Disease, we have seen in this chapter, is likely behind much of the human disgust response, so it's fitting that such revolting rhetoric should appear in a play so thoroughly committed to presenting an image of the diseased state. And *Henry IV, Part 2* is only one of many examples that illustrate Shakespeare's continual concern with the dramatic and thematic possibilities of disease disgust; it is a theme that he found consistently compelling.

6

Coriolanus

The circuit of disgust

I began this book with the image of Caius Martius Coriolanus vomiting: Shakespeare's most emotionally volatile Roman, I suggested, is a character defined by the extent to which he is disgusted. In *Coriolanus*, disgust is a key component of the relationship between Rome's citizens and Rome's protector, though this affective node has not received much scholarly attention. Stanley Cavell comes closest, noting that 'the value of attending to this particular play' involves mapping 'the pervasive images of food and hunger, of cannibalism and disgust' that dominate it.[1] But his assertion may be pushed further: *Coriolanus*, I argue in this chapter, is a play fundamentally about the experience of being disgusted.

In Chapter 1, we surveyed how the modern affective sciences understand the dynamics of disgust; these dynamics, I suggest in what follows, correlate with the stylistic, thematic and dramaturgical investments of *Coriolanus*. Disgust is an emotion about boundaries, about entries and expulsions, about the regulation of bodies, both literal and symbolic; it is an emotion about blood and guts, about disease and illness, about the incorporation and elimination of food. These are, it should be immediately clear, concepts essential to Caius Martius and his tragedy – and as such, disgust functions as a master trope in *Coriolanus*, variously guiding the action and manner of the play.

In the introduction to his Oxford edition of *Coriolanus*, R. B. Parker details the variety of 'image-clusters' that dominate the text: these include, he suggests, images related to *food-eating* (and *cannibalism*), *animals, perversions . . . of sex, bodily fragmentation* and *the body as diseased*.[2] This catalogue correlates almost exactly to the list of conceptual objects that, we've seen earlier, researchers have identified as the elicitors of human disgust: a list that includes *food, bodily products, animals, sex, body envelope violations* and *disease*. Though such categories, this book demonstrates, variously contribute to the imagery of Shakespeare's plays, their concentration here is telling: *Coriolanus* is overwrought with images associated with disgust, from the 'stinking breaths' (2.1.233) of the 'beastly plebeians' (93) to the 'large cicatrices' (146) and 'unaching scars' (2.2.149) that mark the bloody body of Rome's hero. In constructing *Coriolanus*, Shakespeare seems to have taken his cue from the lexicon of disgust, missing little opportunity to deploy language associated with that which makes us sick.[3] The cumulative effect of such images underscores a central facet of the play: the world of *Coriolanus* is inhabited by ill, compromised bodies, unsettled by the pangs of hunger, the soldier's blade or the moral disgust experienced so viscerally by its title character.

When discussing the play's interest in fragmented, anatomized bodies, scholars of *Coriolanus* have deployed Bakhtin's familiar paradigm of bodily construction; Michael D. Bristol, for example, grids the play's corporeal politics within the battle of Carnival and Lent, the 'central event of popular festive life' in early modern Europe.[4] Yet, despite the obvious value of Bakhtinian approaches, we must be careful to avoid formulaic notions of the classical and carnivalesque body: *Coriolanus* is not, as Zvi Jagendorf notes, a play of 'Rabelaisian abundance', but is instead populated by starving plebs, rotund senators and an abundance of porous bodies, confounding any easy class distinction.[5] The concept of disgust, I suggest, is one such way to advance a more nuanced account of the body in *Coriolanus*. Given the intimate connection of visceral and sociomoral disgust, revulsion provides a useful way of integrating a discussion of the physical body (and its various tortured forms) with the play's larger conceptual issues, such as matters of political incorporation, self-sufficiency and popular participation. To consider the *disgusted* body is to think of a body that is capable of being violated both physically and morally – often from the same root cause. *Coriolanus* depicts this association throughout, taking a wide cue from the spectrum of disgust.

This chapter traces tropes of food, disease and wounded bodies in *Coriolanus*, showing how this constellation of disgust-invoking concepts provided Shakespeare with a poetic, thematic and dramatic vocabulary in the play. Ultimately, I argue that *Coriolanus* stages a circuit of revulsion, as both Caius Martius and his enemies become locked in a mutually reinforcing cycle of disgust. This motif, I suggest further, has a concrete correlate, as the play's insistent depiction of both the protection and violation of physical boundaries (in the form of city gates and walls) can be seen as a literal analogue to the 'gatekeeping' function of the human disgust system. Disgust, it seems to me, is at the heart of *Coriolanus* – it underwrites the play in a way that has not yet been fully appreciated.

* * *

If *Coriolanus* is a play about disgust, it follows closely that it's a play about food; the emotion, as we've seen, originated as a governor of oral incorporation, and its visceral sensation is located primarily in the digestive tract. Kenneth Burke famously emphasized 'the last two syllables of the hero's name', and there is indeed a way that the play is preoccupied with all things alimentary, from food entering the mouth to exiting the anus.[6] The action of *Coriolanus* is framed by issues related to food: it begins with the starving plebeians of Rome, rioting for corn, and ends with the plebs of Antium, devouring Coriolanus in a symbolic feast.[7] Other key moments of the plot concern food and its consumption. When the banished Coriolanus arrives at the house of Aufidius, he finds his rival 'feast[ing] the nobles of the state' (4.4.8); conversely, Coriolanus's ill-reception of Cominius is attributed to the fact that 'he had not dined', and that 'veins unfilled . . . are unapt / To give or to forgive' (5.1.50–3). Stylistically, the rhetoric of food, digestion and cannibalism overwhelms the play: there's no dearth of references to gnawing teeth and growling stomachs, and it's telling that its governing metaphor, the trope of the body politic, is introduced by Menenius's celebrated 'fable of the belly'. Furthermore, for a contemporary audience, the play likely spoke to a set of relevant issues from their own gustatory experience: *Coriolanus* has been linked topically to several food-related social phenomena, such as the Midland Enclosure Riots of 1607, or the Great Dearth of 1593–7.[8] And if there's any remaining doubt that Shakespeare emphasized food, we need only look to the alterations of his source: in Plutarch's account, the plebeians rise primarily to end 'the sore oppression of vserers', while in *Coriolanus* they instead resolve 'rather to die than to famish' (1.1.4–5).[9]

Die, famish or perhaps something else: to kill Caius Martius, suggests the First Citizen in the play's opening lines, is to 'have corn at our own price' (10–11). Immediately denounced as the embodiment of the patricians – whose ruthless agrarian policy is to hoard the harvest – the hero of Rome is precariously cast as the cause of its citizens' empty stomachs, an irony made all the more cutting by his own 'surplus' of faults and vices (43), which cannot help but mock the 'leanness' of the plebs (19). Although the eruption against Martius and the patricians is clearly symptomatic of a deeper fault line in Rome's social organization, the plebeians are careful here to couch their action not in the language of political opposition, but rather that of naked sustenance; 'I speak this in hunger for bread', claims the First Citizen, the primary agitator of the riot, 'not in thirst for revenge' (22–3). With this pat distinction (*hunger* for *bread* / *thirst* for *revenge*) Shakespeare introduces a central preoccupation of *Coriolanus*: the Roman body as a site of both visceral sensation and metaphoric possibility, a semantic range that accounts for the play's pervasive interest in how bodily matters function as both literal and figurative signifiers. In these opening moments, when the plebeians control the linguistic terrain, the focus remains overwhelmingly visceral: though Martius may be cursed as 'a very dog to the commonalty', it is the multitude, more accurately, who in their hunger are reduced to the barest form of animal life (26).[10]

But despite this early focus on Caius Martius, it is Menenius who first takes up the patrician case. He does so, quite crucially, by transforming the body into a different kind of rhetorical object: one that conveys information not in the sensual experience of its pangs and aches, but in the potency of its symbolic application. This entails, of course, his famed 'fable of the belly', the long-standing trope of political theory that forms one of the most memorable moments in *Coriolanus*. The familiar allegory details 'a time, when all the body's members / Rebelled against the belly', spiteful of the latter's apparent leisure (93–4); the situation is defused when the belly reminds us that it is he who receives and distributes 'that natural competency / Whereby they live' (136–7). For Menenius, the fable has clear enough bearing on the republic's current troubles: 'the senators of Rome are this good belly,' he suggests helpfully to the plebs, 'And you the mutinous members' (145–6). With good reason, the fable of the belly has inspired considerable commentary from scholars of the play, who routinely deem it a rhetorical failure; James Houlston, for example, calls it an 'almost contemptuously inappropriate' response to the plebeian rising, while Arthur Riss observes that Menenius 'does not merely fail to restrain the revolt, he actually legitimizes it'.[11] While I am in full agreement with this assessment, I think that the contemptuousness of Menenius has even been understated: though perhaps a reflection of his rhetorical naïveté, the form of the allegory equally reveals the deep disgust he harbours towards the plebeians.

The fable of the belly is, of course, a story about digestion, and as such, it has natural affinity with the domains of disgust. As Frank Whigham has revealed, images of the alimentary tract were inscribed with a rich 'social coding' in the early modern period, fraught with anxieties concerning 'class ingestion, retention, and evacuation'; surely this machinery is also active in the famous fable, which is, fundamentally, an attempt to justify Rome's rigid social hierarchy.[12] As the bodily system devoted to incorporation and elimination – and thus to food, faeces and vomit – digestion thus offers a material cognate to the social disgust that implicitly defines Menenius's response to the plebeians – and that will find explicit expression in Caius Martius. But the stuff of literal disgust is equally active here: though the fable, Anny Crunelle notes, 'does not explicitly mention elimination', there is still a series of scatological puns on *tale/tail, pretty/prat* and *but/buttock*.[13]

Indeed, in the stunted digestion of this allegorical body, the stomach is said to deliver the 'flour' to its members, who in return 'leave [him] but the bran' (142–3) – that is, the inedible waste of the distribution process, which receives no further mention in the fable. As Jonathan Goldberg suggests, this crucial incompleteness codes the belly as 'undeniably anal': the stately stomach, he argues, 'assumes the position of the anus, receiving what is normally expelled; a closed economy is imagined in which waste is consumed'.[14] For Peter Holland, the belly is thus a 'vision of a hyper-efficient system', in which 'there is no waste to be disposed of, no excess to the consumption, no outside to which the waste is turned' – an assertion to which, I imagine, Menenius would assent, insofar as it substantiates the rhetorical fiction of his fable.[15] But there is also, I think, a way in which this image undoes itself, much to the detriment of Menenius and his senatorial interests. Though the fable's stomach indeed receives the body's waste, there's nothing in the passage to indicate that it is further consumed: perhaps instead it remains unprocessed, a heap of slowly spoiling refuse, much like the musty grain in the patrician's silos. Rather than a finely tuned fantasy of Roman engineering, the patrician's stomach may well be an overburdened midden, housing waste but doing little to dispose it further. This is the reading of the Second Citizen, who deems the belly 'the sink o'th' body' (119) – and there is certainly a way that Menenius may be seen as a partly constipated figure, swollen with the bloat of his own rhetoric.

Shakespeare intensifies this excremental association, by portraying Menenius as an explicitly *digesting* body. In the midst of his fable, the senator is famously interrupted by a flare-up of his own belly, providing a convenient opportunity for some meta-commentary:

> 2 CITIZEN   Well, sir, what answer made the belly?
> MENENIUS   Sir, I shall tell you. With a kind of smile,
> Which ne'er came from the lungs, but even thus –
> For, look you, I may make the belly smile
> As well as speak. (103–7)

Though slightly obscure, Menenius breaks some kind of wind here – either *vpward* or *downeward*, as the early moderns put it.[16] There are two things to be emphasized about this moment. First, Menenius's attempt to co-opt his body's (potentially embarrassing) intrusion, and incorporate it into his fable, is perhaps the most naked example of his rhetorical obtuseness in this sequence: quite remarkably, he thinks it wise to stress that his body is literally processing food directly in front of the starving plebs. But given the gravity of the moment, it is also worth considering that the 'belly smile' might be rather disgusting – as a reminder both of his grotesque corporality *and* his grotesque contempt for the plebs. Menenius here unites two modes of the signifying body: by drawing attention to his own senatorial belly, he provides the visual correlative to the Senate's role in the famous fable: he exemplifies the stomach, through and through, offering it to the plebs – quite perversely, in these circumstances – as an object of both literal and figurative contemplation.

But what, more specifically, does it mean to associate Menenius with the stomach, or to say generally that 'the senators of Rome are this good belly' (145)? Besides activating this network of digestion and disgust, the patricians' linkage with the stomach equally invokes a variety of other associations within the humoural discourse of the early modern period. As has been well documented, early modern concepts of the embodied self were not governed by a Cartesian binary of body and mind; in the early seventeenth century, physiology and psychology were endlessly entangled, just as the body itself was thought to experience a more porous engagement with its environmental context than is customary in a post-Enlightenment framework.[17] Accordingly, to speak of the belly, as Menenius does, is to unlock (in this case, perhaps, unwillingly) a set of dispositional associations as well. In early modern usage, the word *stomach* entailed not only 'the pipe wherby meate goeth dowen' but also the sentiments like 'indignation, anger, vehement wrath, hatred, displeasure, abhorring of anie thing that liketh not'.[18] These are, of course, all emotions with a clear linkage to disgust – and indeed, some current researchers have argued that *indignation* is simply verbal shorthand for the feeling of moral disgust.[19]

The stomach, then, was a festering pool for a host of angry, hostile eruptions. Within the humoural framework of the early modern period, this emotional set forms a taxonomy of choler, and it's probably not surprising that nowhere in Shakespeare does the word *choler* appear more than in *Coriolanus*. Yet while the usage of the term indeed invokes the now-familiar physiological theory of the early modern period – with the elaborate sociocultural and dispositional implications it entails – there is also a more direct way that *choler* circles back to matters of the stomach and disgust. In contemporary usage, *choler* also denoted what is now usually referred to as *cholera* – that is, the affliction of the bowels that 'purgeth vncessantly both vpward and downeward'.[20] Though distinct, both senses of the word are nonetheless entangled by their shared roots in the Latin *cholera*, tellingly defined by one sixteenth-century lexicon as 'The humour called Choler. Also a sicknesse of the stomacke, with a troublous flixe and vomite ioyned wyth great daunger.'[21] To complicate matters further, this network of meaning must also include the etymologically distinct, but phonetically proximate, *colic* – the 'wynde of the great Guttes' that is, we will see, later invoked by Menenius.[22]

Choler, the humour, induces a figurative stomach that erupts with temperamental anger; *choler*, the infirmity, induces a literal stomach that erupts with vomit and faeces. Both expressions are intimately related, and both correlate to the spectrum of disgust: rage and indignation form the basic expression of moral disgust, while the bodily wastes function as indicators and elicitors of visceral disgust. The opening scene of *Coriolanus*, I suggest, enacts this range of meaning, by staging both senses of *stomach* in progression. That is to say: by casting the Senate as the *stomach* of his fable, Menenius equally assigns it a dispositional orientation towards his plebeian audience – one that finds imminent expression in the tongue of Martius, whose venomous rhetoric amplifies the implicit force of his comrade's allegory.

The indignation of Caius Martius, it follows, makes good on the rhetorical groundwork installed by Menenius, by excavating the latent disgust of the belly fable. Despite the inappropriateness of his attempt, Menenius at least tries to partly hide his contempt for the plebeians; he enters the scene with a reputation of 'one that hath always loved the people' (49–50), and he doesn't denounce Rome's 'rats' until after the obvious failure of his fable (159). Coriolanus, however, has little time for such niceties: his choler, his disgust and his *stomach* are evident from the moment he takes the stage. Though his opening invective draws widely on the lexicon of disgust – with images of illness, animals and bodily fragmentation – it is most ripe with images of food and digestion: a thematic cluster apt for those plebs who would 'feed on one another' (185) and with whom he would gladly 'make a quarry' (195).[23]

In fact, Martius seems to be disgusted by the very fact that Rome's citizens are hungry at all:

They said they were an-hungry, sighed forth proverbs –
That hunger broke stone walls, that dogs must eat,
That meat was made for mouths, that the gods sent not
Corn for rich men only. With these shreds
They vented their complainings. (202–6)

Contempt drips from this passage, as do the images of visceral disgust, which cast the plebs as *dogs* and their plaints as *shreds*. But most telling is the remark that they rioters *vented* their complaints to the senators – to *vent*, as Holland notes 'can mean to fart, to shit or to piss'.[24] Martius, quite perversely, attaches a scatological weight to their hunger pangs; unable to excrete food from their empty bellies, they instead excrete words from their mouth, the site of the dirty teeth and rotten breath that so repulse him.[25] Indeed, for Coriolanus, the commoners are the refuse of the republic, an association confirmed by his reaction to the pending Volscian assault: 'I am glad on't,' he exclaims, 'Then we shall ha' means to vent / Our musty superfluity' (222–3). Recalling what we saw in the earlier discussion of *Timon*'s vagrants, Coriolanus sees the war as a fine way to process Rome's overflowing wasteheap: it is not just the Senate but Rome itself which is constipated, overburdened with the festering waste of the common mobs.

* * *

It is a remarkable image: plebeians as the waste of the Roman body politic, an impacted mass which must be expelled for the good of the republic. In crafting this, perhaps the preeminent social fantasy of Caius Martius, Shakespeare takes a cue from his source in Plutarch. In the comparable passage, the patricians respond similarly to news of the Volscian assault:

> So the wise men of ROME beganne to thincke . . . howe by this occasion it was very mete in so great a scarsitie of vittailes, to disburden ROME of a great number of cittizens: and by this meanes as well to take away this newe sedition, and vtterly to ryd it out of the cittie, as also to cleare the same of many mutinous and seditious persones, being the superfluous ill humours that greuously feede this disease.[26]

As noted earlier, Shakespeare's use of the word *vent* enables a specifically scatological reading of this moment; this is consistent with the larger thematic agenda of the play's opening movement, which explores Rome's social conflict via the class-inflected rhetoric of digestion and disgust. But while the excretory context is not explicit in the source-text, North's rendition is nonetheless suggestive for the related discourse that it activates: by comparing the common mob to a humour that must be purged, the passage is indebted to early modern medical practices, casting the plebeians as a kind of social pathology. Unsurprisingly, the rhetoric of disease is closely associated with the bodily matters we have thus far explored, and illness and contamination, we have seen, are key domains under the umbrella of disgust. If the healthy body is disgusting in its natural functions of excretion, the pathologized body is even more disgusting in its disintegration and decay – and as such, images of disease and illness form the second crucial component of how *Coriolanus* establishes its affective mode.

In his opening speech, Martius deploys the rhetoric of disease to express his contempt for the multitude:

> What's the matter, you dissentious rogues,
> That, rubbing the poor itch of your opinion,
> Make yourselves scabs? (161–3)

With this introduction, Shakespeare activates a variety of thematic concerns associated with disease and disgust. Yoking an image of physical degradation with one of sedition, Coriolanus presents a multitude that is both materially and politically compromised – and he is disgusted in both terms, visceral and sociomoral. The notion of scabbiness itself bridges the literal and metaphoric senses of disease: in this ambiguous phrasing, Coriolanus presents the multitude as physically covered in scabs and as the scabs of the body politic. For Coriolanus, popular political action is self-defeating, and even rather indulgent: unable to restrain themselves, the plebeians scratch their bodies bloody, inviting further discomfort in the act of seeking relief. This implicit image of self-consumption – participating in the play's larger motif of cannibalism – is made more explicit in Martius's next salvo: 'your affections are / A sick man's appetite, who desires most that / Which would increase his evil' (174–6). The multitude is again cast as diseased – and, more importantly, as driven mad by their illness. Coriolanus continues to deflate the political seriousness of the uprising, by dismissing it as something like a fever-dream – not to be heeded, and more harmful than helping. And given the context, this medical advice is all the more perverse: while Martius speaks metaphorically of a 'sick man's appetite', the plebeians before him really are hungry, and their appetites really are being ignored by the patricians.

News of the Volscian assault pre-empts further discussion. In battle, however, Martius finds renewed cause to lament Rome's ailing body politic, denouncing his comrades as a social plague:

> All the contagion of the south light on you,
> You shames of Rome! You herd of – boils and plagues
> Plaster you o'er, that you may be abhorred
> Farther than seen, and one infect another
> Against the wind a mile! (1.4.31–5)

These are the 'common file' of the Roman army – those who fled to the trenches while Martius penetrated the gates of Corioles alone (1.6.44). Recalling Timon's invective, Coriolanus here deploys the rhetoric of disease with a remarkable concentration – one that is only matched, as we will see, in reaction to his own banishment. Again, visceral and sociomoral forms of repulsion intermingle, as Martius conjures a vision of physical revulsion to match the offence occasioned by the soldiers' shameful retreat. In the context of combat, his metaphors are particularly apt; the waves of panic that overtake a breaking rank mirror the trajectory of a plague-wind, and there is an obvious justice in casting an incurable blight on those who fled their appointed death by an enemy's blade. Though Coriolanus was disgusted enough by the plebeian uprising, he is, given his own martial investments, supremely repulsed by the pleb's execrable conduct in the field.

But it is not simply the plebeians who elicit the rhetoric of disease from Coriolanus and the aristocratic party: as proxies for the multitude, Sicinius and Brutus are equally painted as a source of contamination and infection. A notable example inaugurates the second act, in which Menenius and the tribunes, waiting for news of the Volscian assault, turn their discussion to matters of state. In the midst of their banter, Menenius attacks the tribunes with a particularly strange elaboration: 'When you are hearing a matter between party and party, if you chance to be pinched with the colic, you make faces like mummers, set up the bloody flag against all patience and, in roaring for a chamber-pot, dismiss the controversy bleeding, the more entangled by your hearing' (2.1.71–6). While editors routinely note that the passage conflates a variety of the play's stylistic investments (images of disease, warfare, legality, etc.), I think a simple question must be asked: Why, when mocking the tribunes for their parochial scope, would Menenius jump to a vision of their violent, bloody evacuation? Menenius makes a clear thematic linkage: in his fantasy, proximity to the plebeians – here specifically, entanglement in the daily rhythms of their life – correlates with the onset of a painful illness, the force of which loosens the boundaries of continence and turns the body inside-out. Though a Bakhtinian account may explain the image of the boundless plebeian body, I think the larger issue here is one of contagion: the tribunes are compromised by the dealings with the plebs, whose social repulsiveness finds a correlate in their bodily ailments. And quite appropriately, the illness is coded as specifically excretory – the disease of the plebeians is one that manifests the raw material of disgust, a fetid reminder of its origin in the common mob. Given the perennial fullness of his own belly, it's unsurprising that Menenius distances himself from the tribunes, now a source of contagion themselves: 'More of your conversation,' he dismisses, 'would infect my brain, being the herdsmen of the beastly plebeians' (91–3).

It's no surprise that Coriolanus and his colleagues thus cast the plebs and their representatives as 'measles' on the body politic (3.1.80): Rome is 'sure of death', Coriolanus rails, lest this popular influence be purged 'with a dangerous physic' (155–6). Yet, despite the obvious ferocity of this rhetoric, it is equally important to recognize that Caius Martius has no monopoly on being disgusted: the tribunes also rely on disgust-based imagery in their attempts to agitate the populous against the military hero. In fact, it is Coriolanus's very disgust for the plebs that enables this rhetorical strategy: guided by the tribunes, the citizens are incited by the very disgust response that they themselves elicit in their protector.

We have already seen how disgust for the rabble manifests in Coriolanus – this visceral response, I have argued, underpins his characteristic indignation, a term synonymous with moral disgust. The tribunes identify this 'soaring insolence' as the key to toppling Coriolanus, and it is indeed the posture of *insolence* – associated by one contemporary dictionary with 'pride, hautinesse, stomacke' – that is invoked to enflame the moral anger of his opponents (2.1.251).[27] In their first moments on stage, Sicinius and Brutus lay the groundwork for this strategy: contempt for the plebeians, they note, is virtually encoded in Coriolanus's bodily expression, seated in his 'lips', 'eyes' and 'taunts' (1.1.251–2). (We may think here of the 'disgust face' identified by Darwin and modern researchers.) It is this famous pride, swollen with class-based contempt, that enables the tribunes to orchestrate his undoing:

> BRUTUS   I heard him swear,
> Were he to stand for consul, never would he
> Appear i'th' market-place nor on him put
> The napless vesture of humility,
> Nor, showing, as the manner is, his wounds
> To th' people, beg their stinking breaths. (2.1.228–33)

The concentration of imagery in this passage suggests the proximity of visceral and sociomoral disgust elicitors. Coriolanus is sickened both by the populace and by the notion of submitting himself to them: the implications of humility, it follows, are as stomach-turning as the smell of the unwashed masses. The central charge of insolence encompasses both registers: when Sicinius implores the masses to 'forget not / With what contempt . . . he scorned you', he asks them to acknowledge their status as both materially and politically repulsive (2.3.218–20).

But once the tribunes establish Caius Martius's indignation, they are able to wrench free the rhetoric of disgust and fashion it to their own purposes. Coriolanus is cast as a disease of the state, a figuration *enabled* by his own constant professions of disgust: by announcing himself as sickened by the commoners, Coriolanus unwittingly enables the tribunes to construe his insolence as a dangerous infection, which itself must be purged for the sake of the state's social harmony. In Shakespeare's elegant construction, Coriolanus and the plebs are thus locked in what might be called an affective feedback loop. Martius, to start, is doubly disgusted by the plebeians: viscerally, by the grotesqueness of their bodies, and morally, by their cowardice, ingratitude and presumption. He consequently casts them as a pox on Rome's body – crafting a metaphor that, by emphasizing illness and decay, perversely reflects the material circumstances of their lived experience. But Coriolanus's social arrogance inflames its own populist resentment in the plebeians – who, with the help of the tribunes, themselves diagnose this very snobbery as its own disease of state. What's evident here, above all else, is the fluid relationship between forms of disgust; matters of pride and indignation effortlessly inspire images of illness and disease, while being associated with such elicitors is enough to arouse contempt in even the most powerless subjects. In this manner, disgust and indignation become trapped in a mutually reinforcing emotional circuit: the plebs are disgusted by Martius's flagrant dismissal of their political voice, while Coriolanus is himself disgusted that they are bold enough to want one at all.

For their part, the tribunes insistently cast Coriolanus as a sickness of the state, aping the rhetoric with which he condemned the populace. Recalling Timon's fantasies for Athens, Coriolanus becomes a one-man social plague, threatening to 'depopulate the city, and / Be every man himself' (3.1.266–7). As self-appointed physicians of the state, Sicinius and Brutus work to ensure that Coriolanus's damning influence 'shall remain a poison / Where it is, not poison any further' (88–9). When Menenius urges a temperate approach to Coriolanus, Brutus assures him that the case is far too severe: 'Sir, those cold ways / That seem like prudent helps are very poisonous / Where the disease is violent' (221–3). This rhetorical motif culminates in the conclusion to scene 3.1, in the final moments before Coriolanus and his allies retreat from the mob. Here, Sicinius most nakedly denounces Coriolanus as an infection of the state: 'He's a disease that must be cut away' (296). Despite the attempts of Menenius to disarm the metaphor – 'O, he's a limb that has but a disease: / Mortal to cut it off, to cure it easy' (297–8) – the tribunes stand by their diagnosis:

> SICINIUS: The service of the foot,
> Being once gangrened, is not then respected
> For what before it was.
> BRUTUS: We'll hear no more.
> [*to the Citizens*] Pursue him to his house and pluck him thence,
> Lest his infection, being of a catching nature,
> Spread further. (307–12)

Are the citizens, then, pathogens or antibodies? It depends on who you ask. It's hard not to associate this violent, angry mob with the spreading infection that Brutus describes, and Coriolanus and his party surely perceive their assault as requiring a healing 'physic' (3.2.34). But, co-opted by the tribunes, the pathologizing discourse has equally been turned against Coriolanus, and he too is transformed into a diseased subject.

In the showdown between plebs and patricians, the central political question may thus be framed in strikingly material terms: Who, the play asks, has the greater right to be disgusted? As both parties stake claim to the politics of disgust, they paint their enemies as a blight on the body politic, to be healed only by their own purging physic. Shakespeare makes much, I think, of this fundamental similarity, which is revealed especially in the moments following Coriolanus's banishment. Here, Martius unloads a barrage of disgust-based rhetoric:

> You common cry of curs whose breath I hate
> As reek o'th' rotten fens, whose loves I prize
> As the dead carcasses of unburied men
> That do corrupt my air, I banish you. (3.3.119–22)

Though anchored in the familiar metaphor of contamination, the explosive imagery of this passage correlates remarkably with the disgust elicitors I reviewed in Chapter 1: Coriolanus runs the gamut of disgust, framing his revulsion in terms of hygiene, animalism, dead bodies and, of course, illness. But even more telling, I think, is his famed declaration of reciprocal banishment. Having lost the current battle – and by extension, being condemned as the source of Rome's illness, at least in the court of plebeian opinion – Coriolanus makes a final effort to invert the sentence of the tribunes, just as they inverted his own pathologizing discourse. Though intended as a distancing move, confirming his own fantasies of self-sufficiency, the manoeuvre ironically confirms his proximity to the tribunes, with whom he shares a central rhetorical premise.

In *Coriolanus*, the clash between plebeians and patricians manifests largely in the struggle to affirm one's repulsion. Yet, while both parties attempt to pathologize their adversaries – in order to distinguish Rome's healthy body from its diseased counterpart – the effect of this rhetorical mirroring, I suggest, ultimately works to undermine the class difference in which the play's characters are so invested. Accordingly, when the banished Coriolanus famously takes his leave like 'a lonely dragon [to] his fen' (4.1.30), a simple question lingers: does he set off to the same rotten fen in which he earlier located the plebs?

* * *

Disgust, we have seen, is known by many theorists as the 'gatekeeper emotion'; it oversees the boundaries of the self and the social order, guarding the integrity of both from internal disruption and from foreign contamination. It is thus finally unsurprising that disgust is of central importance to *Coriolanus*, a play that is, if nothing else, about the opening and closing of gates. In our discussion of *Timon of Athens*, I made much of characters being expelled from Athens's walls; *Coriolanus* returns to this theme of boundary regulation, and considers it with a new intensity. The play, I have already argued, involves Shakespeare's vast deployment of disgust-related imagery – most notably (but by no means exclusively) images of digestion and disease – and his positioning of disgust as an affective touchstone in the rhetorical conflict between the plebeians and the patricians – each party struggling to assert just how much it is repulsed by its counterpart. In this concluding section, I want to expand my focus, by exploring how some of the conceptual issues associated with disgust – matters of incorporation and purgation, integrity and violation – manifest in the larger structural features of the play. *Coriolanus* is preoccupied with thresholds, and its dramatic architecture is dominated by a series of ritualized entries and expulsions. For much of his time on the stage, Coriolanus is entering or exiting a city gate – sometimes forcing, sometimes forced, but always with profound consequence for those inside and out. To consider these concerns in an affective framework provides means for aligning the play's stylistic and structural features: the abundances of images associated with disgust elicitors find dramatic expression in the shape of the narrative, which ultimately enacts an allegory of disgust.

As noted earlier, readers of *Coriolanus* have long viewed Caius Martius as a character enchanted by the fantasy of his own completeness; in this sense, he perhaps exemplifies the Bakhtinian notion of the classical body, that 'strictly completed, finished product . . . isolated, alone, fenced off from other bodies'.[28] For Coriolanus, it is the plebeian body that is marked by its fundamental incompleteness: he spends a great deal of the play railing in this manner against 'the mutable, rank-scented meinie' (3.1.68), whom he tellingly denounces as 'fragments' during the climax of the food riots (1.1.219). Yet this dichotomy is also routinely challenged by the play, in the sense that the body of Coriolanus is far from pristine: it is one that wounds, and scars, and bleeds, sometimes to a shocking extent. Coriolanus's commitment to notions of the bounded self is further compromised by his own role as guardian of Rome's social order: as the republic's war machine, he is fundamentally tasked with puncturing and penetrating the wholeness of once-firm boundaries, whether cleaving apart an enemy soldier or breaching the gates of an enemy compound. In structural terms, Coriolanus spends a great deal of his play as an invading force, trying to encroach upon a place where he's not wanted – be it Corioles, Antium or, in the final sequence, Rome itself.[29] Accordingly, he regularly assumes the status of a foreign body – a term that, with its saliency in multiple discourses, helps account for Coriolanus both as a political and symbolic subject.

It is, of course, in the assault on Corioles that Martius wins his greatest renown, and it is in this initial action that Shakespeare establishes the narrative pattern of invasion and entry that dominates the play. Many readers, especially those with psychoanalytic interests, have associated the gates of Corioles with female genitalia, variously reading immersion in the symbolic vagina/womb in terms of rape and rebirth – a sequence thought, with good reason, to reflect Coriolanus's ambivalent bond to the overbearing Volumnia.[30] While this approach is certainly suggestive, I do think that it might be usefully expanded, by associating the assault on Corioles with the play's larger interest in the violation of bodily integrity. My basic suggestion here is that, in breaching the Volscian walls, Martius mirrors the trajectory of a contaminant that corrupts a body – that is, the same mechanism through which one is disgusted by a noxious substance, be it spoiled food, a dangerous pathogen, or a morally offensive sentiment. With the declaration that 'the gates are ope' (1.4.44), Rome's premier soldier clears the lane for his entry into foreign ground; in the moments that follow, he is incorporated into the body of Corioles, 'himself alone / To answer all the city' (55–6). Despite his comrades' cowardice, Caius Martius undoes the Volscians from the inside-out, gutting the defenders within their walls before welcoming his fellow Romans. In this moment, he is the infection – the spoiled blood and rotten humours that Corioles would expel, if only it possessed a suitable purgative.

And it is crucial, I think, that Martius is injured in the siege. Despite the victory, his own body is not preserved intact, and Lartius insists that the conquering hero retire from subsequent engagement: 'Worthy sir, thou bleed'st. / Thy exercise hath been too violent / For a second course of fight' (1.5.14–16). Despite his fantasy, Martius's is no classical body; it is subject to the same intrusion and violations that it inflicts upon its unfortunate opponents. But this is hardly an impediment: the quick-thinking Martius is able to appropriate the injury – to own his wounds, so to speak – by exploiting the features of early modern medical discourse, and casting the blood as restorative: 'The blood I drop', he assures Lartius, 'is rather physical / Than dangerous to me' (18–19). Unlike those of the unfortunate Volscians, these wounds merely enliven him for the next round of combat. Yet at the same time, blood is blood, and there is equally a sense in which the source of spillage is ultimately indistinguishable, comingled as it is on his Roman body. This is the effect of his subsequent entry in the camp of Cominius, where he arrives as a bloody spectacle: 'Who's yonder', the general asks, 'That does appear as he were flayed?' (1.6.22–3). Not only a source of amazement, Martius appears here as an object of disgust: soaked in gore, it is he who is now turned inside-out, in the manner of a skinned deer. Though much of the blood is Volscian, its effect is to make him the anatomy; Martius is again the defiler and the defiled, consistent with the struggle for disgust displayed elsewhere in the play.

In fact, the success of Coriolanus in the field is explicitly measured by the degree of injury to his own body; Volumnia and Menenius eagerly anticipate cataloguing his new wounds, 'every gash . . . an enemy's grave' (2.1.153–4). In the action of war, Martius is distinctly not disgusted by the blood and gore of violated flesh; his fantasies of integrity are temporarily suspended, replaced by a moral standard that rewards the shedding of blood and tearing of bodies, both his enemies' and his own. Yet after the din of war has faded, and Coriolanus has donned civilian garb anew, he reassumes a classical orientation of the body – incessantly defending his own corporal boundaries, and thoroughly repulsed by the common mob. Coriolanus, it seems, embraces injury as a visceral sensation – one suspended in the time-bending action of combat – but cannot assess its meaning in the aftermath; his injuries only smart when they 'hear themselves remembered' (1.9.29), and he'd rather suffer his 'wounds to heal again / Than to hear say how [he] got them' (2.2.69–70). Coriolanus is thus particularly unnerved by the electoral procedure of the consulship – a populist gauntlet that demands he peddle his punctured body, placing it in nauseating proximity with the garlic-eaters. In Plutarch, the returning hero embraces Roman custom, displaying his 'many woundes and cuttes' without the protest of his dramatic counterpart.[31] Shakespeare's rendition insists upon Coriolanus's inability to tolerate this contact: not only a reflection of social antagonism, it reveals a deep anxiety about the proximity of the plebeian body to his own.

Why is Coriolanus repulsed by the idea of exposing his body to the rabble? Disgust is primarily a guardian of boundaries, and we know that Coriolanus fiercely asserts the social distinction that separates him from the multitude. Yet in its current state, his war-ravaged body might actually be thought to resemble that of the plebs: it is compromised by sores, cuts, and a fundamental state of rupture. Coriolanus, we have seen, casts the rabble as *scabs* during his initial moments on the stage – but he, we must assume, is literally scabby, the open and half-healed wounds of Corioles set in relief by the faded scars of battles passed.[32] To expose himself, it follows, is to reveal physical affinity with the plebeians – a material congruence that equally implies social cohesion. For obvious reasons, Coriolanus works to disavow any notion that he and the citizens enjoy a transactional parity:

> To brag unto them 'Thus I did, and thus',
> Show them th'unaching scars which I should hide,
> As if I had received them for the hire
> Of their breath only. (2.2.148–51)

Yet there is another sense of exposure, entailing not display, but communicability – that is, not exposure *of*, but exposure *to*. If his current state makes Coriolanus resemble the plebeians, it also makes him more susceptible to them: here, the openness of his wounded body threatens both physical and social contamination. We saw in the last chapter how pathogen avoidance is a fundamental motive of the human disgust system, and it seems that Coriolanus intuitively recoils from placing his compromised body in proximity to the disease-ridden plebs – a reluctance that modern researchers might see as a function of the BIS. Perhaps the most naked testament to the frailty of corporal boundaries, a scab is the threshold between injury and integrity; it is an extension of the body proper, under continual threat of rupture or infection. Fearful of plebeian contagion on his best days, Coriolanus is particularly repulsed by the notion of subjecting his open body to an interaction with the rabble. Assaulted by enemy steel, the gates of his body have been unfastened; to offer it to the plebeians as such is to grant them access unopposed. '[W]e are', tellingly remarks one citizen, 'to put our tongues into those wounds' – a statement that, I think, captures a disgusting fear of Martius (2.3.6–7). Popular political action, Coriolanus later exclaims, 'bereaves the state / Of that integrity which should become't'; these common tongues, with their rotten teeth and stinking breath, equally undermine the integrity of his own self (3.1.159–60).

Yet such attempts to inoculate himself against the plebs are unsuccessful; after his failure in the political arena, Coriolanus is himself diagnosed as a pathogen to Rome, an invading body that must be purged for the good of the state. Though ostensibly antithetical, his return to Rome – the play's second crucial entry – thus proves to be analogous to the capture of Corioles: he is ultimately cast as a foreign agent in both cities. A basic problem of *Coriolanus* is one of (military) incorporation; the play explores the fate of the war machine in times of peace. But unlike Cincinnatus – the other preeminent solider-statesman of early republican Rome, who was successfully reintegrated into civilian life – Coriolanus ultimately proves to be indigestible by the Roman body politic: chaff of the senatorial belly, he is a necessary ingredient of peacetime living, but one that ultimately must be disposed of and expelled after serving its purpose. In her perceptive reading of the play, Paster suggests that, 'in banishing Coriolanus', Rome effectively 'devours' its hero.[33] But this, I think, is only half the story, and the analogy must be pressed further. Rome does not simply devour Coriolanus, it also excretes him out – expelling that which, now exhausted, resists any further incorporation into the healthy state. That his banishment is a popular action only amplifies the scatological implications: progression through the alimentary tract is inherently democratic, as that which is differentiated at the time of oral incorporation finds itself homogenized by the anus.[34] In this manner, Coriolanus is declared utterly abject by the plebeians, an object of repulsion even to them. This is the ultimate humiliation for Martius, who has strived endlessly to guard against such social contamination.

In banishing Coriolanus, the Roman citizens are said to 'have pushed out [the] gates the very defender of them' – and much is made of this irony as the narrative continues (5.2.39–40). Indeed,

Coriolanus is a play thoroughly devoted to the collapsing of apparent opposites – be it attacker/defender, patrician/pleb, Roman/Volscian and, of course, disgusting/disgusted. Ultimately, I think that such an opposition defines the role of Coriolanus in Rome's political body, as an agent ultimately undone by the nature of his own utility. To extend the bodily metaphors, Coriolanus functions like pus – matter that, in being expelled, bears witness to the body's own defence – or like the curing purgative – a remedy that, we have seen, is expelled in the process of generating expulsion. In other words, he becomes an object that, by virtue of being purged, is no longer distinguishable from the very threats he once himself repelled.

This trajectory is immediately literalized, when Coriolanus enters the gates of Antium, his third-such symbolic entry thus far in the play. After humbling himself before his rival, Coriolanus is readily incorporated into the Volscian political body, thus confirming his new identity as Rome's enemy. Unsurprisingly, he deploys the rhetoric of disease and disgust when denouncing his former home, vowing to 'fight / Against [his] cankered country with the spleen / Of all the under-fiends' (4.5.92–4). This is quite appropriate, I think, because the manner of his revenge serves as another metaphor of infection. Having been cast away as refuse, Coriolanus is transformed into a pure contaminant: now literally a foreign body to Rome, he acquires the ability to tear down his former home from without, through the same means of violent incorporation that undid Corioles. Rome is, in effect, now contaminated by its own filth. The folly of its ways is confirmed by the symbolic reversal that follows, in which Coriolanus now assumes the role of gatekeeper – first ejecting Cominius, then Menenius from the presence of his warcamp. By initiating this assault on Rome, Coriolanus is (as Volumnia notes) effectively 'tearing / His country's bowels out' – he aims to destroy the symbolic organ that expelled him, as well as a conceptual metaphor of the play (5.3.102–3). By concurrently activating associations of food, disease and bodily violations, this image exemplifies the play's structural debt to the dynamics of disgust in a way unlike any other.

Coriolanus, we know, never orchestrates this infection of Rome; his plans for violent invasion are pre-empted by the offer of congenial incorporation, through which he is to be reintegrated into both his familial and civic roles. A Roman messenger celebrates the news, tellingly cast in the language of purgation:

> The Volscians are dislodged and Martius gone.
> A merrier day did never yet greet Rome,
> No, not th'expulsion of the Tarquins. (5.4.43–5)

Yet things aren't so happy in Antium. Aufidius and his conspirators prepare for the return of Coriolanus – the final of the play's long progression of entries, and the one that will bring ruin to the Roman hero. As Aufidius reveals his plot, Shakespeare tellingly balances images of incorporation and expulsion:

>   Him I accuse
> The city ports by this hath entered and
> Intends t'appear before the people, hoping
> To purge himself with words. (5.6.5–8)

In the final moments of the play, the status quo is restored: Coriolanus is once again cast as an invading pathogen. This time, however, he threatens to undermine the city with the spirit of reconciliation – a danger that Aufidius must neutralize, before he contaminates the Volscian plebs with his pacifying rhetoric. Indeed, the returning Coriolanus begins his address to the Antiates by declaring himself innocuous:

> Hail, lords! I am returned your solider,
> No more infected with my country's love
> Than when I parted hence. (71–3)

Yet, for his immediate audience, it is difficult to square this claim with his subsequent celebration of peace. And while mercy may have bought Coriolanus re-entry into his native land, it does little to endear him to the Volscians, who took him for a strand of ill far less susceptible to remedy. As the articles of treason are revealed, Coriolanus is indicted for failing to exhibit (what is thought to be) the characteristic brutality that fuelled his assault on Corioles, and that occasioned his banishment from Rome: the Volscians were sold a bill of goods, and the man before them – who 'at his nurse's tears . . . whined and roared away' the conquest of Rome – does not live up to the 'stolen name' of Coriolanus (99–100; 91). It is clear that Aufidius is disgusted by the accommodating behaviour of Coriolanus, whom he famously denounces as a 'boy of tears' (103). This, the final blow, triggers the Roman's familiar indignation – a violent outburst that, in a crippling irony, only provides the final pretext for the Volscian coup. In witnessing the rage of Coriolanus, the plebeians are at last reminded of the violence to which it was once directed: 'He killed my son! My daughter! He killed my cousin Marcus! He killed my father!' (121–3). In this bloody spectacle – which is also clearly a symbolic feast – the Volscian citizens 'tear him to pieces', sentencing Coriolanus to the same fate as his many unfortunate victims in the field (121). Blood, wounds, stomachs, indignity – this is the stuff of raw disgust, and it is present as ever in the play's final moment.

7

Body envelope disgust

Soaked in the gore of his fallen adversaries, Coriolanus returns to the Roman camp appearing to have been *flayed*; for a brief moment, it seems as if his body has been gruesomely turned inside-out. And though he is awash with the blood of others, that very body has itself been partly compromised by enemy swords, rewarding him with the gashes and scars that so titillate the hero's hungry countrymen. *Coriolanus* thus shows a particular interest in violations of the human body's corporeal integrity, what disgust researchers have deemed the *body envelope*. Violence against our bodies seems to be a widely reliable trigger of revulsion; when trying to elicit disgust (even in studies not ostensibly on the emotion), researchers often show video clips of the human form under visceral duress, such as 'the treatment of burn victims' or 'a close-up of the amputation of an arm'.[1] Shakespeare, of course, made good dramatic use of such bodily violations – as we saw most vividly in *Titus Andronicus* – and it is thus important for us to consider the disgust that is evoked by the traumatized human shell.

In their initial work outlining common triggers of disgust, Haidt, McCauley and Rozin noted that responses to a disgust questionnaire showed a persistent concern with 'gore, surgery, puncture wounds, deformity, and other situations in which the normal exterior envelope of the body is breached or altered'; this led them to conclude that *body envelope violations* form a stable category of disgust elicitors that account for our revulsion at the compromised human body.[2] As we saw in Chapter 1, such triggers were understood in the larger context of animal-reminder disgust:

> Humans are like other animals in having fragile body envelopes that when breached, reveal blood and soft viscera. For all our

efforts to distinguish humans from animals (e.g. language, morality, two-legs-no-feathers), on the inside we are almost indiscriminable from other mammals. Body envelope violations may therefore be disgusting because they are direct reminders of the fragility and animality of our bodies.[3]

Subsequent research has similarly found envelope violations to be associated with animal-reminder disgust – but this is certainly not the only way to account for the phenomenon.[4] This is because disgust has been linked to numerous forms of bodily irregularity, including 'less attractive or atypical bodily features that mimic signs of infectious disease' (such as acne), features that 'trigger concerns about genetic or reproductive quality' (such as obesity), or those that 'involve violations of an idealized and desirable exterior body shape' (such as disfigurement).[5]

Given what we've already seen about disgust's vital role in disease prevention, it's not surprising that body envelope violations have been consistently associated with pathogen transmission in more recent thinking. At the most basic level, of course, a torn or open body is a body more likely to transmit whatever pathogens are lurking within, so it makes sense that a disgust response to wounds and blood signals that 'potential infectious contaminants carried in the bloodstream [are] now exposed by a violation of the body envelope'.[6] This envelope disgust, however, goes even further than bloody wounds, because in humans it is not unusual for 'contagious diseases [to be] accompanied by anomalous physical features'.[7] Accordingly, we seem to have developed 'a tendency for people to implicitly associate the risk of infection with a broad range of superficial cues', meaning that 'any gross deviation from species-typical morphological norms may be interpreted as evidence of [an] infection, triggering an aversive response'.[8] As we discussed earlier, it is theorized that 'humans have an evolved predisposition to avoid individuals with disease signs, which is mediated by the emotion of disgust' – and, because of the hypervigilance of the BIS, this 'implicit avoidance occurs even when [we] know explicitly that such signs... result from a noncontagious condition'.[9] Thus any 'benign object *resembling* an agent of disease can assume the infectious threat value of the actual repugnant stimulus', meaning that not only are people repulsed by bodily variations that 'pose a genuine disease risk (e.g. pustules)'; they are 'also disgusted by things that pose no risk at all but which simply resemble genuine disease risks (e.g. psoriasis)'.[10] Accordingly, it has been suggested that 'the emotion of disgust may play a key role in disability prejudice', because the hair-trigger sensitivity of the pathogen avoidance system means that 'the non-conforming bodies and behaviors of people with disabilities (PWD) may be mistaken for pathogen cues'.[11] (And unfortunately, this is only the first instance we'll encounter in which the BIS's reactivity seems to contribute to social marginalization.)

Disgust, then, helps shape how we respond to bodies – the bodies of others, and the bodies we inhabit ourselves. Researchers have explored this linkage in a variety of contexts. Most immediate is that of *blood-injury-injection* (BII) *phobia*, which is defined as extreme 'fear and avoidance . . . triggered by the anticipation or presence of blood, injury, injections, and conceptually similar stimuli'; experimental results indicate that disgust is the 'primary emotion' involved in this condition.[12] But there are many more domains where disgust has been shown to guide our response to traumatized or non-normative human bodies. As mentioned earlier, people with high disgust-proneness 'tend to report greater negative reactions and visual attention to photos of disfigured faces', and evidence suggests that 'facial disfigurement . . . can trigger the same set of emotional and behavioral responses as a contagious disease'.[13] The same basic response has been recorded towards obese persons, whose bodies can be 'heuristically perceived as a sign of disease that trigger[s] a disgust and avoidance response'.[14] As 'an emotion that is felt when the body border is violated', disgust is also thought to be 'intimately linked to body image' concerns, and a wealth of research has examined how feelings of disgust shape perceptions of our own bodies.[15] Self-disgust is an important measure of negative body image, and is particularly elevated in people with body image disturbance and body dysmorphic disorder.[16] Prosthesis use, which 'helps to maintain the amputated limb in the body schema', leads to significantly less self-disgust in amputee patients.[17] Conversely, people with body integrity identity disorder (BIID) – a disorder 'characterized by the overwhelming desire to amputate one or more healthy limbs or to be paraplegic' – respond with 'a selectively reduced disgust response to violations of the body envelope', when shown images of limb amputation.[18]

Bodily disgust also has important health-care implications, in terms of both how patients respond to their own injured bodies and how caretakers respond to the compromised bodies they must heal. For example, patients with high disgust sensitivity are at greater risk for being non-compliant with home self-care wound management, leading to a host of potential medical complications.[19] The emotion has also been linked to mental health outcomes in colostomy patients, while sensitivity to disgust seems to increase the likelihood that a person with a skin condition will develop depression.[20] More broadly, disgust shapes how people think about organ transplants and organ donation; more specifically, those who are not registered as posthumous organ donors show more investment in 'emotionally valenced factors relating to disgust (ick factor) and bodily integrity' than those who are willing to donate.[21] Finally, even bodies augmented by plastic surgery have been shown to elicit disgust and moral condemnation, apparently because of underlying 'perceptions of plastic surgery as fundamentally unnatural'.[22] Considered together, there seems to be ample evidence supporting the claim that disgust features heavily in how we respond to injuries and alterations to the human body, particularly when those bodies are perceived as abnormal.

This is very important for our current discussion – because as Jeffrey R. Wilson notes, Shakespeare was 'keenly interested in the abnormal body'.[23] We saw in Chapter 2 how early modern England had an ambivalent fascination with those inhabiting non-normative bodies, and Shakespearean drama is in this sense reflective of its culture; still, it seems that Shakespeare was especially captivated by the literary possibilities of such individuals, and recent scholars (particularly those working in disability studies) have devoted much attention to his portrayals of them.[24] Wilson has worked extensively on this topic, valuably framing it within a sociological concept of *stigma*.[25] It seems to me, however, that body envelope disgust can also provide useful insight into how the process of stigmatization works, given the empirical evidence linking it to numerous forms of discrimination against the physical form. And for Shakespeare, those who inhabit stigmatized, non-normative bodies are more often than not presented as morally suspect.

There is no doubt that Shakespearean drama routinely draws a connection between body envelopes and morality: in both comic and tragic contexts, individuals with abnormal bodies are consistently associated with villainy. The classic example, of course, is Richard III, whose deformity prompts comment in three different plays; one telling barb, deploying the language of visceral disgust, declares him a 'foul indigested lump, / As crooked in thy manners as thy shape' (*Henry VI, Part 2*, 5.1.157-8).[26] This assessment anticipates Prospero's indictment of the deformed Caliban, who he describes being 'as disproportioned in his manners / As in his shape' (*The Tempest*, 5.1.291–2). *Twelfth Night's* Antonio, thinking himself betrayed by Sebastian, cannot believe that such bad behaviour could emerge from such a beautiful body; 'thou hast . . . done good feature shame', he tells his friend, because 'none can be called deformed but the unkind' (3.4.270;72). In *King John*, Constance gives a somewhat bizarre explanation, again couched in the language of disgust, of how Arthur's currently threatened royal birthright is tied to his physical integrity:

> If thou that bid'st me be content wert grim,
> Ugly, and slanderous to thy mother's womb,
> Full of unpleasing blots and sightless stains,
> Lame, foolish, crooked, swart, prodigious,
> Patched with foul moles and eye-offending marks,
> I would not care, I then would be content;
> For then I should not love thee, no, nor thou
> Become thy great birth, nor deserve a crown.
> But thou art fair, and at thy birth, dear boy,
> Nature and Fortune joined to make thee great.
> Of nature's gifts thou mayst with lilies boast
> And with the half-blown rose. (3.1.43–54)[27]

Elsewhere in the play, John claims that his own mind was actually drawn to murderous thoughts by Hubert's apparent deformity:

> How oft the sight of means to do ill deeds
> Makes deeds ill done! Hadst not thou been by,
> A fellow by the hand of nature marked,
> Quoted and signed to do a deed of shame,
> This murder had not come into my mind.
> But taking note of thy abhorred aspect,
> Finding thee fit for bloody villainy,
> Apt, liable to be employed in danger,
> I faintly broke with thee of Arthur's death. (4.2.219–27)

This is quite a remarkable testament to the corrupting power of the non-normative body. And it recalls what we saw earlier of Falstaff's diseased, obese shell, which serves as an index to his social vices, and ultimately necessitates his purgation from the social body surrounding the king.[28]

Of course, villains don't simply possess a compromised, disgusting body envelope – they also attempt to inflict revolting trauma to the body envelopes of others. Perhaps the most obvious case is the blinding of Gloucester in *King Lear*. This act, Samuel Johnson famously declared, is something 'too horrid to be endured in dramatick exhibition'; centuries later, this assessment was echoed by John D. Staines, who notes that 'Cornwall's revenge against the most sensitive of human organs can shock even the eyes of modern spectators accustomed to the graphic gore of Hollywood film'.[29] Gloucester is himself first described as a 'filthy traitor' before the act occurs (3.7.33) – but Shakespeare most firmly establishes himself as a genius of poetic disgust with Cornwall's infamous command 'Out, vile jelly', a phrase I cannot read without experiencing a visceral shudder (83). As Robert B. Pierce frames it, the trauma inflicted to the body's integrity here is existential: 'loss of sight, loss of power, induced physical helplessness, and violation of his body are the motifs of the transformation that Gloucester undergoes, and loss of sight is the symbolic nexus of this horror.'[30] There is also, somewhat perversely, a moral valence to Gloucester's punishment, in the sense that blinding functions as a symbolic castration for the crimes of fornication and adultery; Jay Halio reminds us that there was for early modern audiences a historical linkage of blinding and punishment for sexual offences, as when the homily 'Against Whoredom, and Adultery' observes that 'emonge the Locreusyans, the adulterers had bothe theyr eyes thrust oute'.[31] Conversely, the non-blinding of Arthur in *King John* functions (in retrospect) to increase our moral sympathy with Hubert – despite his own alleged deformity, he refuses to alter the shape of Arthur's pristine body. We have already seen the traumatic violence of *Titus Andronicus*; in no other play of Shakespeare are body envelopes so thoroughly violated. The horrors inflicted on Lavinia render her an object of both sympathy and disgust, while it's interesting that the often flippant way bodily injury is vocalized in the play ('Bear thou my hand, sweet wench, between thy teeth' [3.1.283]; 'Lavinia 'tween her stumps doth hold / The basin that receives your guilty blood'

[5.2.182–3]) seems to uncomfortably delight even as it repels, reflecting the play's overall dynamic that I discussed in Chapter 2.

It is also notable that the violence to Lavinia and Titus is orchestrated by racial outsiders (Goth and Moor), because I would be remiss to neglect *The Merchant of Venice* – a play in which a notorious threat to bodily integrity is manufactured by a character who is himself marked as Other. We will see in Chapter 9 how the Jewish body was portrayed as an object of disgust in early modern England, and it is likely that Shylock would be understood by contemporaries as corporeally non-normative, whether or not he wore the exaggerated prosthetic nose that was used to signify Jewishness in other plays of the era.[32] *Merchant,* writes Clayton Koelb, is a work that 'puts into question commonplace notions about what belongs together and what may come apart', and I think that the discourse of bodily disgust is a primary means through which this inquiry occurs.[33] Of course, Jews were already associated with body envelope violations through the ritual of circumcision, and James Shapiro has argued that 'an occluded threat of circumcision informs Shylock's desire to cut a pound of Antonio's flesh'.[34] There is also some suggestion that the flesh is desired for a symbolic act of cannibalism, given Shylock's earlier vow 'to feed upon / The prodigal Christian' (2.5.14–15) and the later characterization of his desire as 'wolvish, bloody, starved and ravenous' (4.1.137). To this end, François-Xavier Gleyzon emphasizes that 'Shylock's attempt to open the body [and] make an incision into the Christian body of Antonio represents and reproduces a willingness to attack and to profane the Eucharist'.[35] Whatever the case, the play's horror is amplified by Shylock's refusal to fully account for his interest in 'a weight of carrion flesh' (40), as there is nothing (besides villainy and sadism) to contextualize or rationalize the threat to Antonio's bodily integrity ('I'll not answer that . . . I give no reason, nor I will not' [41; 58]). Finally, it's especially interesting that Shylock appeals to the collective experience of having a bodily shell in his most famous speech; by asking 'if you prick us do we not bleed', he attempts to leverage body envelope disgust by activating in his enemies an awareness of their shared (corporeal) humanity (3.1.58–9). While this logic may be rejected by those internal and external to the playworld – David S. Katz reminds us that in the period 'not only was Jewish blood fundamentally distinct from that of Christians, [but] the bodily orifices from which it issues might be uniquely Jewish as well' – the larger point is that *Merchant* clearly has a sustained interest in the opening of bodies, a reflection of the fact that disgust seems to innately keep (most) people squeamish about such matters.[36]

But to conclude this chapter, I'd like to consider a play that consistently explores the dramatic and thematic potential of body envelope violence: *Julius Caesar*. The play begins, of course, with Caesar's opponents famously framing his deaf and epileptic body as compromised; Cassius cannot believe that 'a man of such a feeble temper should / So get the start of the majestic world / And bear the palm alone' (1.2.130–2).[37] But I am most interested in the portrayal of Caesar's bloody, wounded corpse – and indeed, Maurice Charney argued long ago that the 'central issue' of the play's interpretation concerns 'the imagery of blood'.[38] Gail Kern Paster agrees, noting that 'one way of phrasing the play's central political struggle up to the point at which civil war breaks out is to say that it occurs discursively as a struggle over kinds and meanings of blood and bleeding'.[39] But while Paster focuses her analysis on the gendered implications of this struggle – arguing that the assassination 'discloses the shameful secret of Caesar's bodiliness . . . a womanly inability to stop bleeding' – I suggest that we can equally view this contest as one to control whether or not Caesar's violated corpse elicits visceral and moral disgust.

Even before the murder, the play insistently asks us to imagine extreme violence against Caesar's bodily integrity. Ironically, these images are first evoked through negation; Brutus envisions the conspirators as 'sacrificers but not butchers' (2.1.165), 'purgers, not murderers' (179), and suggests that they 'carve him as a dish fit for the gods, / Not hew him as a carcass fit for hounds' (172–3). Antony is spared, because 'he can do no more than Caesar's arm / When Caesar's head is off' (181–2) – and it would 'seem too bloody . . . to cut the head off and then hack the limbs' (161–2). Brutus, in fact, attempts to deny Caesar's corporality all together, vowing that 'we all stand up against the spirit of Caesar, / And in the spirit of men there is no blood' (166–7). But this is distinctly not the case, as we are reminded by Calphurnia's prophetic dream – in which Caesar's statue, 'like a fountain with an hundred spouts, / Did run pure blood; and many lusty Romans / Came smiling and did bathe their hands in it' (2.2.77–9). Decius attempts to reinterpret – assuring that the 'many smiling Romans bathed / Signifies that from you great Rome shall suck / Reviving blood' (86–8) – but we know better: the play ominously insists upon the fragility of the body's boundaries, a theme quietly furthered both by Portia's 'voluntary wound' (2.1.299) and by the augurer who, 'pucking the entrails of an offering forth . . . could not find a heart within the beast' (2.2.39–40).

But it is after the murder that comes the more crucial moment of interpretation, for the conspirators must convince their countrymen that the trauma they just inflicted on Caesar's body is not cause for alarm. Quite curiously, Brutus does so by fully embracing the gory matter they have just turned inside-out:

> Stoop, Romans, stoop,
> And let us bathe our hands in Caesar's blood
> Up to the elbows and besmear our swords.
> Then walk we forth even to the market-place,
> And waving our red weapons o'er our heads
> Let's all cry, 'Peace, Freedom and Liberty'. (3.1.105–10)

Flush with the righteousness of their deed (and, we must imagine, with adrenaline), Brutus and Cassius have already decided how their actions will be judged by posterity; 'how many ages hence / Shall this our lofty scene be acted', they wonder, 'how many times shall Caesar bleed in sport?' (111–12; 114). For now, however, it is Caesar's allies who must be convinced, leading to Brutus's attempt to reframe the murder for Antony:

> Though now we must appear bloody and cruel,
> As by our hands and this our present act
> You see we do, yet see you but our hands
> And this the bleeding business they have done:
> Our hearts you see not. (165–9)

It seems to me that this suggestion reveals a rather stunning obliviousness on Brutus's part – because while he can abstractly conceive of how the situation appears, he doesn't seem to fully register just how horrifying his bloodied form must be to the shocked onlookers. One cannot simply ignore the carnage and peer into his heart; this is indicated, I think, by Antony's telling remark that 'your purple hands do reek and smoke' (158). While Arden editor David Daniell suggests that *reek* here is a simple synonym for *smoke* (OED, 'reek, *v*.1, 1.a), I think it more likely means 'a powerful, unpleasant smell' (ibid., 4b) – as when Coriolanus in the last chapter compared the plebeian's noxious breath to the 'reek o'th' rotten fens' (3.3.120). In other words, Antony experiences the blood-soaked scene as viscerally disgusting, just as he will later portray it as morally repulsive. Expedience demands that he embrace the murderers in the moment, but he cannot help but comment on the trauma that has been inflected on Caesar's still-leaking body:

> If then thy spirit look upon us now,
> Shall it not grieve thee dearer than thy death
> To see thy Antony making his peace,
> Shaking the bloody fingers of thy foes?
> Most noble in the presence of thy corse,
> Had I as many eyes as thou hast wounds,
> Weeping as fast as they stream forth thy blood,
> It would become me better than to close
> In terms of friendship with thine enemies. (195–203)

But it is after the conspirators leave that he can fully acknowledge the horror of what has happened to Caesar, where he actually invokes the open wounds as the occasion for prophecy:

> O pardon me, thou bleeding piece of earth,
> That I am meek and gentle with these butchers.
> Thou art the ruins of the noblest man
> That ever lived in the tide of times.
> Woe to the hand that shed this costly blood.
> Over thy wounds now I do prophesy
> (Which like dumb mouths do ope their ruby lips
> To beg the voice and utterance of my tongue)
> A curse shall light upon the limbs of men. (254–62)

And if there's any doubt about how he feels, Antony concludes the speech by casting the conspirator's action in the rawest language of explicit disgust: 'this foul deed', he vows, 'shall smell above the earth / With carrion men, groaning for burial' (274–5).

What I'm suggesting, then, is that Brutus and his allies are fundamentally disconnected from how the murder would be reasonably construed by onlookers: it does not occur to them that

Antony might be viscerally and morally repulsed by their bloody ramblings in front of Caesar's leaking corpse. And when it comes time to sway the citizens, Antony does so by evoking in them the same disgust that he so powerfully experiences. The plebeians in *Caesar* are notoriously fickle, and it is true that they initially call for Brutus – but when Antony gets his turn, things quickly alter. Though Antony's famous speech is, of course, multifaceted, one thing that he surely does is make salient the raw materiality of Caesar's opened, bloody carcass. 'Make a ring about the corpse of Caesar', he declares to the onlookers, inviting them to ritually gaze upon the body (3.2.158). He then draws their attention to Caesar's cloak, narrating the tear made by each conspirator's knife:

> Look, in this place ran Cassius' dagger through:
> See what a rent the envious Caska made:
> Through this, the well-beloved Brutus stabbed,
> And as he plucked his cursed steel away,
> Mark how the blood of Caesar followed it. (172–6)

But the climax occurs when Antony shockingly removes the cloak, exposing 'Caesar's . . . marred as you see with traitors' (194–5). As Daniell notes, 'Caesar's stabbed corpse is suddenly present, a reality that is dramatically explosive'; the plebeians are shocked by this 'most bloody sight', and quickly vow revenge (198). Antony's recitation of Caesar's virtue primed them to reinterpret the murder as a moral crime – but their exposure to his mangled corpse makes their offence visceral. Antony, I suggest, leverages body envelope disgust to harness the crowd, as he is ultimately able to control how the violation of Caesar's corporeal integrity is experienced somatically and spiritually by his countrymen.

8

Othello

The disgusting outsider

The human mechanism of disgust, working on behalf of the hypervigilant BIS, is designed to guard against substances that might cause our bodies harm – and, as we have seen, it errs on the side of caution. But while this reactive tendency is an evolutionary measure designed to keep us safe, it also, unfortunately, seems to have rather dire social consequences, in terms of how it inadvertently shapes human relations in the world. In the last chapter, we saw how the sensitive calibration of disgust can lead to discriminatory practices against those who inhabit bodies that seem abnormal. In this chapter, I will engage *Othello* to demonstrate how the disgust system promotes dehumanization and discrimination of another kind: that targeting racial and ethnic outgroups.

While few would deny that jealousy and envy are the dominant (and most explicitly articulated) emotions in *Othello*, I suggest in what follows that the affective mode of disgust plays an equally important role in the tragedy. More specifically, I argue that racialized disgust is what precisely animates Iago's plot to undo his master, serving both as a personal motivator and as an instrument by which he poisons how Othello is perceived by others. In this sense, the circulation of racial meaning in Shakespeare's Venice is intimately tied to the circulation of affective meaning – and the inscription of racial identity onto Othello by the inhabitants of Venice is fundamentally an emotional process.

The ongoing development of premodern critical race studies (PCRS) is perhaps the most exciting intellectual current in early modern studies today.[1] In this chapter, I attempt to put the vital insights of this research in conversation with scholarship on disgust from the affective sciences.[2] I am thus informed by recent work that broadly treats the connection between race and emotion – such as the essays gathered in Carol Mejia LaPerle's groundbreaking collection *Race and Affect in Early Modern English Literature* – as well as on more specific research that has begun to explore how disgust becomes racialized.[3] Mira 'Assaf Kafantaris, for example, persuasively demonstrates that disgust is a component of how foreign queens are racialized in *The Faerie Queene*, Gitanjali G. Shahani, we will see, reveals how disgust towards foreign food marked the European response to other cultures in contemporary travelogues and Ian Smith has briefly remarked upon the 'racial disgust' that Othello's Black skin elicits in Brabantio.[4] I build on this important scholarship, not only by drawing upon a historicized account of early modern racial disgust but also by engaging modern psychological research on how disgust seems to contribute to racial discrimination. I take this approach because modern scientific studies of both race and emotion make one thing clear: disgust is central to how outgroup prejudice and racial discrimination function in everyday life. That is, a compelling body of evidence demonstrates that we cannot fully account for the workings of racism without accounting for the role that disgust plays in its operation; because of this, the description and analysis of racial formations in early modern England can be valuably informed by considering how the dynamics of disgust feature in the forms of marginalization, discrimination and violence that we find in the historical and literary record.

In *Othello*, the central character's status as a racialized subject comes to be underpinned by his status as a *disgusting* subject.[5] Racial discourses, I suggest, are thus entwined with affective discourses: while jealousy is the mechanism through which Iago first attacks his master, it is disgust that underwrites how Othello is broadly understood throughout Venice, and it is the circulation of disgust that underwrites the forms of racial violence that are depicted in *Othello*. The terms through which Othello is racially encoded are consistently drawn from the lexicon of disgust – and they importantly anticipate the findings of the modern scientific research tradition, which consistently shows that disgust is a central component of racial discrimination. The case study of *Othello*, it follows, suggests how sensitivity to the workings of disgust might help elucidate some of the specific forms that early modern racist violence takes.[6] Finally, it is vital to acknowledge that recent scholarship has crucially underscored the connection between premodern constructions of race and the world we inhabit today; Arthur L. Little, Jr. observes that the study of early modern race is invested in the way that 'Western modernity is *intimately* bound to early modern race formations', while Margo Hendricks notes that PCRS 'actively pursues not only the study of race in the premodern . . . but [also] the way those studies can effect a transformation of the academy and its relationship to our world'.[7] Because of this, I conclude the chapter by suggesting that there is a linkage between the patterns of racial disgust depicted in *Othello* and the mechanisms of racist violence that still plague our contemporary moment. Viewing the play through this lens, we will see, reveals another striking continuity between the racial and racist formations of the past and the present, and will, I hope, further demonstrate how this model of racial disgust might serve as a valuable tool for analysing both premodern and modern race.

* * *

While disgust's gatekeeping functions have undoubtedly helped the human species navigate both its physical and cultural worlds, they also have introduced some very unfortunate side effects: the emotion, scientific findings suggest, is integral to the workings of outgroup discrimination, including racism. Indeed, since 2004, over sixty psychological studies have examined the association between disgust and xenophobia, with results reliably suggesting that 'disgust sensitivity [is] a relatively standard predictor of prejudice'.[8] In one experiment, for example, having a high disgust sensitivity on interpersonal matters (such as 'not wanting to wear clean used clothes or to sit on a warm seat vacated by a stranger') has been shown to predict 'negative attitudes toward immigrants, foreigners, and socially deviant groups'.[9] Furthermore, research suggests that outgroup disgust is *essentializing* – that is, 'when a person says "group X is disgusting" s/he conveys a belief that this group possesses a negative inherent *essence* (as opposed to merely being associated with a negative outcome or behavior, or possessing a negative characteristic that is incidental/fleeting)'.[10] In this sense, disgust towards outgroups suggests that members of that group, fundamentally, have an 'impure essence' with 'a biological basis [that] is immutable and fixed'.[11] When outgroups are essentialized as disgusting, it makes them subject to discrimination and violence – and indeed, it has been suggested that those prone to outgroup discrimination and hate 'may actually see themselves as the immune system of a wider "body politic" which must be defended from dangerous social pathogens'.[12]

That the object of disgust becomes construed as something like a pathogen is important, because the emotion 'appears to have the unique capacity to foster the social-cognitive dehumanization of outgroup members' – and dehumanization, the process of thought and action through which another is construed as not fully human, is a consistent feature of the literature on disgust and prejudice.[13] Experimental participants primed with disgust cues are more likely to subsequently dehumanize an arbitrary outgroup than those primed with other emotions or neutral stimuli, and subjects who already possess a higher sensitivity to matters of disgust are also more inclined to dehumanize an outgroup.[14] Unsurprisingly, dehumanization most often occurs 'in relation to ethnicity, race, and related topics such as immigration and genocide' – and in fact, 'the inclination to view members of other ethnic groups as not quite human' has been called 'a persistent theme in ethnographic and historical literatures that record the dynamics of intergroup relations'.[15] Accordingly, when thinking about how the character of Othello is increasingly stripped of his humanity as the play unfolds, it is important to remember that it is the emotion of disgust that is fuelling this dehumanization – disgust, I'll argue in the second part of this chapter, that is weaponized by Iago, who uses it to infect not only third parties but also Othello himself.

Modern scientific research thus suggests that disgust plays a central role in how racial outgroups are perceived. And indeed, we find this mechanism at work in early modern racial discourse, as racial outsiders – particularly Black racial outsiders – are regularly associated with disgust elicitors like dirt and disease. According to Sir Thomas Brown, 'things become blacke by a sootish and fuliginous matter proceeding from the sulphur of bodies torrified'; because of this, it was said that 'Aethiopians or Negroes become coalblacke from fuliginous efflorescences and complexionall tinctures arising from such probabilities'.[16] The terms *sootish* and *fuliginous* ['covered or blackened with soot'] here are crucial, because they link Black skin – like Othello's so-called 'sooty bosom' (1.2.70) – with the notion of dirt, a crucial element in how disgust has been cross-culturally theorized.[17] Mary Douglas, whose comments on monstrosity we considered earlier, importantly traces cultural understandings of dirt in terms of both pollution and taboo; she influentially theorized that dirt signifies 'matter out of place', that which threatens order and propriety in a social environment.[18] For this reason, dirtiness is associated both with the visceral elicitors of somatic disgust (notions relating to pathogens, hygiene, filthiness, etc.) and with the social violation of moral and symbolic disgust, insofar as that which is fundamentally dirty becomes marked as that which is not integrated into the social order, or even welcomed in it. We may think, in *King Lear*, of how Poor Tom becomes dirty in his abjection – and indeed, Benjamin Minor and Ayanna Thompson have shrewdly suggested that Edgar's begrimed disguise functions like a form of blackface.[19] In early modern England, Black bodies are thus, in their alleged dirtiness, inherently 'out of place'; they are always an implicit object of disgust, and often (as we will see in a moment) become so explicitly. This association between Blackness and dirt is evident in the period's commonplace proverb about the impossibility of *washing* the pigment out of Black skin; writers frequently refer to the fact that '*Black-moores* will not change their hue, though you wash them with Sope'.[20] Indeed, Kim F. Hall notes that 'the whitewashed Ethiopian is a ubiquitous image in Renaissance literature, appearing often in emblem books and proverbs as a figure of the impossible'.[21]

The association of Black skin and disgust is amplified when we consider that the early modern period advanced what Jonathan Gil Harris calls a 'quasi-scientific discourse of blackness as a hereditary infection'.[22] George Best, contemplating 'the *Ethiopians* great blacknesse', decides that 'this blacknesse proceedeth of such naturall infection of the first inhabitants of that Countrey, and so all the whole progenie of them descended, are still poluted with the same blot of infection'.[23] That Blackness is conceptualized as an *infection* is very telling: proximity to disease is one of the fundamental elicitors of disgust, and we have seen throughout how scientists theorize that the human disgust response partly originated as a system of disease and pathogen avoidance. Calling the Ethiopians *polluted* furthers this association with disease-based disgust, but it also links them to broader matters of symbolic impurity – in other words, the domain of regulatory, sociomoral disgust. For it was said in the period that 'the blackness of the *Negroes* proceeded from the curse upon *Cham*'s posterity', providing an apparent biblical justification for linking Black skin to violation and wickedness.[24] In Best's telling of this tale, Cham violates his father Noah's commandment by engaging in 'carnall copulation' with his wife on the ark; as punishment for this transgression, God willed that 'a sonne shuld be borne, whose name was *Chus*, who not only it selfe, but all his posteritie after him, should be so blacke & lothsome, that it might remaine a spectacle of disobedience to all the World'.[25] The phrase *black & lothsome* instantly activates the register of disgust; *loathsome*, we've seen, functions as a synonym of *disgusting*, as a word that can refer to both that which triggers visceral nausea and that which triggers moral offence. Furthermore, it is telling that this punishment resulted from the breaking of a sexual taboo, because the violation of perceived sexual norms is a primary category of disgust elicitors. As Sujata Iyengar observes, Best's account associates Blackness with a 'polluted and polluting' sexual violation, ultimately signalling English 'fears about sexual commixture, the horrifying fantasy of racial pollution'.[26] Racial disgust is thus very much invoked in this fantasy of original Blackness, which entails what Joyce Green MacDonald calls a 'sinister moral taint'.[27]

Given the centrality of food to the human disgust system, it's unsurprising that food disgust also plays a role in how racial and ethnic outgroups are designated as repulsive. As Shahani has demonstrated, contemporary travelogues reveal that disgust towards unfamiliar foods was a common component of how European travellers interacted with non-white persons in their native regions. In particular, Shahani focuses on narratives describing the Cape of Good Hope, where the 'dietary habits of the native inhabitants provoke the expression of unmitigated disgust': the indigenous people of the region were said to participate in a host of customs that repulsed their European observers, including eating raw entrails and using animal dung as a form of relish.[28] This 'ethnographic disgust' is apparent in many accounts of indigenous eating practices, to the extent that there may be said to be 'an evolving tradition of ethnographic observation seemingly interrupted by disgust or culminating in disgust, inscribing disgust itself as a textual convention of the travelogues and protoethnographies that proliferated in the seventeenth century'.[29] Disgust is a thus crucial component of how African peoples were racialized in the early modern period, as the emotion's obvious contribution to outgroup othering is readily apparent in contemporary records.

Finally, the evidence for early modern racial disgust is sometimes quite explicit: as Smith has documented, both literary and non-literary texts suggest that the sight of Black skin elicited a 'general revulsion' in at least some Renaissance English subjects.[30] The most notable example is Dudley Carleton's reaction to Jonson's *The Masque of Blackness* (1605), in which courtly ladies were painted black on their faces and arms; Carleton registers his disgust at their appearance in a series of letters, advising his correspondents that it 'was a very lothsome sight' and that 'you cannot imagine a more ugly Sight, then a Troop of lean-cheek'd Moors'.[31] Indeed, Carleton's response has helped shape how modern commentators understand the literary features of the masque; Hardin Aasand, for example, argues that the disguised Queen Anne becomes 'a royal grotesquery' that 'presents the grotesque and all its implications', including susceptibility to 'the contagion of physical defilement'.[32] This is not, of course, to say that Black skin was universally considered repulsive by white English subjects; though the ladies of *The Masque of Blackness* were offensive to Carleton, scholarship by Mejia LaPerle and Bernadette Andrea suggests that the literary dynamics of that performance may actually explore a more ambivalent, if not positive, association between Blackness and beauty.[33] But Smith does record that Carlton's adverse response is representative of a more widespread phenomenon (overlapping with fear), which he characterizes as a 'propensity for black panic' in the minds of contemporary white English subjects.[34] Racialized disgust was thus actively experienced in early modern England, and Shakespeare represents a parallel experience in the Venice of *Othello*.

Critical race theory is not simply concerned with the outlook of individuals, but also with how racism is perpetuated by deep legal and social structures, and I will have more to say herein about the systemic relation between disgust and race in the Venice of *Othello*. But because human psychological architecture helps contribute to the shape of sociocultural systems – and because literary drama has an inevitable investment in the interactions of individual characters – it is worthwhile to also think about how meanings of race are formulated at the level of subjective psychology.[35] And here, research shows, the emotion of disgust is a central component of how discrimination and racism operate in individuals. I turn now to *Othello*, which I see as a case study of how racial disgust leads to tragic violence: it is disgust, I suggest, that comes to characterize how Othello is perceived by other characters in the play, and it is disgust that determines how he comes to understand himself. By attending to racial disgust, we can freshly analyse both the affective and the racial dynamics of *Othello*, ultimately seeing how these two discourses are intimately connected.

* * *

In a recent study of the 'process of marking' in *Othello*, Patricia Akhimie observes that Othello's Black skin serves as an 'immutable somatic mark' that signals not only his difference but also his association with 'a set of undesirable behavioral tendencies'.[36] This process is compounded, I'll now argue, by the way that Iago uses the essentializing function of racial disgust to transform Othello into an object of fear and repulsion, conferring on him an identity that then seems to other characters to be inevitable and immutable. In his plot to ruin his master, Iago causes racial disgust to circulate throughout the playworld – and the way that it increasingly defines Othello reveals the extent to which affective and racial discourses are entwined in this dramatic universe.

This process begins mere minutes into the play, as Iago (aided by Roderigo) successfully works to enflame the racism of Brabantio. The means through which he accomplishes this is crucial, because the association of outgroup members with animals is a prominent way that disgust dehumanizes racial outsiders. Researchers agree that 'animal metaphors offer a revealing window into human prejudice and social judgment', and studies indicate that 'disgust and revulsion feature prominently in images of animalistically dehumanized others'.[37] The play stages such animalistic dehumanization in its opening scene, as Iago, using a series of vivid animal metaphors – Othello is 'an old black ram . . . tupping [his] white ewe' (87–8), a 'Barbary horse' covering his daughter (110) and one with whom she 'mak[es] the beast with two backs' (115)

– insists that Othello's coupling with Desdemona is a disgusting violation. 'Plague him with flies', he commands Roderigo, as the pair proceeds to infect Brabantio with the same racialized disgust that, we will see, ultimately motivates Iago (70).

Because, as noted above, matters associated with sex are also a reliable category of disgust elicitors, the revulsion activated by the animalization of Othello is compounded by the terms in which Iago presents it: Iago wants Brabantio to be disgusted by the image of a Black man sexually violating his white daughter, and it seems to work.[38] (Because 'interracial romance has historically been viewed as a moral affront to purity', it is perhaps unsurprising that modern research suggests that disgust plays 'an important role in bias against interracial romance'.[39]) Iago, I suggest, attempts to specifically elicit a disgust response in Brabantio by using a series of animalistic sex metaphors to convey the alleged unnaturalness of the union. In this sense, it is not simply Blackness that is portrayed as disgusting at the level of essence; it is also *proximity* to Blackness, by which the father comes to see his daughter as symbolically tainted. It's vital, I think, that Brabantio apparently once 'loved [and] oft invited' Othello into the life of his daughter (1.3.129); his bigotry is not absolute, but is rather stoked by Iago, triggered particularly by the apparent sexual corruption of his daughter. But once it is activated, it becomes totalizing, as suggested by Brabantio labelling Othello a 'foul thief' (1.2.62) and referring to his 'foul charms' (73). That which is *foul*, we have seen, is that which elicits some form of disgust (visceral or moral) – and for Brabantio, Othello is thus marked as a revolting object, so much so that he cannot fathom his daughter coupling with such a man willingly. He says as much to Othello, when he expresses his disbelief that 'she, in spite of nature, / Of years, of country, credit, everything, / [could] fall in love with what she feared to look on' (1.3.97–9). In a case of obvious projection, Brabantio assumes that the disgust that he now feels for Othello's Black skin must also reside within his daughter. Brabantio's invocation of *nature* here – repeated several lines later, in his claim that their match is 'against all rules of nature' – is crucial, blurring the lines between the domains of visceral and moral disgust; the marriage, which he sees as a violation of the social order, becomes construed as a violation of the natural order as well (102).

Indeed, I believe that Iago himself is personally sensitive to these alleged violations, because of what we shortly learn about how he perceives his own marriage: Iago projects disgust onto Othello and Desdemona's union, because disgust seems to characterize his own sexual jealousy. I'm referring, of course, to his suspicion that 'the lusty Moor/ Hath leaped into my seat, the thought whereof / Doth like a poisonous mineral gnaw my inwards' (2.1.293–5). It's hard to know what exactly to make of this surprising admission, which is first made in 1.3.384-85 ('it is thought abroad that 'twixt my sheets / He's done my office') – but we know that it is not simply a fleeting thought, as Emilia later reveals that he has charged her with this violation directly ('some such squire [has] turned your wit the seamy side without / And made you to suspect me with the Moor' [4.2.147–9]). I do think, however, that Iago's affective relationship to his own suspicion is made salient by his tactics in the opening scene. When agitating Brabantio, Iago suggests that interracial coupling is an act that offends the social and natural order. If Iago understands an interracial union to be particularly offensive, then it seems likely that he is especially aggravated by the notion of being cuckolded by a Black man – the violation to the sanctity of his marriage compounded by the particularities of who's doing the violating, which turns the transgression into an object of disgust. As we have seen, Blackness – and particularly, Blackness and sexuality – was associated with revulsion and infection in the early modern mind, and, as Iago tells it to Brabantio, Desdemona is essentially polluted by her union with Othello. Emilia would thus equally be rendered disgusting by her contact with Othello's offending body: the imagined transgression is not just symbolic for Iago, but somatic as well. To this end, it is impossible to ignore the suggestive difference in how Iago responds to the prospect of Emilia sleeping with Othello, and how, in the same soliloquy, he responds to the thought of her sleeping with Cassio. While he neutrally mentions that 'I fear Cassio with my night-cap too' (2.1.305) in a casual remark set off grammatically from his main thought, he is, by his own account, viscerally tormented by imagining Othello with Emilia, which prompts a gnawing pain in his stomach – the core domain of disgust. Given his earlier characterizations of Othello as an object of animalized revulsion, it seems that Iago's jealousy here may be fuelled by a deeper kind of outgroup disgust towards the racial Other – this, I think, may actually constitute the *hatred* that Iago feels for Othello (1.1.6; 1.3.383).

Thinking about an Iago who is disgusted by his adversary also allows us to recontextualize his actions in the play's first scene: while his agitation of Brabantio's racism is indeed strategic, it also reveals something of his own orientation towards Othello, and something about the way that both racial and affective meaning operate in Shakespeare's Venice. If we grant my suggestion about Iago's motivation, then we may see his strategy towards Brabantio as a process by which he activates in another the same affective outlook that he feels himself: this is how disgust circulates in the play. I have argued in Chapter 6 that Shakespeare stages a circuit of disgust in *Coriolanus* – the emotion is widely transmissible – and I believe that the opening sequence of *Othello* depicts a similar phenomenon: here, affective meaning becomes mapped onto racial meaning, as Iago induces in Brabantio the disgust that he feels for Othello, just as he will attempt to do with others in the play. And it is this circulation, I will ultimately argue, that transforms racism into a structural feature of Shakespeare's Venice: it constitutes the very fabric of social interaction.

When speaking to the heartbroken Roderigo, Iago consistently characterizes Desdemona's love for Othello in gastric terms. He first notes that a wife's 'eye must be fed' by the appearance of her husband – and incredulously wonders 'what delight shall she have to look on the devil?' (2.1.223–4). Iago's strategy here closely resembles the one he used with Brabantio: he convinces Roderigo that Desdemona could not genuinely be attracted to a Black man, and, consequently, that she will ultimately discard her infatuation and come to see her husband as he does, as an object of disgust. He similarly declares that there is nothing in Othello to give Desdemona a 'fresh appetite' – again recalling the earlier reservation of her father, Iago implies there is an offensive unnaturalness in their union, owing to the lack of 'sympathy in years, manners, and beauties' (226–8). But the invocation of disgust becomes most explicit when he concludes his thought: 'now for want of these required conveniences', Iago predicts, 'her delicate tenderness will find itself abused, begin to heave the gorge, disrelish and abhor the Moor' (228-31). In Iago's metaphoric fantasy, Desdemona will eventually come to vomit at the thought of her husband, finding herself disgusted by that which she once desired. Ben Saunders – whose work on anality and purgation in *Othello* touches briefly on disgust – argues that Iago, 'expressing disgust at what he portrays as Desdemona's excessive desire . . . also betrays his own excess – excessive disgust *at* her desire – by rendering its object abject'.[40] I very much agree, but would suggest that Iago's disgust at Desdemona's desire must be seen as a consequence of his fundamental disgust for Othello himself: he is disturbed that Desdemona could be attracted to what he perceives as a repulsive object, so he once again projects his own disgust onto another, by assuming that she too will inevitably come to feel what he feels. In a perceptive reading of Iago's psychology, Paul Cefalu speaks of the character's 'exaggerated mind reading [that] often misleads and disconcerts him' – and we can certainly see that in this sequence, insofar as 'it is one thing to assume that Desdemona might long for a younger man, but another to posit that she will eventually abhor Othello and cuckold him'.[41] It is Iago's disgust for Othello, I think, that underwrites this cognitive error, as the intensity of his own feeling overloads his capacity to read Desdemona's mind, and makes him misattribute his emotion to her. But while he may fail with Desdemona, we have seen that Iago is able to make disgust circulate in Venice: through a process of association, he induces in Brabantio a revulsion similar to his own, and this quality will ultimately be responsible for his undoing of Othello.

When describing the plan to destroy his master, Iago vows to 'pour . . . pestilence into his ear', and thus to infect Othello with the same jealousy that eats at his own innards (2.3.345); as Cristina León Alfar observes, 'Iago tells the same story about Othello that he imagines is being told about himself', and thus 'forces his enemy and rival to experience identical and equivalent anxiety, pain, and anger'.[42] But this is not the only matter of emotional circulation at play here: in a much larger sense, the activation of this jealousy is contingent on convincing Othello to see *himself* as a disgusting object, just as Iago sees him. To realize this plan, Iago first intimates that his suspicions of Desdemona are too disgusting to reveal – they are 'foul things' and 'uncleanly apprehensions' (3.3.140; 142). This, of course, only provokes Othello further, starting a sequence that culminates in Iago's declaration that jealousy is a 'green-eyed monster, which doth mock / The meat it feeds on' (168–9). We have seen earlier how Iago links his own jealous feelings to matters of the stomach, so it's no accident that his metaphor includes a gastric tag; insofar as jealousy, like envy, feeds upon itself, the image of self-consumption is also apt, given that Othello will soon come to see himself in the same terms of disgust that Iago strategically invokes throughout the sequence. Iago is repulsed by the thought of being cuckolded by a racial outsider, and he leads Othello to believe that his wife's alleged infidelity is a consequence of his disgusting outsider status.

'In *Othello*', Dennis Austin Britton writes, 'Shakespeare positions pity as the emotion that inspires the love between a Venetian woman and a Moor'; as the play unfolds, I suggest that it is actually the emotion of disgust, not jealousy, that inspires the dissolution of that love.[43] Having primed Othello with thoughts of jealousy, Iago next works to poison the very foundation of the match with Desdemona, by portraying her interest in her husband as a disgusting perversion of nature:

> Not to affect many proposed matches
> Of her own clime, complexion and degree,
> Whereto we see, in all things, nature tends –
> Foh! one may smell in such a will most rank,
> Foul disproportion, thoughts unnatural. (233–7)

Othello has already heard this rhetoric from Brabantio, and the audience has further seen it in Iago's conversation with Roderigo – but here, in such an intimate setting, coming from such a trusted source, it is particularly pernicious. Iago reminds Othello of the social conditions that preceded his elopement with Desdemona: she turned down many proposals from men to whom (it is said) she would naturally be suited, in favour of the unnatural one with a Black man. But in emphasizing the unnaturalness of the union, Iago also insists that Desdemona's desire for Othello is viscerally repulsive, as the image of a *rank smell* suggests the essential rottenness of their marriage. There's no doubt that Iago's choice of words recalls the nauseous feeling of bodily disgust; we saw in Chapter 5 that *rank* is often paired with disgust elicitors in early modern English. And to confirm the point, he continues by again invoking the term *foul*, which has been reliably associated with disgust throughout the play. The logic of this argument clearly resonates with Othello, who has been already made vulnerable by Iago's chilling manipulation at the beginning of the scene; he dismisses his ensign immediately after this speech, and in a soliloquy decries that 'she is gone, I am abused, and my relief / Must be to loathe her' (271–2). Othello, of course will ultimately require further proof, but he seems to accept Iago's suggestion that there is something disgusting about Desdemona's love for him – and he, in turn, must *loathe* her for it. By entertaining this premise, I suggest, Othello equally seems to accept what it implies about his own identity: if Desdemona's love for him is disgusting, it is because *he*, at his core, is disgusting.

The concept of internalized racism is relatively familiar in discussions of *Othello,* but I think that this process could also be more specifically called one of internalized disgust – Iago, himself repulsed by the idea of being cuckolded, spends the play convincing others that Othello is an object of disgust, and Othello eventually adopts that viewpoint of himself. Othello's internalization of disgust is most apparent later in the scene, when he declares that Desdemona's 'name, that was as fresh / As Dian's visage, is now begrimed and black / As mine own face' (389–91). Recalling Brabantio's earlier emphasis on *soot*, the notion of Othello's *begrimed* face is one that presents Blackness as an uncleanliness, a filth, a stain – in other words, as an object of disgust. The fact that Othello is begrimed physically and Desdemona is begrimed morally suggests the different registers, variously of material and of symbolic purity, in which disgust operates. If Desdemona's disgusting infidelity has rendered her Black, then Blackness itself must inherently be raw material for disgust. As Ambereen Dadabhoy notes, 'Iago attacks Othello precisely on the points where natural and cultural identities collide and compete – his body'.[44] I think that the alleged disgustingness of that body is one of the (ostensibly) natural and cultural identities that Iago leverages, an identity that, once activated, begins to infect how Othello understands his own relationship to others. In this way, Othello comes to see himself as somatically 'marked', just as he is perceived by other characters in the play.

Commenting on his own villainy earlier in the scene, Iago cheekily deploys the explicit language of early modern disgust: his manipulation, he says, is 'scarce found to distaste / But with a little art upon the blood / Burn[s] like the mines of sulphur' (330-32). But while Othello may not taste it going down, it certainly has a crucial effect, as Iago's command of disgust shapes how other characters see him, how he sees himself, and how he ultimately sees Desdemona. When further goading Othello, Iago continues to paint Desdemona's actions as fundamentally repulsive:

OTHELLO	I will chop her into messes! Cuckold me!
IAGO	O, 'tis foul in her.
OTHELLO	With mine officer!
IAGO	That's fouler. (4.1.196–9)

For this reason, he demands that Desdemona be strangled in 'the bed she hath contaminated' (204) – a remark that anticipates the relevance of disgust to the play's terrible final scene.

As Michael Neill has argued, revulsion is a key component of *Othello*'s conclusion: drawing upon Lodovico's remark that the bloody spectacle 'poisons sight', as well as Samuel Johnson's horrified critical response to it, Neill notes that 'the tableau on the bed announces a kind of plague, one that taints the sight as the deadly effluvia of pestilence poison the nostrils'.[45] After Iago's horrific suggestion of strangulation is realized, Othello first adopts the language of disgust when justifying the murder – 'O', he tells Emilia, 'she was foul' (5.2.198) – because after having been made to see himself as an object of revulsion, Othello comes to see his wife this way as well. Emilia's response to the shocking crime also demonstrates how the discourse of disgust and the discourse of race are perilously entwined in the play. After Desdemona's death, Emilia rails against her murderer, denouncing Othello as a 'blacker devil' (129); according to Edward Berry, this 'startling' explosion of 'suppressed racial hatred' reveals that Emilia had 'apparently masked a revulsion against Othello's blackness'.[46] I think that Berry is quite right to emphasize her *revulsion* – for in their subsequent encounter, Emilia attacks Othello using several images from the lexicon of disgust, calling him both 'ignorant as dirt' (160) and Desdemona's 'most filthy bargain' (153). Though her horror at Othello's action is quite understandable, her sudden deployment of this imagery is a telling example of how the circulation of disgust operates on the stage: the language of racial disgust that Iago introduces into the playworld is here adopted in this moment of crisis, the activation of a potentiality that was always latent in Othello's Otherness. This process demonstrates my basic understanding of the play: Iago, repulsed at the thought of being cuckolded by Othello, spreads his own disgust throughout Shakespeare's Venice, eventually infecting even those who he does not explicitly induce. We cannot, it seems to me, fully account for the tragedy of Othello without acknowledging the role that disgust plays in his undoing: this emotion comes to define the character's identity, and fuels that racist action that comes to destroy him.

In his reading of *Othello*, Saunders argues that 'the primary rhetorical means by which Iago (and others) force Othello back to his "true" marginalized "black" position involves an emphasis on filth, dirt, and excrement' – a statement, it should be clear, with which I largely agree.[47] But while Saunders focuses on cleanliness and anality, I suggest that this list – to which disease, animalization and sexuality must be added – should be more broadly understood as harnessing the affective power of *disgust* in general – a power that accounts not only for the insistent bodiliness of the play's rhetoric but also for the symbolic system through which othered, racialized subjects like Othello are policed within and ultimately expelled from the social order. The success of Iago's plotting is founded on a manipulation of disgust; he is able to harness the disgust that he feels towards his master and induce it in other characters, including, most importantly, Othello himself.

In the final analysis, this process both defines and is enabled by the racial structure that governs Venice more broadly. As scholars of the early modern period increasingly come to engage critical race theory, there is a growing sensitivity to how racial meaning and racism do not simply emerge from the will of individuals, but are instead built into larger structures and institutions; Mary Janell Metzger, for example, emphasizes 'the construction of whiteness as a form of social power' in her teaching of *The Merchant of Venice*, while Ruben Espinosa draws on the methods of critical race theory and ethnic studies to interrogate 'the power structures that define Shakespeare [and that] also define and often oppress Chicanxs'.[48] I think that we see such institutional work at play in how easily the citizens of Venice adopt the disgust-based outlook of the racial Other – that is to say, the ease with which disgust circulates in Shakespeare's playworld. To be sure, this process originates in Iago's individual malice – but as he slowly passes his racial disgust on to other characters, there emerges a sense in which Venice itself comes to construct Othello as the disgusting other, 'matter out of place' in the social order. In this way, racial meaning is partly created by affective meaning, and its consequences define not only relations between individual characters but also the identity of the entire social community.

Though the connection between racism and disgust was first explicitly articulated by twentieth-century affective scientists, it is clearly anticipated by imaginative works like *Othello*, which show how the workings of disgust become weaponized in the service of racial animus. One of the many ongoing achievements of PCRS is demonstrating how the racial (and racist) logics of the past inform our present moment; indeed, Smith and Justin Shaw have recently begun essays on *Othello* with a discussion of American police killing unarmed Black men.[49] Tending to the operation of racialized disgust similarly provides linkage between the past and present by showing continuity in how the human disgust system contributes to forms of outgroup discrimination like racism: in *Othello*, Shakespeare depicts an emotional phenomenon that affective scientists have independently found to be active today, and the play thus reflects cultural and political forces that have created and continue to create situations in which this emotional phenomenon does racist work. In her discussion of *The Faerie Queene*, 'Assaf Kafantaris argues that Spenser's engagement with racial disgust 'contributes to a nascent white supremacist discourse' by 'foreground[ing] the kind of dehumanizing ideological work that justifies the expulsion of non-white people, and later on, their enslavement as means of production only'; it is hard not to suspect that a similar process is operating in *Othello*, especially in the sense that Shakespeare showcases the logic of racial disgust in a form that is endlessly replicated in subsequent readings and performances.[50] While cultural understandings of disgust are indeed shaped by specific historical circumstances, the persistence of certain social structures enables us to talk about broad continuities in how some aspects of emotion operate – and in terms of revulsion and prejudice, the racialized disgust depicted in *Othello* is still, unfortunately, very much with us today. To stay with Smith and Shaw's example: in a recent experiment, a computer program that simulates how police officers respond to ostensibly threatening situations has shown that white participants with a higher general disgust sensitivity are more likely to fire their hypothetical weapon at the image of an unarmed Black person than they are at the image of an unarmed white person.[51] While more work is needed in this area, these tentative results suggest that racial disgust may play a factor in the epidemic of modern police violence against Black Americans – just as an analogous process of racial disgust, portrayed by Shakespeare in literary form, plays a prominent role in the undoing of Othello.

9

Racial disgust

Disgust towards an outgroup has been shown in even the most arbitrary, trivial matters: in a laboratory setting, for example, undergraduate students show more disgust when smelling a sweaty T-shirt with the logo of another university than they do when smelling a sweaty T-shirt with the logo of their own university.[1] But as we saw in the last chapter, outgroup disgust is particularly pernicious in the way it contributes to racial and ethnic prejudice, an unfortunate feature of the emotion that has a considerable social impact. While I have argued that this process of racial disgust underwrites Othello's destruction, the disappointing truth is that it more broadly affects, to varying degrees, all manner of encounters between majority and minority populations, in both the early modern period and today.

As noted, the discriminatory effects of outgroup disgust seem to be an evolutionary by-product of disgust's biologically protective functioning. We saw earlier how evolutionary theorists have proposed the existence of a BIS, a social mechanism designed to safeguard against pathogen transmission – and this process apparently underpins much racial and ethnic prejudice. Some propose that this is because 'in ancestral environments, interaction with members of the in-group will generally have posed less risk of disease transmission than interaction with members of an outgroup, as individuals will have possessed antibodies to many of the pathogens present in the former, in contrast to those prevalent among the latter'.[2] Others are sceptical that 'outgroup members have recurrently carried more dangerous pathogens than ingroup members over human evolutionary history', and thus believe that the BIS is not 'designed for avoiding outgroup members *per se*' –

instead, it encourages us to 'avoi[d] people from one's extended social network' more broadly.[3] But whatever the case, most readily acknowledge the unfortunate fact that the BIS undoubtedly 'contributes to ethnocentrism and xenophobia'.[4] When unchecked by other moderating factors, BIS mechanisms seem to 'encourage the endorsements of socially conservative beliefs, which promote social exclusivity, tradition, and negativity toward outgroups'; a meta-analysis of published research on the BIS concluded that having a high 'fear of contamination and disgust sensitivity' is correlated with higher tendencies towards 'right-wing authoritarianism, social dominance orientation, religious fundamentalism, ethnocentrism, collectivism, and political conservatism'.[5] In fact, psychologists have actually developed a measure for assessing an individual's 'intergroup disgust' sensitivity, which is thought to fundamentally entail '(a) negative affect, especially revulsion and disgust toward outgroups; (b) contamination concerns (i.e., outgroup is dangerous, can invoke change in the self/ingroup); and (c) sense of ingroup superiority and purity (i.e., "we" are better in nature than "them")'.[6]

It is important to note, however, that the association between disgust, pathogen avoidance and outgroup prejudice does not necessarily mean that the pathogen avoidance aspect of the disgust system is *designed* to promote the kind of outgroup prejudice that it seems to foster today; on the contrary, it has been argued that this is another 'misfiring' of pathogen detection, by which the disgust system mistakenly interprets human difference as a sign of potential infection that must be avoided.[7] The BIS, we have seen, is necessarily hypervigilant and will thus err on the side of 'misclassify[ing] an unfamiliar person or other stimulus as a pathogen threat'.[8] But the fact that modern racial prejudice is the result of misfiring does not make its consequences any less real: disgust is central to the othering of racial outgroups, an affective process with undeniable social consequences.

The connection between racism and disgust, then, is not simply academic, or merely an intellectual curiosity: it has very real, and often dire, consequences for people's lived experience. While laboratory experiments give us one set of data on this front, literary constructions like *Othello* provide complimentary evidence for how notions of revulsion play a role in the social construction of racial outgroup members. And the linkage between disgust and racism, in fact, is consistent throughout Shakespeare: almost every time we find the depiction of racial outsiders in his plays, the concept of disgust is not far behind. Oftentimes, the exploration of this theme is not substantial, but members of racial outgroups are nonetheless casually linked to words from the lexicon of Shakespearean disgust. In *Love's Labour's Lost*, for example, the dark complexion of Berowne's Rosaline is compared to the dirtiness of 'chimney-sweepers' and the Blackness of 'Ethiops' (4.3.262; 264). On a similar note, in *A Midsummer Night's Dream*, the charmed Lysander quickly denounces Hermia not only as 'Ethiop' and 'tawny Tartar' but also as 'vile thing' and 'loathed medicine' (3.2.257; 263; 260; 264). And as we saw in Chapter 3, the revolting Welsh leek delineates ethnic boundaries in *Henry V*, as food disgust or appreciation defines the boundaries of ingroups and outgroups.

Unsurprisingly, in plays more specifically concerned with matters of race, we find a more concentrated exploration of racial disgust. In *Antony and Cleopatra*, where, we have already noted, discourses of race and sex entwine, Cleopatra's 'gipsy's lust' is portrayed as unnatural and dangerous (1.1.10); it is no surprise, then, that Antony eventually laments that 'this foul Egyptian hath betrayed me' (4.12.10).[9] On a similar note, in *Titus Andronicus* Bassianus attributes Tamora's sexual interest in the racial outsider Aaron to 'foul desire' (2.2.79); their biracial child is described as 'loathsome as a toad' (4.2.69), and their union is dismissed as 'her foul proceedings' (5.3.8). And we find racial disgust especially deployed in *The Tempest*, where Caliban – who is tellingly described as 'not honoured with / A human shape' (1.2.283–4) – is routinely portrayed as an object of revulsion. He is said to be descended from a 'vile race' (359); his mother Sycorax is called a 'foul witch' (258), whose 'charms' involve a litany of animals linked to disgust ('toads, beetles, bats' [340-41]). It is thus impossible to separate Caliban's disgusting features from his indigeneity, a fact that becomes apparent when he attempts to curse Prospero; harnessing his native association with the island, he prays that 'All the infections that the sun sucks up / From bogs, fens, flats, on Prosper fall, and make him / By inchmeal a disease' (2.2.1–3). But Caliban's connection to racial disgust is most nakedly displayed in Trinculo's immediate response to encountering him: recalling the fact that disgusting objects can also compel our attention, Caliban's repulsive features (he is 'a strange beast' that 'smells like a fish') are entwined with his racial otherness (he is 'an islander that hath lately suffered by a thunderbolt') to make him a source of fascination that, as we saw earlier, is worthy of public display (2.2.31; 26; 36–7). It is no accident, I think, that Ariel eventually leaves Caliban and his new friends in a 'filthy-mantled pool . . . dancing up to th' chins, that the foul lake / O'erstunk their feet' – the island's native monster becomes washed with the raw material of disgust, a reminder of his racialized status in the playworld (4.1.182–4).

But after *Othello*, it is *The Merchant of Venice* that offers Shakespeare's most concentrated engagement with the rhetoric of racial disgust. As we have seen, Black bodies were construed as sources of revulsion in early modern England, and anti-Blackness is indeed present in *Merchant*; Morocco begins his selection speech by anticipating Portia's race-based rejection – asking her to not 'mislike me . . . for my complexion' (2.1.1) – while Portia nakedly reveals that, in matters of marriage, even an exemplary character isn't enough to outweigh a disqualifying racial otherness – noting that if a suitor has 'the condition of a saint and the complexion of a devil, I had rather he should shrive me than wive me' (1.2.126–8). (Portia's disdain recalls Claribel in *The Tempest,* who is said to have had a 'loathness' to marry the African King of Tunis, and only did so out of filial 'obedience' [2.1.132]). Matters of disgust are perhaps more pointedly invoked in Lancelet's 'getting up of [a] negro's belly' (3.5.35); as a comic aside, it is telling that the clown figure puts pressure on social boundaries with the act of miscegenation, and Imtiaz Habib notes that this 'inexplicable impregnation' may refer to the fact that 'one of the recommended Renaissance cures for venereal disease [was] sexual intercourse with a black woman'.[10]

It is Shylock, however, who is the figure most targeted by racial invective in the play – and he is the figure most painted by the brush of racial disgust. Because it was not only the peoples of Africa who elicited disgust in early modern racial discourse: as Brett D. Hirsch outlines, there was a widely popular anti-Semitic discourse 'linking the Jews to excrement and filth, plague and disease'.[11] Hirsch notes that early modern culture 'frequently depicted Jews as physically abject', portraying them 'with large hooked noses, red or dark curly hair, goatlike beards, and dark skin and features, [including] monstrous attributes such as cranial horns, prehensile tails, a foul sulfurous stench, and menstruation in men'.[12] Most commonly, Jewish people are linked to the notion of filthiness, as in reference to 'Iewes blynded wyth filthye desyres' or the 'filthie rable of *Iewes*':

Daniel Dyke, for example, suggests that '*Iewes,* but filthie swine that they are, after they haue washed themselues . . . returne presently to their wallowing in the mire of their former filthinesse'.[13] The alleged disgustingness of Jews was epitomized by a moment in the Biblical Passion, when Christ is 'besmeared with the filthy spettle of the Iewes'; early modern authors relentlessly recalled the image of Jesus 'dunged, soiled with the filthy excrements of the Iewes' and 'slabbered and bespalled with the loathsome spittle and filthy driuell of the Iewes'.[14] The association between Jews and excrement even developed into an urban legend, as in the tale of a thirteenth-century Jewish man from Tewkesbury that was much repeated in chronicles and sermons throughout the early modern period.[15] Foxe offers one account, recording how 'a certain Iew . . . fell into a priuy at Tewkesbury vpon a sabboth day', and 'for the great reuerence he had to his holy sabboth, would not suffer him selfe to be plucked out'; thus the 'wretched superstitious Iewe remain[ed] there tyll mondaye, [and] was found dead in the doung'.[16] Besides rendering the Jew as an object of disgust, this story was also said to be indicative of the 'preposterous and hypocriticall zeale' that Jews were thought to exhibit in their strict adherence to the 'Ceremonies' of scripture.[17] But the strict Jew dying in toilet filth was actually a more widespread anti-Semitic trope in the period: writers also tell of 'a *Jew* of *Magdeburg,* who falling on a *Saturday* into a Privy, would not be taken out [and] was poisoned with the very stink'.[18]

The notion of *stink* here, in fact, connects to a larger aspect of anti-Semitic discourse, because it was commonplace in the period that Jews had a disgusting, rancid smell (the *foetor judaicus*).[19] Thomas Browne extensively considers the claim 'that Jews stinck naturally' in *Pseudodoxia Epidemica,* and it is easy to find contemporary authors referring to 'filthy and stinkinge Iewes' and affirming that 'Iewes have a loathsome and stinking smell'.[20] According to John Weemes, this alleged smell was a hereditary curse, 'as the Lord set a marke upon *Cain*' – a divine punishment 'since they killed the Lord of glorie and shed his innocent bloud'.[21] Alternately, Robert Heath wonders if it is 'because their Noses . . . so long and great, and therefore full of Mucre and Stink?'[22] Some authors, to be sure, refuted this suggestion; Browne, in fact, writes extensively against it, and Edward Kellett suggests that there 'is no proofe that the Jewes were naturall stinkards; or inwardly had noysome, mal-odorous bodies'.[23] But, as Hirsch observes, the fact that this discourse needed to be regularly disputed suggests the hold it had on the early modern imagination.[24] To conclude, this and other features of disgust-based anti-Semitic discourse are particularly illustrated in Nashe's *The Unfortunate Traveller*, where the diabolic Jew Zadoch describes his plan for revenge against an enemy:

> I haue a leg with an issue, shall I cut it off, and from his fount of corruption extract a venome worse than anie serpents? If thou wilt, Ile goe to a house that is infected, where catching the plague, and hauing got a running sore vpon me, Ile come and deliuer her a supplication, and breathe vpon her. I know my breath stinkes so alreadie, that it is within halfe a degrée of poyson. Ile pay her home if I perfect it with anie more putrifaction.[25]

The constellation of associations here – infection, disease, stink, poison, plague – all emphasize the affective component of early modern anti-Semitism: Jewish people, like those from Africa, were understood as fundamentally disgusting by many English subjects, a reflection of how disgust features in outgroup prejudice and discrimination.

And in *Merchant*, Shylock is relentlessly portrayed as disgusting, in both body and soul, as his moral character is consistently conflated with his status as an outsider Jew.[26] As we saw earlier, dehumanization is a primary means through which racial disgust operates, and characters in the play relentlessly deploy epithets that symbolically strip Shylock of his humanity. While this is accomplished through labels like 'stony adversary' and 'inhumane wretch' (4.1.3), it is, like in the case of Othello, through the language of animalization that Shylock is most insistently attacked. The disgust that fuels racial animalization, I think, is why we find Shylock cast as 'dog Jew' (2.8.14), 'impenetrable cur' (3.3.18), 'currish Jew' (4.1.287) and 'damned, inexecrable dog' (4.1.127). Furthermore, as we saw in Chapter 7, this animalization becomes associated with the disgust-based category of food, when his desires are deemed 'wolvish, bloody, starved and ravenous' (4.1.137) – a characterization that inflects how we must understand Shylock's boast that the flesh of Antonio will 'feed [his] revenge' (3.1.48). Insofar as Shylock is human, what is invoked is a disgusting act of cannibalism; insofar as he has been dehumanized, the image equally recalls that of a dangerous animal.

Finally, on multiple occasions Shylock links being construed as a non-human animal with having another's disgusting bodily fluids cast upon him: he first notes that Antonio called him 'cut-throat dog / And spit upon my Jewish gaberdine' and then reminds us that 'you spat on me on Wednesday last [and] another time, / You called me dog' (1.4.109–10; 123–5). (This construction seems to reverse the image of Jews spitting on Christ.) Consistent with what we saw from Othello, Shylock eventually internalizes this racial disgust, rhetorically embracing his own identity as less than human: 'Thou call'dst me dog before thou hadst a cause', he retorts, 'But, since I am a dog, beware my fangs' (3.3.6–7). In his racial otherness, Shylock is thus regularly portrayed as something less than human – an association only amplified by the apparent moral violations of his behaviour. Given that animalistic dehumanization, we have seen, is a key component of racial disgust, I think we must understand this portrayal in affective terms: it is ultimately fuelled by revulsion.

10

Hamlet

Death and disgust

Pretty much everyone, I think, would agree that something is very rotten in the state of Denmark. It thus seems appropriate to end my study of revulsion in Shakespeare with an analysis of *Hamlet*, the play that contains perhaps the most extensive engagement with disgust of any in the canon. In terms of staged horrors, I argued earlier that *Titus Andronicus* is Shakespeare's most explicitly disgusting work – but *Hamlet*, at a more global level, is so thoroughly soaked in an atmosphere of disgust that it is hard to understate the emotion's influence on the unfolding tragedy.

Readers have long found occasion to comment on the disgust that pervades both the play and its central character. Nowhere else in Shakespeare, A. C. Bradley observed a century ago, do we find anything quite like 'Hamlet's disgust at his uncle's drunkenness, his loathing of his mother's sensuality, his astonishment and horror at her shallowness, his contempt for everything pretentious or false, his indifference to everything merely external'.[1] (The one possible exception, Bradley notes, is 'the rage of the disillusioned idealist Timon', which we examined in Chapter 4). Several decades later, G. Wilson Knight argued that Hamlet's mind is 'drawn to images in themselves repellent, and he dwells on the thought of foulness as the basis of life'.[2] Much more recently, William Tanner has seen Hamlet in terms of the 'representative Elizabethan malcontent', the figure who feels a 'nauseating disgust for self and species'.[3] And an interesting bit of trivia: when a group of researchers in the 1960s attempted to quantify *Hamlet*'s 'elementary impulses', they found disgust to be the fourth most frequent sentiment (out of sixty-six total) detected by readers coding the play.[4]

But while disgust is self-evidently acknowledged to be a central component of *Hamlet*'s affective universe, there has been surprisingly little critical work that centres disgust as an analytical target. Scholars have occasionally framed the play in terms of carnival grotesqueness, with Claudius representing the spirit of festivity and Hamlet the spirit of restraint; more pointedly, Chikako D. Kumamoto has performed a Kristevan analysis of abjection in the play, while Duncan A. Lucas has used the work of Silvan Tompkins to explore Hamlet himself in terms of a 'disgust-shame dyad'.[5] In what follows I will thus attempt to develop a reading of *Hamlet* that finds disgust at the centre of the play's dramatic and thematic action. I do so by anchoring my analysis in a psychological model that views disgust as a fundamental component of the human existential experience. In *Emotion in the Tudor Court*, I explored the dreadful emotional atmosphere of the 1590s through the lens of Terror Management Theory (TMT), a modern framework that sees human psychology as eternally bound in a struggle to contend with the inevitability of death.[6] In a subsequent essay, I took the initial steps to extend this thinking to the most iconic literary work of late Elizabethan England – *Hamlet*, a play that is of course supremely concerned with the existential terror of mortality.[7] But what that essay did not do is account for the role of disgust in Terror Management processes – a role that has been empirically demonstrated – and this was a notable flaw in my argument, given the equally important role of disgust in *Hamlet*. In this chapter, I will use the broad findings of TMT to generate a reading of *Hamlet* that foregrounds disgust, and that gives one possible explanation for the play's profound concern with all things repulsive.

First developed in the 1980s by the social psychologists Jeff Greenberg, Tom Pyszczynski and Sheldon Solomon – who themselves took a cue from the cultural anthropologist Ernest Becker – TMT begins with the premise that human beings, 'by virtue of the awareness of death and their relative helplessness and vulnerability to ultimate annihilation', must exist 'in constant danger of being incapacitated by overwhelming terror'.[8] Accordingly, TMT argues that 'a great deal of human behavior can be understood as an attempt to gain psychological equanimity in the face of this awareness' – and it proposes that the response to this existential crisis of individual psychology is the creation of socially constituted meaning:

> Homo sapiens solved this existential quandary by developing cultural worldviews: humanly constructed beliefs about reality shared by individuals in a group that serves to reduce the potentially overwhelming terror resulting from the awareness of death. Culture reduces anxiety by providing its constituents with a sense that they are valuable members of a meaningful universe. Meaning is derived from cultural worldviews that offer an account of the origin of the universe, prescriptions of appropriate conduct, and guarantees of safety and security to those who adhere to such instructions – in this life and beyond, in the form of symbolic and/or literal immortality.[9]

TMT maintains that 'it is through this culturally derived system of meaning and value that people can begin to manage their existential fears'; it is thus cultural participation that allows people 'to construe the self as a valuable contributor to a meaningful existence rather than a mere material animal fated only to obliteration upon death', because 'adhering to the tenets of specific belief systems permits humans to feel that they are valued members of their respective cultures'.[10] And though this may seem abstract, there is actually a wealth of experimental evidence that suggests a linkage between a person's awareness of death (mortality salience) and their investment in cultural world views. In the typical TMT experiment, participants are asked to answer an essay question either about death (to prime thoughts of mortality) or about a neutral topic; after a brief delay, in which an irrelevant distraction task is performed, the researchers then measure how participants respond to a reading that disagrees with their world view. A meta-analysis assessing 277 experiments across decades of TMT research found that the effect of such mortality salience manipulation is 'robust': people who are primed to think about death are indeed more likely to defend their cultural beliefs, religious or otherwise.[11] Or, as one of the theory's founders put it in 2008, 'hundreds of published studies to date have demonstrated that mortality salience leads people to favor and defend their cultural worldview and to demonstrate that they possesses socially valued attributes and skills.'[12]

So what, you're probably wondering, does this have to do with disgust? Quite a lot, actually, because in the course of their research TMT psychologists have consistently found a linkage between revulsion and mortality, leading them to conclude that 'the disgust reaction is a . . . symbolic means of coping with the problem of death'.[13] Individuals who score high on disgust scales also tend to be more fearful of mortality; accordingly, it seems that 'highly disgust sensitive people appear to be guarding themselves from external threats: they are more anxious, more afraid of death'.[14] The reason for this, TMT argues, owes to the troubling notion of human creatureliness. It will be remembered from Chapter 1 that one of the primary theoretical models of disgust combines certain revulsion elicitors under the category of *animal-reminder disgust*; these are things that make uncomfortably salient humanity's fundamentally animal nature. For Terror Management theorists, this category of animal-reminder disgust reflects our existential psychological dilemma: 'things that remind humans of their animal nature disgust them because their animality reminds them of their vulnerability to death.'[15] Jamie L. Goldenberg and colleagues elaborate:

> By showing disgust toward such things, humans can psychologically distance themselves from the material, creaturely reality these things represent. From this perspective, disgust can be viewed as an emotional response that enables humans to elevate themselves above other animals and thereby defend against death. . . . Disgust can be understood as the emotional protest against any reminder of our creatureliness, an affective assertion that says 'I am fundamentally better than that.'

This outlook is equally supported by laboratory research, which demonstrates a connection between disgust and death in multiple directions: experiments have shown both that reminders of mortality lead 'people to respond with increased disgust sensitivity to a variety of specific disgust elicitors' and that 'priming participants with graphic explicit images that elicit animal-nature disgust (feces, urine, vomit, etc.) increased death-thought accessibility scores'.[16] In sum, these results have led TMT researchers to believe that 'disgust, at least in response to direct reminders of creatureliness, may function as a protest against death'.[17]

With this in mind, in this chapter I advance a reading of Hamlet that views his character and its progression in terms of Terror Management. The death of King Hamlet, I suggest, creates an existential crisis for his son, by making mortality intensely salient; Prince Hamlet's profound disgust at the world (including at his mother's sexual life) functions as a compensatory protest against these mortality fears, in the anxiety buffering manner predicted by TMT and described in the previous paragraph. The subsequent unfolding of the play, however, entwines him in a series of events that force him to reckon ever more closely with death – and eventually demands that he takes consolation in a meaningful cultural world view, as TMT suggests. The adoption of this world view, which accounts for his transformation of outlook in the play's final scene, provides a buffer to his characteristic fear of death, allowing him to take revenge at the cost of his own life.

While we obviously must be careful when analysing literary characters in terms of psychological models, I will nonetheless argue that the basic framework of TMT can help account for how certain key themes of *Hamlet* are presented. I am not, of course, suggesting that Hamlet's character is a strict, vulgar or transparent reflection of Terror Management processes – but rather I will try to show how the core features of the TMT model can be seen to shed light on the remarkable things that happen in *Hamlet*. This is a play that is legendarily concerned with mortality, and it is a play brimming with the stuff of disgust; TMT provides one compelling way to explain how these two themes are entwined, at the level of psychological functioning.

* * *

I began this chapter by noting the widespread agreement that *Hamlet* is a play concerned with rottenness, corruption and, above all, disgust. Long ago, Derek Traversi argued that 'the action of *Hamlet* is, in its inner logic, the progressive revelation of a state of disease'; Eric S. Mallin, building upon this, suggests that '*Hamlet*'s plot is a virtual schematic of plague . . . a progressive dispersal of weakness, delusion, passion, and violent physical decomposition among a growing number of susceptible bodies'.[18] Caroline Spurgeon, in her analysis of the play's imagery, similarly finds 'a feeling of horror, disgust and even hopelessness not met before', leading to a 'general sense of inward and unseen corruption [that] is very strong'.[19] Much of this, of course, is established through the perspective of the central character, whose systematic revulsion at Denmark cannot help but colour the audience's perception of the playworld.

Hamlet's opening appearance in 1.2 provides an easy in-road for thinking about this disgust in terms of Terror Management processes. I hardly need to rehearse his state of mind during his first moment on stage; before we encounter a disgusted Hamlet, we encounter a Hamlet profoundly broken by the death of his father, paralysed by an 'obstinate condolement' and 'unmanly grief' that concerns both king and queen (1.2.93; 94).[20] King Hamlet's death, it seems clear, has severely traumatized his son – and I suggest, more specifically, that it has made mortality grimly salient for the young Hamlet, initiating the existential crisis that grips him for the rest of the play. Given that revulsion, TMT predicts, is a psychic defence against death, it is fitting that we then immediately witness Hamlet, in his first soliloquy, revealing his disgust at the condition of the world: not only is it 'weary, stale, flat and unprofitable' but more importantly has been reduced to 'an unweeded garden / That grows to seed, things rank and gross in nature / Possess it merely' (133; 135–7). *Rank,* I noted in Chapter 5, is a word associated with disgust – as in Claudius's admission that his 'offense is rank [and] smells to heaven' (3.3.36) – and though *gross* in Shakespeare's time was not an exact synonym of disgusting (as it is for us), the descriptor was nonetheless used in multiple contexts that invoke repulsive excessiveness.[21] As the speech continues, Hamlet reveals that the disgust he feels is both visceral and moral – particularly targeting his mother, as described herein – and, as the first act continues, we see the extent to which he is consumed by it. To this end, Hamlet's famous revulsion at the king 'tak[ing] his rouse' is symptomatic of his outlook more generally (1.4.8); given that Hamlet is sickened by gustatory indulgence, the core domain of food disgust is activated, but he is even more offended by the moral implications of Danish custom, which allow others to 'soil' the nation with 'swinish phrase' (20; 19). (This recalls what we saw in Chapters 8 and 9 on animalization and disgust.)

Of course, the most important encounter in Act 1 is Hamlet's visitation with the ghost, and here Shakespeare insistently presents King Hamlet's murder as an act that is (to his son, at least) understood as a disgusting violation of the natural and moral order. This is most readily accomplished by the motif of *foulness*, a word we have seen throughout this book to trigger both visceral and symbolic disgust. Immediately after hearing of the ghost, Hamlet imagines 'foul play' and suspects that 'foul deeds' will be revealed (1.2.254; 255); his thoughts are substantiated by the ghost himself, who in quick succession refers not only to his own 'foul crimes' but more importantly to 'foul and most unnatural murder', 'Murder most foul' and his 'foul, strange and unnatural' death (1.5.12; 25; 27; 28). As commentators have observed, the foulness of the king's demise has multiple components. Michael Cameron Andrews suggests that some Elizabethans would understand the term *foul play* to be 'alluding to adultery', meaning that Gertrude's union with Claudius alone would be enough to 'give [his] spirit cause to walk'.[22] Compounding this, Patrick Colm Hogan argues that King Hamlet characterizing his murder as *foul* indicates revulsion at the unnaturalness of Claudius's fratricide: 'his bond of attachment broken, [he] now feels a surge of disgust at the thought of his brother.'[23] And even the circumstances of the murder may contribute: because poisoning was considered a particularly treacherous act, Piotr Sadowski reminds us that the manner of Hamlet's death would generate 'moral revulsion' for many early modern English audience members.[24] But while all this is undoubtedly true, I think that the crime's particular repulsiveness is signalled by the visceral trauma that is inflicted on the victim's unfortunate body – a trauma that is described in chilling detail. As the ghost tells it:

> Upon my secure hour thy uncle stole
> With juice of cursed hebona in a vial
> And in the porches of my ears did pour
> The leperous distilment whose effect
> Holds such an enmity with blood of man
> That swift as quicksilver it courses through
> The natural gates and alleys of the body
> And with a sudden vigour it doth possess
> And curd like eager droppings into milk
> The thin and wholesome blood. So did it mine
> And a most instant tetter barked about
> Most lazar-like with vile and loathsome crust
> All my smooth body. (62–74)

There is no doubt that *vile* and *loathsome* are words intimately tied to the notion of disgust: Shakespeare demands that we (and Hamlet) understand that the poison's work rendered King Hamlet's body an object of revulsion. This is, I think, crucial to Hamlet's developing investment in disgust, because the ghost's description makes mortality salient in a way far more horrific than it was before: Hamlet is forced to imagine his father's corpse as a piece of animal meat, rotting from the inside-out. After the ghost's visit, death is thus made even more salient to a man already in existential crisis, and his outlook becomes ever more consumed by thoughts of disgust.

* * *

As the play unfolds, Hamlet increasingly sees his world in terms of disgust, and his thoughts become consumed with images of corruption, disease, rot and decay. We can point, for example, to his outburst in the closet encounter with his mother, when he memorably compares Claudius to 'a mildewed ear / Blasting his wholesome brother' (3.4.62–3). When posted behind the praying Claudius, he similarly speaks of his uncle's 'sickly days', and views his decision not to strike then as a temporary 'physic' (3.3.96). And an especially arresting moment occurs when he spars with Polonius, in his comments on human procreation:

> HAMLET For if the sun breed maggots in a dead dog, being a good kissing carrion – have you a daughter?
> POLONIUS I have, my lord.
> HAMLET Let her not walk i'th' sun: conception is a blessing but as your daughter may conceive, friend – look to't.
> (2.2.178–83)

For Hamlet, the generation of human life is best understood by reference to a rotting dog carcass spawning maggots in the sun – a particularly important metaphor, in fact, because Hamlet's engagement with disgust does not simply concern images of physical death. We must also account for the play's considerable investment in the theme that has tellingly been called *sex nausea* – because 'of all of Shakespeare's tragedies', Linda Bamber observes, '*Hamlet* is the one in which the sex nausea is most pervasive.'[25] At the turn of the twentieth century, Freud shined an influential spotlight on Hamlet's apparent 'sexual aversion', and both his contemporaries and subsequent commentators have had much to say on how Gertrude's remarriage seems to have evoked a shockingly intense sexual disgust in her son.[26] 'Why did Hamlet hate his mother's lechery?' Frank Harris asked in 1909; 'most men would hardly have condemned it, certainly would not have suffered their thoughts to dwell on it beyond the moment,' but for Hamlet 'his mother's faithlessness was horrible, shameful, degrading'.[27] Ernest Jones, in his well-known psychoanalytic study of the play, similarly suggests that Hamlet's 'excessive reaction to his mother's conduct' demanded explanation, as it clearly reflected some sort of larger authorial psychodynamic, such as Shakespeare's relationship to his own mother.[28] T. S. Eliot was equally baffled by it, which led to his famous assessment that *Hamlet* was an artistic failure: 'Hamlet is up against the difficulty that his disgust is occasioned by his mother, but that his mother is not an adequate equivalent for it . . . [his] disgust envelops and exceeds her.'[29] But of the early commentators, I think it is Bradley who most elegantly encapsulates the issue:

> It was not his father's death; that doubtless brought deep grief, but mere grief for some one loved and lost does not make a noble spirit loathe the world as a place full only of things rank and gross. It was not the vague suspicion that we know Hamlet felt. Still less was it the loss of crown; for though the subserviency of the electors might well disgust him, there is not a reference to the subject in the soliloquy, nor any sign elsewhere that it greatly occupied his mind. It was the moral shock of the sudden ghastly disclosure of his mother's true nature.[30]

This 'eruption of coarse sensuality' in his mother 'brings bewildered horror, then loathing, then despair of human nature' – 'his whole mind is poisoned'.[31]

Modern commentators, bolstered by feminist theory, have similarly engaged Hamlet's revulsion at sex. Celia R. Daileader describes Hamlet's 'misogynistic anti-carnality' – which entails 'his scapegoating of women and their sexuality for the biological inevitabilities of age, illness, filth, death, and dissolution'.[32] Karl P. Wentersdorf similarly emphasizes 'Hamlet's intense disgust at the thought of what seems to him to be the frailty of womankind'; it is 'this disgust and the desire to avenge his father's death', he argues, that serve as 'the two most powerful forces motivating his behavior throughout the play'.[33] And Hamlet's impulses to this end also seem shared by his father: as Janet Adelman notes in her famous analysis of the play, both King and Prince Hamlet seem to maintain that Gertrude's 'chief crime is her uncontrolled sexuality', which serves as 'the object of their moral revulsion, a revulsion as intense as anything directed toward the murderer Claudius'.[34] In this sense, Mark King suggests that *Hamlet* stages a progressive indictment of feminine sexuality, 'whereby the rot expands from a fixed point in a homosocial male world to a female locus'.[35] The consensus, then, is that Hamlet's sex nausea overwhelms the play, encompassing not only 'disgust at the thought of pandering and prostitution' but 'revulsion against the very processes of generation and gestation, especially the concept of sexual pleasure' – and we cannot, therefore, account for disgust generally in *Hamlet* without accounting for his disgust at all matters sexual.[36]

And here, perhaps surprisingly, we can also turn to TMT, which offers empirical insights into the function of sex disgust. The TMT understanding of this phenomenon is once again based on humanity's existential quandary. Because the 'human species has intercourse and reproduces just as other animals do, the physical aspects of sex make apparent our animalistic creaturely nature'; according to TMT, 'the cultural solution to this problem is to imbue sex with meaning and significance that elevates it from the world of the creaturely and animalistic into the realm of the sacred and sublime.'[37] But the very reason we need this cultural solution, as discussed earlier, is because reminders of our animalistic nature inherently also remind us of our inevitable mortality. To this end, experiments have shown that when individuals were primed 'to associate the physical aspects of sex with an animal act, thinking about physical sex served to prime thoughts about death', and that 'when participants [are] reminded of their creatureliness . . . thinking about physical, but not romantic, aspects of sex increased the accessibility of death-related thoughts'.[38] More importantly, because TMT theorizes that disgust is a shield against mortality, it makes sense that the animalistic properties of sex, by making death salient, have the ability to trigger revulsion as a defensive mechanism. This is particularly true for people with neurotic tendencies, who usually rate high in disgust sensitivity generally; research suggests 'both that physical aspects of sex make death highly accessible for individuals high in neuroticism and that mortality salience leads such people to find the physical aspects of sex particularly unappealing'.[39] Consequently, 'people with neurosis report low sexual satisfaction and perceptions of sex as disgusting', because 'sexuality is a reminder of their creaturely, animalistic nature, which in turn is a reminder of the inevitability of death' – findings that 'further support [the] contention that neurotic individuals' problems with sex are rooted in anxiety surrounding fears associated with death'.[40] I'm not, of course, suggesting that we put Hamlet on the couch, but it seems relevant to note that, starting with Freud, a century of psychoanalytic critics have viewed Hamlet in terms of neuroticism.[41] More generally, it also seems relevant to note that early modern culture similarly acknowledged the connection between sex and mortality, as in the well-known usage of 'to die' as a euphemism for sexual activity – a linguistic wrinkle that Shakespeare exploits on multiple occasions, like when Pandarus in *Troilus and Cressida* sings 'these lovers cry, "O! O!", they die! / Yet that which seems the wound to kill / Doth turn 'O! O!' to 'Ha, ha, he!' (3.1.118–20). TMT provides a possible rationale for this union, by emphasizing how sex makes salient our fundamental animality, and thus underscores the inevitability of our animal death and decay.

It should be clear, I hope, how this thinking can be extended to *Hamlet*: I suggest that Hamlet's overwhelming disgust towards sex is a function of his existential mortality terror, a linkage that can be explained through the Terror Management processes described earlier. It is important, I think, that the onset of both his sex nausea and his obsession with mortality is triggered by the twin-traumas of his father's death and mother's remarriage. Ophelia's reference to the multiple 'ladies . . . that sucked the honey of his musicked vows' indicates that Hamlet was not always repulsed by sex (3.1.154–5), while Claudius's surprise that 'the clouds still hang' on Hamlet suggests that his disposition was not normally morbid (1.2.66). If we indeed view King Hamlet's untimely death as initiating an existential crisis in his son, then the subsequent betrayal of Gertrude's remarriage – for reasons that Hamlet can only attribute to animalistic lust – further activates death anxiety by making salient the creatureliness of sex – an anxiety that must be buffered by a defensive disgust towards raw sexuality at large. Jacqueline Rose notes that, for Hamlet, 'Gertrude's blatant sexuality makes her less than human', and it is telling that one of his first attacks on his mother positions her beneath even an animal; his opening soliloquy opines that 'a beast that wants discourse of reason / Would have mourned longer' than Gertrude, who 'post[ed] / With such dexterity to incestuous sheets' (150–1; 156–7).[42] It is also vital that Hamlet, consistent with his tendency to idealize his father, seems to have no issue with Gertrude's sensual relationship with her former husband – indeed, he declares that 'she would hang on him / As if increase of appetite had grown / By what it fed on' (143–5). This is echoed by the ghost, who contrasts the sublime sanctity of their sexual relationship with Gertrude's debased desire for Claudius: 'Lust, though to a radiant angel linked, / Will sate itself in a celestial bed / And prey on garbage' (1.5.55–7). In TMT experiments, mortality concerns are triggered by the physical aspects of sex but not by its romantic aspects; this is because the romanticizing of sex elevates the act's symbolic and cultural significance and distances us from its raw creatureliness.[43] Accordingly, Hamlet can tolerate the sexuality of his parent's union, because it is imbued with a higher conceptual meaning bestowed by its (partly idealized) romantic context – but Gertrude's marriage with Claudius, which Hamlet sees as defined only by putrid, bestial lust, provokes in him the deepest revulsion.

As Richard Levin importantly notes, our understanding of Gertrude's sexuality is dependent on the suspect analysis of King and Prince Hamlet: 'she and her libido are constructed for us by the two men who have grievances against her and so must be considered hostile and therefore unreliable witnesses, while she herself is given no opportunity to testify on her own behalf.'[44] Whether or not Hamlet actually wrote the Player Queen's lines in 3.2, he certainly seems to endorse the notion that 'the instances that second marriage move [are] none of love'; a second marriage, quite crucially, cannot be subject to the same idealizing measures that elevate his parent's romanticized love, meaning that no buffering process redeems Gertrude and Claudius's union from the taint of animal desire (178–9). Hamlet, in fact, explicitly dismisses this possibility to Gertrude's face: 'you cannot call it love, for at your age / The heyday in the blood is tame' (3.4.66–7). What is there, however, is the alleged lust that Hamlet fixates on, and that strikes him as something that defies normal human functioning: by natural rights, a 'matron's bones' shouldn't have the sexual vigour that Hamlet attributes to his mother (81). When Hamlet gets fully ramped up in the closet scene, it is impossible to discount the raw disgust that his mother's sexual life elicits in him; the play's sex nausea is at its most intense when Gertrude is imagined 'liv[ing] / In the rank sweat of an enseamed bed / Stewed in corruption, honeying and making love / Over the nasty sty' (89–92). Of course, locating the act in the *nasty sty* furthers the animalization of their sex, and it is notable that later in the scene Hamlet envisions his mother as a 'mouse' and Claudius as 'a paddock . . . a bat, a gib' – all vermin that may be customarily thought to evoke disgust (181; 188).[45] Ultimately, the disgust that Hamlet feels at her sexualized, animal body causes him to imagine her body as repulsively compromised more generally; he sees in his mother an 'ulcerous place [where] corruption mining all within / Infects unseen' (145–7). In this way, Hamlet's sex nausea connects to the larger theme of Denmark's fundamental rottenness, in the sense that (as Susan Dunn-Hensley notes) Gertrude's 'sexualized body has the power to contaminate the state'.[46] Finally, we must observe that Hamlet (and the ghost's) insistence on the incestuousness of the Gertrude/Claudius union is a further amplification of the disgust that the pair elicits; though no one else in Denmark seems to object, both father and son see this quality of their marriage as an affront to the social and religious order, and thus morally repulsive.[47] Indeed, Charles R. Forker observes that 'what Hamlet and his father's ghost choose to regard as the blackest of sexual transgressions seems to occasion no great objection in Denmark generally', and the disgust that they both feel thus must be seen as an idiosyncratic feature of their own psychology.[48]

But Hamlet, of course, is not simply disgusted with his mother: his revulsion against female sexuality deeply shapes his interactions with Ophelia. Bradley argued that Gertrude's betrayal has such a profound effect on Hamlet that 'he can never see Ophelia in the same light again' – 'she is a woman, and his mother is a woman'.[49] While it is true that Hamlet adopts a overriding generalized misogyny in response to his mother's behaviour – as in his famous comment on women's frailty (1.2.146) – the unfortunate Ophelia, being the only other woman in the play, is forced to bear whatever excess venom Hamlet cannot direct at Gertrude. Bradley, in fact, further noted that 'the insulting grossness' of Hamlet's speech to Ophelia during *The Mousetrap* is unprecedented; 'it is such language', he suggests, 'as you will find addressed to a woman by no other hero of Shakespeare's.' (Though I, for sure, wouldn't be so quick to identify Hamlet as a hero.) His barbs about 'country matters' and what 'lies between maids' legs' are clearly designed to discomfort Ophelia – a woman he claims to have once loved – and it seems hard to detach the coarseness and violence of his language here from the sex nausea that has consumed him throughout the play (3.2.111; 113).

It is in his earlier encounter with Ophelia, though, that we see Hamlet's sexual revulsion in its most extended form, for here he ultimately cannot tolerate the process of generation more broadly. To be sure, this sequence is flush with conventional misogyny, as in Hamlet's harangue on women's duplicity:

> I have heard of your paintings well enough. God has given you one face and you make yourselves another. You jig and amble and you lisp, you nickname God's creatures and make your wantonness ignorance. Go to, I'll no more on't. It hath made me mad. (3.1.141–5)

But beyond statements like this, Hamlet reveals an even more complex sex disgust. After first denying that he ever gave Ophelia gifts (what we'd now, given the context, call gaslighting), he quickly moves to denounce both feminine virtue and beauty in sexual terms, noting that 'the power of Beauty will sooner transform Honesty from what it is to a bawd than the force of Honesty can translate Beauty into his likeness' (3.1.110–12). From here, he infamously commands Ophelia to 'get thee to a nunnery', a phrase with a well-known double meaning (120). Insofar as *nunnery* is a slang for brothel, the implication (following the statement on honest women turning bawd) seems to be that Ophelia belongs with prostitutes because all women are prostitutes. We may recall Hamlet's earlier claim that his mother is 'common' (1.2.74), and the ghost's insistence that Gertrude was won partly won by 'traitorous gifts' (1.5.43), a statement that anticipates the dumbshow's 'poisoner woo[ing] the queen with gifts' (3.2.131). Equating sex with prostitution obviously aligns with the debased way that Hamlet views eroticism, especially because he can no longer envision the possibility of rarefied love in the wake of his mother's remarriage. But Hamlet's advice to Ophelia is equally suggestive if we take it at face value: a life of chastity is the only worthy life-choice, because to procreate is to inherently be 'a breeder of sinners' (3.1.121). Hamlet's disgust is such that there seems to be no ethical way to have sex, an outlook that reaches its logical conclusion in his closing declaration that 'we will have no more marriages' (145–6). We have earlier explored Hamlet's general disgust with the corruption of the world, and that here links with his sexual aversion; to have sex is to engage in a repulsive act that only engenders the creation of morally rotten souls who will inevitably disappoint. He even acknowledges a self-disgust in this regard: 'I am myself indifferent honest', he exclaims, 'but yet I could accuse myself of such things that it were better my mother had not borne me' (121–3). Generation, for Hamlet, cannot finally be cleansed from either the taint of sexuality or the blight of moral decay, and comes to be a source of intense revulsion for a man already sensitive to matters of disgust. And this, finally, further amplifies the force of his earlier comment to Polonius, where human generation is compared to the breeding of maggots in a dead dog. According to TMT, sex is a source of disgust because it reminds us of our creatureliness, and thus, mortality; it is therefore thoroughly appropriate that the disgusted Hamlet sees human procreation in terms of a rotting animal carcass.

* * *

If we view Hamlet's outlook and behaviour in terms of Terror Management strategies, his sex nausea aligns comfortably with the generalized disgust that causes him to see his world in terms of corruption and rot: both are psychic defences against the existential terror of death. Mortality was made devastatingly salient by the shocking death of his father, and activated Hamlet's well-known anxieties about the human animal's inevitable end. Hamlet does, it is true, show a brazen attitude towards death on two main occasions; in his first soliloquy, he fantasizes about suicide and claims to wish that his 'flesh would melt' (1.2.129), while he later in Act 1 proclaims that 'I do not set my life at a pin's fee' (1.4.65). But given both his actions and behaviour elsewhere in the play, such statements strike me more as spontaneous posturing than reflections of a more considered outlook. Hamlet's famous delay, it seems to me, must surely be at least somewhat a function of his awareness that an act of regicide has a reasonable chance of resulting in the perpetrator's death. (He has the most likely chance of getting away with it during the prayer scene – but because of his antic behaviour during *The Mousetrap*, in which he excitedly narrates a nephew assassinating his royal uncle, it seems likely that suspicion might fall to him if Claudius was discovered murdered.) Of course, for much stronger evidence of this dread, we need only point to the 'To be, or not to be' soliloquy, in which the uncertainties of our ultimate fate are directly explored (3.1.55). This speech, which I interpret as addressing both suicide and the likelihood that an action against Claudius would be fatal, explicitly acknowledges that humanity is paralysed by existential fear: 'for in that sleep of death what dreams may come / When we have shuffled off this mortal coil / Must give us pause' (65–7). Here, Hamlet's overriding disgust for humanity is reframed by his fear of death, for it is only the dreadful uncertainties of what lies beyond that necessitates our suffering in this corrupt world:

> Who would fardels bear
> To grunt and sweat under a weary life
> But that the dread of something after death
> (The undiscovered country from whose bourn
> No traveller returns) puzzles the will
> And makes us rather bear those ills we have
> Than fly to others that we know not of. (75–81)

Thus, 'conscience does make cowards' of us all (82). Hamlet ends the speech with a statement that, it seems to me, can only refer to an attempt on Claudius: he reflects that

> the native hue of resolution
> Is sicklied o'er with the pale cast of thought,
> And enterprises of great pitch and moment
> With this regard their currents turn awry
> And lose the name of action. (83–7)

It's telling that Hamlet sees inaction as a consequence of sickness; the phrase *sicklied o'er*, which seems a Shakespearean coinage, reminds us of Hamlet's investment in the rhetoric of disgust. But the larger point is that Hamlet's ostensible goal – the *enterprise* of honouring his father's command and achieving his revenge – is at this point thwarted by his fear of death.

It's also vital to note that Hamlet's disgust-based attempts at anxiety buffering are not working very well at the moment. TMT, it will be remembered, suggests that people respond to the existential terror of death by taking solace in cultural world views (like religion) that reduce anxiety by affirming the meaningfulness of the larger cosmos. But here, Hamlet gains no relief through such mechanisms, and he doesn't even mention the comforting possibility of a Christian afterlife. This is presumably to some extent a reflection of his experience with the ghost: whether it is a malicious demon or indeed an avatar of his tormented, suffering father, neither option does much to make the thought of what comes after death less horrifying.

Hamlet, however, is not a static character, and his mindset shortly before the play's tragic end indicates a development in his attitude towards death, and a development of the effectiveness of his Terror Management strategies. This happens, I suggest, through a series of further encounters with mortality in the second half of the play – encounters that are indeed partly counterbalanced with the defensive mechanism of disgust, but which nonetheless make mortality so overwhelmingly salient that Hamlet has no choice but to find comfort in an anxiety buffering world view. To conclude this chapter, I'll explore how these events underwrite Hamlet's transformation of outlook, and how this transformation enables him to enact the revenge that ultimately spells his own doom.

After conversing with his father's ghost, Hamlet's next encounter with death is a rather big one: in a confused, sudden moment, he himself becomes a killer. The murder of Polonius, not being premeditated, is perhaps not quite as morally depraved as his uncle's fratricide – but nonetheless, the fact remains that Hamlet has now taken as many lives as Claudius, and in doing so will subject both Laertes and Ophelia to the same unspeakable anguish that torments him. It's notable that Hamlet's first response to the interloper is to label him 'a rat'; this association with a disgusting, vermin animal sets the stage for the dismissive callousness with which he treats the man he has just killed (3.4.23). I myself find it hard not to be off-put by Hamlet's response here – his statements that 'I took thee for thy better', and that his unfortunate victim should 'take thy fortune' strike me as particularly brutal (30). But it is Hamlet's subsequent actions that truly activate the realm of disgust, as he makes horrifying sport out of hiding Polonius's corpse. 'I'll lug the guts into the neighbour room,' Hamlet declares, initiating a sequence in which Claudius and his agents desperately attempt to take some control of the spiralling scandal (210). It is interesting to see here how Claudius casts his own previous laxness to Hamlet's behaviour: he had acted 'like the owner of a foul disease, [who] to keep it from divulging, let it feed / Even on the pith of life' (4.1.21–3).

It makes perfect sense that when Hamlet speaks about the corpse, he stresses its ability to evoke revulsion; little else, we must imagine, would make mortality more salient than taking the life of another. Hamlet thus sees Polonius's body in terms of its animal creatureliness, as when he anticipates its rotting stench; 'if indeed you find him not within this month', Hamlet assures, 'you shall nose him as you go up the stairs into the lobby' (4.3.34–6). It is further compounded when he imagines the decaying corpse being consumed by worms: Polonius lies 'where 'a is eaten', because 'we fat all creatures else to fat us, and we fat ourselves for maggots' (19; 22–3). Indeed, thinking about the disgustingness of your body's inevitable decay was a common trope of early modern memento mori texts – as when Luis De Granada's *Of Prayer, and Meditation* (a possible source of *Hamlet*) describes 'how filthie and lothsome the bodie is after it is dead'.[50] Our final resting place, De Granda reminds us, will be 'obscure, stinkinge, full of wormes, maggottes, bones, and dead mens skulles'; here, in this 'filthie and miserable donghill', our corpses 'shalbe troden vpon, and eaten with fowle wormes, and maggottes, and within fewe daies be of as owglie a forme, as a dead Carrion that lyeth in the feildes, insomuch that the waiefaringe man will stoppe his nose, and ronne awaie in great hast to auoid the stinkinge sauour of it'. The memento mori tradition might initially seem to contradict the predictions of TMT, in the sense that it reminds us, rather than distances us from death – but it is actually perfectly compatible, when we remember that, in its Christian framework, the emphasis on the disgusting qualities of death serves only to strengthen one's faith in the cultural world view that offers salvation beyond our body's decay. Here, Hamlet cannot help but meditate on the bodily decomposition of the man he just killed, as one dead animal becomes food for another. Randall Martin, in fact, declares that 'Hamlet's change in attitude toward revenge comes about by observing the natural phenomena of physical decay and regeneration facilitated by the work of earthworms' – and though I don't think worms per se are the crucial element, I very much agree that Hamlet's engagement with Polonius's rotting animal corpse makes mortality further salient, in a way that will eventually transform his attitude towards death.[51]

Of course, Hamlet's final major engagement with pre-finale mortality is his experience in the graveyard. It is in the graveyard that Hamlet becomes awash with reminders of mortality, his experience with Polonius's corpse now magnified into an experience with countless animal remains. John Hunt argues that much of the play is fixated on Hamlet's 'attempt[s] to be something other than a body', but I think the graveyard sequence most explicitly demonstrates how 'all of his efforts to remove himself from the compromising infection of corporeality only drive him more deeply into the understanding of his dependence on the frail body'.[52] It is no accident that Hamlet seeks expert testimony on the biology of decay: 'how long will a man lie i'th' earth ere he rot', he asks the gravedigger, who answers with a pun ('if 'a be not rotten before 'a die') suggesting the proximity of physical and moral corruption (5.1.154–6). In this setting, one cannot escape the fact that humanity's inevitable end is such rotting, the dissolution of our bodily flesh – and indeed, death's democratizing inevitability is a major theme of the scene. Whether a tanner, a lawyer, a jester or a king, Hamlet is pointedly made aware, all will be reduced to disparate bones. The commentary on Alexander is particularly telling, because it reminds us that part of anxiety buffering entails the desire to imagine gestures of immortality, even symbolically– what does it mean, then, if even the conqueror of the world is reduced to 'noble dust . . . stopping a bung-hole' (194–5)? Hamlet cannot help but acknowledge that 'Alexander died, Alexander was buried, Alexander returneth to dust' – just as we all will (198–9). But Alexander aside, mortality is made most directly salient for Hamlet in his iconic encounter with Yorick's skull, a moment that insists upon the cold materiality of death unlike any other in the play.[53] Rather obviously, what interests me most is how Shakespeare explicitly tells us, in this moment of existential meditation, that Hamlet is disgusted by this occasion: the juxtaposition between his cherished memories and the stinking skull lies 'abhorred in [his] imagination', and causes his 'gorge [to] rise' (178). Here, we see disgust most nakedly as an anxiety buffer against the inevitability of death – it is almost too much for Hamlet to process. I have suggested throughout this book the disgust concerns the regulation of boundaries, and we may turn here to the useful formulation of Susan Zimmerman; 'the fearsomeness of the corpse', she argues, 'resides in putrefication, or *un*becoming ... that is, in the dissolution of those boundaries that mark the body's former union of parts'.[54] There is hardly anything that signals unbecoming more than a floating skull – an object that equally exposes the inescapable reality of our fundamental animal existence. The frailness of these animal bodies is made apparent a final time as the scene concludes, and Hamlet gains the horrific knowledge that Ophelia, to his surprise, is about to begin that process of decay. Though there is much to say about how Ophelia's corpse becomes a site of contest for Laertes and Hamlet – who, in Q1, leaps into her grave with his rival – my primary concern here is how it is yet another way in which, through close proximity to physical decay, Hamlet is made painfully aware of death's inescapable grip.

We may now consider the play's final scene. To sum up my argument thus far: the murder of King Hamlet initiates in his son an existential anxiety about the inevitability of death, an anxiety that cannot at present be assuaged by conventional faith. As a buffering mechanism, Hamlet's world view is pervaded by an overwhelming disgust at both the physical and moral corruption of the world, with targets including his mother's adultery and human sexuality in general. As the play progresses, however, mortality is made ever more salient for Hamlet through a series of extraordinary (and disgusting) episodes – the murder of Polonius, his encounter with Yorick's skull, and the shock of Ophelia's funeral. This brings us to Act 5.2, where we suddenly find that Hamlet has adopted an entirely new outlook on existence. The passage is famous, but I will quote it in full here. When Horatio asks if Hamlet would like to delay the fencing match, he surprisingly replies:

> Not a whit. We defy augury. There is special providence in the fall of a sparrow. If it be, 'tis not to come. If it be not to come, it will be now. If it be not now, yet it will come. The readiness is all, since no man of aught he leaves knows what is't to leave betimes. Let be. (198–203)

The man who once agonized about being and not being has reached a shocking tranquility: *let be*. And, unlike before, it seems premised on an explicitly Christian consolation: the invocation of providence is unmistakable, and the reference to the fall of a sparrow alludes to Matthew 10:29, which asks, 'are not two sparrowes sold for a farthing, and one of them shall not fall on the ground without your Father?'[55] No longer plagued by thoughts of his uncertain fate, Hamlet is content with acceptance of what's to come. He even explicitly dismisses anxiety towards death: 'since no man of aught he leaves knows what is't to leave betimes.' The contrast between this and Hamlet's previous outlook couldn't be more apparent. What, then has changed?

Speaking in terms of Terror Management processes, I would suggest that Hamlet has finally taken existential comfort in the promise of a cultural world view – and he has done this because the events of the play have made mortality so unbearably salient to him. Disgust, we have seen, is one compensatory defence – but ultimately, the forces of mortality were so powerful that they demanded the acceptance of the conventional spiritual outlook that once gave him pause. The play's unending parade of death left Hamlet with no choice but to adopt a cultural world view that provides the necessary psychic relief. His father's murder, his killing of Polonius, his experience in the graveyard, his loss of Ophelia – all were too much to bear. It's also worth noting that, at the moment of this speech, Hamlet's own mortality has been made particularly salient: he is now aware that Claudius is actively trying to kill him. If, as is usually believed, the *it* in this speech refers to Hamlet's death, then he approaches the fencing match with a premonition of his own fate – he earlier acknowledged that 'thou wouldst not think how ill all's here about my heart' (191–2) – but he importantly did not delay the action. Bradley calls Hamlet's attitude here 'fatalism rather than . . . faith in Providence', but it doesn't really matter; the crucial point is that Hamlet has found a way to buffer his existential terror, which allows him to face Laertes and ultimately achieve his revenge.[56] This transformation, it seems to me, is consistent with the processes described in Terror Management research. To conclude, we might point to the dying Hamlet's insistence that Horatio remain alive and 'tell [his] story' (333): this, to me, anticipates the TMT finding that 'people must believe that some valued aspect of themselves will continue, either literally or symbolically, after cessation of their biological body'.[57] Hamlet, in the final moments of life, takes comfort in the thought of his name enduring.

Though scholars today are often sceptical about the application of psychological models to literary characters, I do think, in the broadest terms, that the principles of TMT can offer some intriguing insights into Hamlet's dilemma: *Hamlet* is a play about death, it is a play about disgust, and TMT provides some empirical evidence for how these two concepts may be linked in the human psyche. This model, I suggest, can help us make sense of the play's disparate elements – Hamlet's anxiety towards death, his obsession with corruption and decay, his puzzling sex nausea – and it provides another example of how Shakespeare may have intuitively anticipated features of disgust that have been articulated in the modern research laboratory.

11

Sex disgust

'It is a fact', Darrell Figgis wrote over a century ago, 'that throughout the great tragic period of Shakespeare's work, one of the prevailing notes towards the whole sex-question is of an absolute nausea and abhorrence.'[1] J. Dover Wilson, writing decades later, couldn't help but note the 'strain of sex-nausea which runs through almost everything he wrote after 1600'.[2] *Hamlet*, we just saw, contains Shakespeare's most famous depictions of sex as revolting – but we analysed a similar theme in Timon's misanthropic railings, and these are not the only examples. Researchers agree that sexuality is a major elicitor of disgust, but sex (at the species level) is obviously a biological necessity – a crux that leads to 'the intriguing question of how people succeed in having pleasurable sex at all?'[3]

As outlined in Chapter 1, theorists have attempted to account for sex disgust in somewhat different ways. Rozin, Haidt and McCauley's cultural evolution model views it within the category of *animal-reminder disgust*, in the sense that the inevitable corporeality of sex makes salient the fact that we share this behaviour with so many other creatures. The Terror Management outlook analysed in the last chapter is obviously premised on this fact, but others not in the TMT tradition have similarly argued that 'sexual disgust functions to motivate rejection of reminders that human bodies are similar to animal bodies'.[4] Tybur's adaptationist model, in contrast, sees sexual nausea as one of the three major categories of disgust; in this evolutionary account, sexual disgust promotes 'the avoidance of sexual behaviors with partners imposing potentially high fitness costs', by encouraging us to avoid low-value mates with poor genetic compatibility. It seems most likely, however, that some combination of these factors is involved, and more recent work is beginning to suggest that sexual disgust likely entails 'multiple concerns about pathogens, mates, animality, and morality'.[5]

Because while sex is necessary for species reproduction, 'it carries several direct costs' – including 'tissue damage during intercourse, the risk of pathogen transmission, and social risks in the form of reputational damage and direct aggression from intrasexual competitors'.[6] Insofar as disgust is a mechanism of regulation and avoidance, 'sex as a procreation stance and disgust as a defensive mechanism' therefore have a 'paradoxical and possibly obstructive' relationship, meaning that in practice humans must balance two competing impulses.[7] In light of this, disgust priming has been shown both to 'reduce subsequent sexual arousal' and to 'diminish sexual arousal in individuals who are already in a state of heightened sexual excitation'.[8] It is thus clear that the inhibiting quality of disgust needs to be downregulated in order for sex to occur, and experiments indeed suggest that higher levels of arousal lead both men and women to be less disgusted by sex-related stimuli.[9] Furthermore, there is evidence that 'mating strategy calibrates sexual disgust', because 'short-term mating orientation is associated with reduced sexual disgust sensitivity'; a willingness to engage with many partners for a short duration obviously entails a willingness to put oneself at higher pathogen exposure risk, which is enabled by a dampening of sex disgust's inhibitory impulses.[10] As noted in Chapter 1, women are consistently shown to be higher in disgust sensitivity than men, and it may be because the unique features of their reproductive and gestational cycle require vigilance against both pathogens and low-value mates; women's disgust sensitivity increases during pregnancy, presumably because it is paramount to avoid dangerous pathogens when carrying a child. But for women especially, 'sexual arousal . . . significantly reduce[s] sensitivity to sexual disgust' – arousal, in other words, facilitates an 'organism's willingness to engage in high-risk, but evolutionarily necessary, reproductive behaviors, an effect that could be particularly important for women'.[11]

Besides its impact on the basic dynamics of reproduction, sex disgust exhibits a variety of other intriguing features. For one thing, there is a fascinating way that it may fold into disgust's core domain of food: findings suggest that food neophobia is linked not only to pathogen disgust but to sexual disgust as well.[12] This leads to the hypothesis that 'a willingness to try novel and unfamiliar foods may be, in part, a mating display that signals immunological competence' – in the sense that 'individuals with more robust immune systems may be better able to withstand the potential costs of eating unknown foods', and 'a willingness to expose oneself to new and unfamiliar foods conveys important information about one's health and the strength of one's immune system'.[13] (Men interested in short-term mating showed a particular willingness to eat novel foods.) Disgust may play a role in a whole host of sexual dysfunctions, and researchers have created the Sexual Disgust Questionnaire to help assess sex disgust sensitivity and help with treatment.[14] Sex is also a good reminder of how disgust thresholds change across the lifespan, because children are often repulsed by the idea when it's first introduced: '[they] can not believe that their parents would do such a thing and insist that they themselves could never find such activities appealing.'[15]

But most notably, and most unfortunately, sex disgust is yet another instance in which the hypervigilance of the BIS seems to lead to the marginalization of vulnerable populations. Sexual acts dubbed 'abnormal' routinely elicit moral disgust in laboratory participants, and studies have amply demonstrated how disgust leads to prejudice and discrimination against multiple identity groups, particularly gay men. Indeed, a recent meta-analysis confirmed that 'disgust, in its induced states, amplifies homonegativity toward gay men', though it is not clear precisely why.[16] Presumably this has something to do with notions of morality; studies suggest that higher disgust sensitivity predicts more negative feelings towards groups who seem to threaten sexual morality (i.e. *young people who are sexually active, gays and lesbians, pro-gay activists, pro-choice activists* and *feminists*) and positive feelings towards groups associated with traditional sexual morality (i.e. *young people who wait until marriage to have sex, Evangelical Christians, anti-gay activists* and *pro-life activists*).[17] Thus homophobic disgust is not just about alleged 'contamination concerns', but 'rather is partially accounted for by conservative sexual ideology'.[18] And socialization, of course, is another important factor; in one experiment, heterosexual American men who scored low on a sexual prejudice scale demonstrated the same physiological stress response to an image of two men kissing as those with higher levels of prejudice, leading researchers to speculate that there may be a widespread 'socialised disgust response to same-sex PDA' active even in whose unaware of having explicit prejudice.[19] Whatever the case, somehow or another the connection between repulsion and sex contributes to a very real social crisis – a fact that has led some psychologists to advise that the 'initiation of policies that attempt to sever the link between disgust and homosexuality could prove to be effective in promoting acceptance of individuals who are gay, particularly among those with more conservative views'.[20]

Modern disgust research, then, offers many ways of looking at the phenomenon that literary scholars have called sex nausea. But what of Shakespeare? His interest in sex disgust, we have seen, intensifies in later works, but there are traces of it in his early career; we can point to Adriana in *The Comedy of Errors*, who asks (who she thinks to be) her unfaithful husband,

> How dearly would it touch thee to the quick
> Shouldst thou but hear I were licentious?
> And that this body, consecrate to thee,
> By ruffian lust should be contaminate? [. . .]
> I am possessed with an adulterate blot;
> My blood is mingled with the crime of lust:
> For if we two be one, and thou play false,
> I do digest the poison of thy flesh,
> Being strumpeted by thy contagion. (2.2.138–41; 148–52)

In Adriana's expression, the moral offence of infidelity is construed in terms of a corrupting internal disease, linking multiple domains of disgust elicitors. But, as Jonathan Gil Harris reminds us, her language also suggests the more literal spread of sexually transmitted infection – and indeed, syphilis functions as a 'virtual leit-motif' in *The Comedy of Errors* evident in various comments about how 'wenches will burn' (4.3.58) and 'love-springs rot' (3.2.3).[21] Scholars have given considerable attention to the presence of syphilis in Shakespeare's work, which becomes particularly concentrated in his mature plays; some, going further, actually suggests that Shakespeare's 'clinically exact' knowledge of the disease seems to indicate that he himself was infected with it.[22] Whatever the case, we can say that his work is filled with off-colour references to burning sores, baldness and aching bones, the typical symptoms of the pox. We saw in Chapter 4 how syphilis was a central theme of Timon's rantings, and we can point to its presence in many other plays; in *As You Like It,* for example, we hear of the 'embossed sores and headed evils' that Jaques would 'disgorge into the general world' (2.7.67; 69), in *A Midsummer Night's Dream,* Quince mentions 'French crowns [that] have no hair at all (1.2.89–90) and in *Much Ado About Nothing,* the sexually disgraced Hero is portrayed as a 'contaminated stale' with 'foul-tainted flesh' who is cruelly dismissed as a 'rotten orange' (2.2.24; 4.1.144; 4.1.31). A particularly interesting example is *Pericles,* which speaks of 'good as rotten' prostitutes who made an unfortunate client 'roast meat for worms' (4.2.8-9; 23–4); as Margaret Healy notes, there are no references to syphilis in any of the play's sources, yet in Shakespeare's 'discussion of the Pox and its consequences are rife and nauseatingly explicit'.[23]

Earlier, we briefly noted the malady of Falstaff – a man who has been described as 'the world's most famous syphilitic'.[24] Johannes Fabricius thoroughly records Sir John's engagement with the disease. In *Henry IV, Part 2,* Falstaff and Doll Tearsheet have an extended dialogue on the pox, in which his memorable conflation of military and sexual danger 'twist[s] her comment into a grim jest about syphilitic lesions':

> DOLL: Yea, Jesu, our chains and our jewels.
> FALSTAFF: [*Sings.*] 'Your brooches, pearls and ouches!' – For to serve bravely is to come halting off, you know; to come off the breach with his pike bent bravely, and to surgery bravely, to venture upon the charged chamber bravely. (2.4.47–52)[25]

Doll, we find out in *Henry V,* eventually succumbs to the disease; after learning that she was treated in 'the powdering-tub of infamy' (2.1.75), we are told at the end of the play that '[Doll] is dead I'th' spital / Of malady of France' (5.1.82–3).[26] In *The Merry Wives of Windsor,* Falstaff receives a parodic treatment for his own infection, as the 'unclean knight' (4.4.57) with 'dissolute disease' (3.3.184) comes to suffer what Fabricius calls 'a venereal burning in Windsor Forest'.[27] This prank, in which Falstaff is ritually burned with candles, simultaneously reflects his 'wicked fire of lust' (2.1.60), the searing pain of venereal disease and contemporary treatments for syphilis, which included both mercury suffumigation and the cauterization of chancres.[28] This punishment, Falstaff reflects, is 'enough to be the decay of lust and late-walking through the realm' (5.5.143–4). But, as Fabricius reminds us, Falstaff doesn't ultimately get a happy ending, and his final moments of life fixate on sexual corruption. On his deathbed, it was reported, he was 'rheumatic and talked of the Whore of Babylon' (*Henry V,* 2.3.35–6) – his 'feverish rantings centering on the scarlet, archetypal prostitute in the Bible', apparently underlying 'a conviction that Lucifer would take his soul as punishment for his immoral dealings with women'.[29]

Of course, Shakespeare's sex nausea is not only about syphilis, and we can point to many plays that show a broader interest in presenting sexuality as a source of physical and moral corruption. For starters, we must surely agree with Gillian M. E. Alban's assessment that *Measure for Measure* is a 'sexually fraught play' – it is 'not just authority (justice) that is tried', Marilyn French argues, 'it is sexuality itself that is on trial'.[30] In the main plot, Angelo, Isabella and the Duke enact various degrees and kinds of sexual repression or withdrawal, while the underplot is raucously populated by bawds and prostitutes; conflicts repeatedly centre around the evaluation of sexual morality, whether it be in Claudio's criminalized relationship with Juliet, Angelo's broken engagement with Mariana, the horrifying bargain proposed to Isabella, or the erotic licentiousness of Vienna more broadly. (Indeed, the play has been associated with rape culture, and has taken on a new urgency in the light of international #MeToo movements.[31]) Carolyn E. Brown, in fact, argues that *Measure* 'focuses on the passions, one of the main themes being the impossibility of eradicating the libido'.[32] But libido, obviously, has a dire cost in this world. Only minutes into the first act, Lucio speaks of having 'purchased . . . many diseases' in Mistress Overdone's brothel, and affirms that his interlocutor's 'bones are hollow [from] impiety' (1.2.44; 54–5); in *Measure for Measure,* Catherine I. Cox suggest, 'syphilis possesses . . . a mysterious power of contagion', a literalization of the 'moral pestilence' that Angelo associates with sexuality more broadly, and that would seemingly doom Claudio.[33] Speaking of the prisoner, it's worth noting that the Terror Management processes we explored in the last chapter may contribute to the play's linkage of sex and death, especially given Claudio's existential reluctance 'to lie in cold obstruction and to rot' (3.1.123); as Fabricius reminds us, *Measure for Measure* 'presents sexuality as existing under the shadow of death and damnation'.[34] While the play's ultimate attitude towards sex is hard to settle, there's no denying the lasting power of how Angelo characterizes his own sexuality as an object of disgust: 'it is I', he says 'that, lying by the violet in the sun, / Do as the carrion does . . . corrupt with virtuous season' (2.2.167–9). This is an appropriate reflection of *Measure for Measure* more broadly, a play that presents (in the words of director Peter Brook) a 'base world . . . the disgusting, stinking world of medieval Vienna'.[35]

Though the theme is somewhat less prioritized, *Measure*'s fellow problem play *Troilus and Cressida* shows an equally troubling concern with matters of sexual revulsion. As mentioned earlier, *Troilus and Cressida* is a work generally seeped in disgust; indeed, if I had the space to add an additional chapter to this book, I would offer a full analysis of it. But for now, it's enough to note its insistently deprecating view of sex, which comes to reduce the foundational conflict of Western civilization to 'an argument [about] a whore and a cuckold' (2.3.71–2). When Thersites links 'war and lechery', he is identifying the major themes of the play (74); as the conflict unfolds, the apparent abandonment of romantic love for debased sex leads to bloodshed and violence on the battlefield.[36] ('Lechery, lechery, still wars and lechery', he repeats at the end of the play [5.2.201–2].) As Marvin Krims observes, the play offers us a few 'tender love scenes', but 'just as we begin to care about the lovers, their romance abruptly vanishes into the morass of mutual betrayal, heedless lust, and cynical expediency'.[37] Of course, the presence of Pandarus – the 'bawd' and 'broker-lackey', who's linked to 'traders in the flesh' (1.2.278; 5.11.33; 45) – ensures that the theme of prostitution is never far from our mind; 'elsewhere in Shakespeare', Joseph Lenz argues, 'the world is a stage', while 'in *Troilus* . . . it is a brothel'.[38] Syphilis is equally present; Pandarus mentions his 'aching bones' on multiple occasions (5.11.35; 50), while Thersites concludes that 'the Neapolitan bone-ache . . . is the curse dependent on those that war for a placket [i.e. vagina]' (2.3.18–20). Reflecting what we saw above about sex disgust and discrimination, the play also traffics in some of the most explicit homophobia that we find in Shakespeare; Patroclus is described as 'Achilles' brach' (2.1.114), 'male varlet' (5.1.15) and 'masculine whore' (17), before being condemned for his 'preposterous [i.e. sexual] discoveries' (23). But it is finally the romantic disillusion of Troilus, through which he is forced to exchange love for 'venomed vengeance' (5.3.47), that provides the play's final commentary on the corruption of sex. Thersites narrates his conflict with Diomedes with typical disgust, directing particular poison towards Cressida:

> That dissembling abominable varlet, Diomed, has got that same scurvy doting foolish young knave's sleeve of Troy there in his helm. I would fain see them meet, that that same young Trojan ass that loves the whore there might send that Greekish whoremasterly villain with the sleeve back to the dissembling luxurious drab, of a sleeveless errand. (5.4.2–8)

Given that Ulysses, a source of relative wisdom in the play, expressed an earlier disgust at Cressida's 'wanton spirits' (4.5.57) – which led him to dismiss her as a 'sluttish spoil [of] opportunity' (63) – it's hard not to think that we're at least partly invited to share Thersites's assessment. *Troilus and Cressida* thus recalls *Measure*'s willingness to construe sex as an elicitor of both physical and moral disgust, another instance of the sex nausea that seems so prevalent at this stage of Shakespeare's career.

And I cannot conclude without considering *King Lear*, another play notoriously pessimistic about sex – and this sex nausea is particularly interesting, Wilson notes, because 'there is no dramatic reason for it at all'.[39] The play shows a consistent engagement with the language of disgust – the disinheritance of Cordelia is initially framed by Kent as a 'foul disease' – but it has a special investment in presenting sex as something repulsive and corruptive (1.1.165).[40] *Lear* opens with a somewhat crude presentation of sex; Gloucester rather callously jokes about the birth of his illegitimate son, noting that 'there was good sport at his making, and the whoreson must be acknowledged' (1.1.22–3). For his part, Edmund's defence of villainous bastardy is partly premised on the fact that adulterous dalliances involve 'the lusty stealth of nature', in opposition to the 'dull stale tired bed' of legitimate matrimony (1.2.11; 13); at the end of the play, Edgar frames his brother's treachery with a poisoned image of female anatomy, proclaiming that his father's 'pleasant vices [in] the dark and vicious place ... cost him his eyes' (5.3.168; 170–1). Even Lear's knights, 'so debauched and bold [with] Epicurism and lust', leave Goneril's court 'infected with their manners' and 'more like a tavern or a brothel / Than a graced palace' (1.4.234–8).

But it is Lear, of course, who most furiously contributes to the theme. As Robert H. West noted decades ago, the king is so incensed by the actions of his children that 'the act of generation has come to seem an inhuman abyss of the human will', and his view of both the act and aftermath of procreation becomes painfully debased.[41] We see this early in his curse of Goneril:

> Hear, Nature, hear, dear goddess, hear:
> Suspend thy purpose if thou didst intend
> To make this creature fruitful.
> Into her womb convey sterility,
> Dry up in her the organs of increase,
> And from her derogate body never spring
> A babe to honour her. If she must teem,
> Create her child of spleen, that it may live
> And be a thwart disnatured torment to her.
> Let it stamp wrinkles in her brow of youth,
> With cadent tears fret channels in her cheeks,
> Turn all her mother's pains and benefits
> To laughter and contempt, that she may feel
> How sharper than a serpent's tooth it is
> To have a thankless child. (1.4.268–82)

Lear's disdain for reproduction and generation mostly emerges from the 'monster ingratitude' of his children (1.5.39) – a morally repulsive offence that shapes how he subsequently perceives physical acts – but it also results from the condition of his declining age, in which (as the Fool tells him) he has 'mad'st thy daughters thy mothers' (1.4.163–4). Despite his plans at the play's opening, he cannot actually embrace the yielding of his natural parental authority, leading him to rail against procreation more broadly. Generation is so corrupt, in fact, that he reframes the child's biological relationship to the father: 'thou art my flesh', he tells Goneril, 'my blood, my daughter, / Or rather a disease that's in my flesh / Which I must needs call mine' (2.2.416–18). What's more, at times Lear severs their relations entirely, as when he calls Goneril a 'degenerate bastard' (1.4.246) and fantasizes to Regan about 'divorc[ing] me from thy mother's tomb, / Sepulchring an adultress' (2.2.326–7). It is in madness, however, that we find Lear's most elaborate comments on the corrupting influence of sex, as he finally has no choice but to embrace its repulsive ubiquity:

> I pardon that man's life. What was thy cause?
> Adultery?
> Thou shalt not die – die for adultery? No!
> The wren goes to't and the small gilded fly
> Does lecher in my sight. Let copulation thrive,
> For Gloucester's bastard son was kinder to his father
> Than were my daughters got 'tween the lawful sheets.
> To't, luxury, pell-mell, for I lack soldiers.
> Behold yon simp'ring dame,
> Whose face between her forks presages snow,
> That minces virtue and does shake the head
> To hear of pleasure's name –
> The fitchew, nor the soiled horse, goes to't with a more riotous appetite. (4.6.108–21)

Lear now sees the taint of lust everywhere he looks, and his experiences thus far have short-circuited any sense of licensed sexual morality. This culminates in his infamous assessment of women, which imagines both their desire and their intimate anatomy in terms of filthy damnation:

> Down from the waist they are centaurs, though women all above. But to the girdle do the gods inherit, beneath is all the fiend's: there's hell, there's darkness, there is the sulphurous pit, burning, scalding, stench, consumption! Fie, fie, fie! Pah, pah! (121–5)

It's impossible to deny the visceral repulsion felt by Lear here; both *fie* and *pah* are interjections signalling the pure experience of disgust.[42] This passage – with its moral emphasis on spiritual corruption and visceral emphasis on noxious, stinking decay – is one of the rawest expressions of disgust in all of Shakespeare – a horrifyingly misogynistic outburst that reflects the play's revolting presentation of sexuality.

Conclusion

In the opening scene of *The Two Noble Kinsmen*, the nuptials of Theseus and Hippolyta are interrupted by a group of grieving petitioners. Clad in black, they announce themselves as

> three queens whose sovereigns fell before
> The wrath of cruel Creon, who endure
> The beaks of ravens, talons of the kites
> And pecks of crows, in the foul fields of Thebes.
> He will not suffer us to burn their bones,
> To urn their ashes, nor to take th'offence
> Of mortal loathsomeness from the blest eye
> Of holy Phoebus, but infects the winds
> With stench of our slain lords. (1.1.39–47)

Seeking 'the bones / Of our dead kings that we may chapel them', the mourners desperately turn to Duke Theseus – addressed as 'purger of the earth', whose 'feared sword ... does good turns to th' world' (49–50; 47–8). In this brief sequence, Shakespeare deploys two descriptors that, we've seen, indicate the register of early modern disgust (*foul* and *loathsomeness*), activates a series of images recalling many of the categorical elicitors that affective scientists have associated with the triggering of disgust (*corpses, body envelope violations, carrion-eating animals, disease, rottenness* and *moral violation*) and finally frames Theseus as a disgust-like agent of social purgation. Though one would probably not claim that disgust is a central theme of *The Two Noble Kinsmen*, this local passage is just one telling example of how the concept of disgust proved a potent compositional tool for Shakespeare, who habitually engaged the emotion with an enormous imaginative flexibility.

I started writing this book because I had a hunch that disgust was, somewhat quietly, an important element of Shakespearean drama; over the course of writing it, and immersing myself in Shakespeare's poetics of disgust, I have concluded that it is far more central to his creative practice than I ever could have predicted at the start. The gatekeeper emotion, I have broadly argued, is used by Shakespeare to explore the fundamental boundaries of human existence – the boundaries between where my body starts and stops, the boundaries between me and you, the boundaries between us and them, the boundaries between what we should and shouldn't do, and the boundaries between life and death. But such a general assessment is almost too reductive and obscures the countless subtleties of how Shakespeare leverages the formal, thematic and dramatic possibilities of disgust. We have learned from modern research that the disgust system is a vital engine of human behaviour, and Shakespeare, I think, understood this intuitively; after reviewing his relentless engagement with the emotion, I now find it impossible to deny that disgust is a centrepiece of his affective universe.

In this book, I have tried to balance in-depth analysis of certain key plays that prominently feature disgust (in the major chapters) with a more ranging, bird's-eye survey of how disgust appears throughout the Shakespearean canon (in the elicitor chapters). I have also attempted to balance the book's two main theoretical influences: historicism and the affective science tradition. More specifically, I have sought to illustrate how the historically situated analysis of early modern emotion can be strengthened by incorporating the insights of modern psychology – because not only are these discourses perfectly compatible, they more importantly have the potential to be mutually informing. For obvious reasons, this book has focused on how the sciences can aid the reading of Shakespeare – but, as noted in the Introduction, as humanists continue to engage the topic of emotion, it is becoming increasingly apparent that literary and historical analysis can equally provide vital context and evidence for affective scientists. Shakespeare, I have argued throughout, often anticipated modern psychological research on disgust, and his plays present compelling case studies that demonstrate many of the emotion's fundamental features. Finally, in the broadest sense, it is my hope that readers of *Shakespeare and Disgust* will have a new appreciation for the fascinating topic of revulsion more generally; though often unrecognized, disgust is a central component of human life and helps shape countless aspects of how we live our lives.

I have thus tried to account widely for Shakespeare's engagement with the dynamics of revulsion. There is, however, still opportunity for further analysis. It is clear, for instance, that there is ample opportunity to develop disgust's role in the comedies. As stated before, I think that Shakespeare's most intensive engagements with disgust occur in tragic contexts, because the emotion's regulatory properties are most salient when boundaries are violated in moments of crisis, rather than when they are transgressed in moments of play. But the comedies, of course, are still flush with examples of less fraught disgust, and it will be valuable to put the insights of psychological research in touch with the more familiar Bakhtinian notions of grotesqueness. The existence of Sir Toby Belch, for example, almost demands to be read in terms of (pleasurable?) revulsion, and we might wonder how *Twelfth Night*'s various forms of bodily and moral excessiveness intersect with a regulatory emotion like disgust. We might equally try to account for the prevalence of disease imagery in *As You Like It*, or how Jaques sees himself as one destined to 'cleanse the foul body of th'infected world' (2.7.60). Furthermore, there is more precise historicist work to be done; it will be fruitful, I think, to explore the ways that these scientific models of disgust do or do not align with early modern discourses of emotion, and we might more thoroughly investigate how aspects of early modern disgust (such as *indignation*) manifest more particularly in the period. (To repeat what I said in the introduction: resources on early modern discourses of disgust are available at earlymodernemotion.net.) Finally, the scientific theories I've explored throughout also need to be integrated into the models of disgust from critical theory and affective post-structuralism – but I'm hopeful that the groundwork I've established in this book can be a starting point for this next phase of analysis.

NOTES

Introduction

1 Quoted in David George, *Coriolanus* (London: The Arden Shakespeare, 2022), 133. This review survives only as a clipping; the title of the periodical is unknown.
2 Plutarch, *The Lives of the Noble Grecians and Romanes* (London, 1579), 245.
3 See *OED*, 'impostume/impostume, *n*'.
4 Roy Porter, *Flesh in the Age of Reason* (London: Allen Lane, 2003), 25.
5 Thomas Dekker, *Iests to Make You Merie* (London, 1607), 15; *The Seuen Deadly Sinnes of London* (London, 1606), 27. This passage is discussed by Amy Kenny, '"A Deal of Stinking Breath": The Smell of Contagion in the Early Modern Playhouse', in *Contagion on the Shakespearean Stage*, ed. Darryl Chalk and Mary Floyd-Wilson (New York: Palgrave, 2019), 51–2. See also Jonathan Gil Harris, 'The Smell of *Macbeth*', *Shakespeare Quarterly* 58.4 (2007): 465–86.
6 The distinction between *affect* and *emotion* is extremely muddled in the humanities. Often, the words are used interchangeably. But for some, 'affect theory' entails a post-structuralist philosophical endeavour in which 'affect' – a kind of latent energy reflecting a body's capacity to affect or be affected – is distinguished from 'emotion' – the specific sociolinguistic fixing of that energy. The 'affective turn' is generally a capacious umbrella term that can encompass both this specific 'affect theory' work and all forms of more general scholarship on emotion, sentiment, feeling, etc. As will become apparent, this book interrogates disgust as a discrete emotion, and does not invest in the specific philosophical concerns of 'affect theory' in its more specific conceptualization. For some overviews to this critical terrain, see, for example, Patricia Ticineto Clough and Jean Halley, eds., *The Affective Turn: Theorizing the*

Social (Durham: Duke University Press, 2007); Melissa Gregg and Gregory J. Seigworth, eds., *The Affect Theory Reader* (Durham: Duke University Press, 2010); Patrick Colm Hogan, *Literature and Emotion* (New York: Routledge, 2018); Patrick Colm Hogan, Bradley J. Irish and Lalita Pandit Hogan, eds., *The Routledge Companion to Literature and Emotion* (New York: Routledge, 2022).

7 Gail Kern Paster, *Humoring the Body: Emotions and the Shakespearean Stage* (Chicago: University of Chicago Press, 2004); Gail Kern Paster, Katherine Rowe and Mary Floyd-Wilson, eds., *Reading the Early Modern Passions: Essays in the Cultural History of Emotion* (Philadelphia: University of Pennsylvania Press, 2004); Douglas Trevor, *The Poetics of Melancholy in Early Modern England* (Cambridge: Cambridge University Press, 2004); Richard Meek and Erin Sullivan, eds., *The Renaissance of Emotion: Understanding Affect in Shakespeare and His Contemporaries* (Manchester: Manchester University Press, 2015); R. S. White, Mark Houlahan and Katrina O'Loughlin, eds., *Shakespeare and Emotions: Inheritances, Enactments, Legacies* (New York: Palgrave, 2015); Amanda Bailey and Mario DiGangi, eds., *Affect Theory and Early Modern Texts: Politics, Ecologies, and Form* (New York: Palgrave, 2017); and Katharine A. Craik, ed., *Shakespeare and Emotion* (Oxford: Oxford University Press, 2020). I offer a relatively thorough survey of early modern emotion studies to 2018 in the introduction to *Emotion in the Tudor Court: Literature, History, and Early Modern Feeling* (Evanston: Northwestern University Press, 2018). For work since then, see, for example, Paul Megna, Brid Phillips and R. S. White, eds., *Hamlet and Emotions* (New York: Palgrave, 2019); Mary Floyd-Wilson and Garrett A. Sullivan, Jr. eds., *Geographies of Embodiment in Early Modern England* (Oxford: Oxford University Press, 2020); Judith Owens, *Emotional Settings in Early Modern Pedagogical Culture: Hamlet, The Faerie Queene, and Arcadia* (New York: Palgrave, 2020); Benedict S. Robinson, *Passion's Fictions from Shakespeare to Richardson: Literature and the Sciences of Soul and Mind* (Oxford: Oxford University Press, 2021); Cora Fox, Bradley J. Irish and Cassie M. Miura, eds., *Positive Emotions in Early Modern Literature and Culture* (Manchester: Manchester University Press, 2021); and Kathleen French, *Shakespeare and Happiness* (New York: Routledge, 2022). See also Susan Broomhall, ed., *Early Modern Emotions: An Introduction* (London: Routledge, 2017).

8 William Ian Miller, *The Anatomy of Disgust* (Cambridge, MA: Harvard University Press, 1997), 5.

9 Robert Rawdon Wilson, *The Hydra's Tale: Imagining Disgust* (Edmonton: University of Alberta Press, 2002).

10 Winfried Menninghaus, *Disgust: Theory and History of a Strong Sensation*, trans. Howard Eiland and Joel Golb (Albany: SUNY Press, 2003); Carolyn Korsmeyer, *Savoring Disgust: The Foul and the Fair in Aesthetics* (Oxford: Oxford University Press, 2011).

11 Martha C. Nussbaum, *Hiding from Humanity: Disgust, Shame, and the Law* (Princeton: Princeton University Press, 2004); *From Disgust to Humanity: Sexual Orientation and Constitutional Law* (Oxford: Oxford University Press, 2010).

12 Debra Lieberman and Carlton Patrick, *Objection: Disgust, Morality, and the Law* (Oxford: Oxford University Press, 2018). On disgust and the law, see also Dan M. Kahan, 'The Anatomy of Disgust in Criminal Law', *Michigan Law Review* 96.6 (1998): 1621–57.

13 Colin McGinn, *The Meaning of Disgust* (Oxford: Oxford University Press, 2011).

14 Rachel Herz, *That's Disgusting: Unraveling the Mysteries of Repulsion* (New York: W.W. Norton, 2013); Valerie Curtis, *Don't Look, Don't Touch, Don't Eat: The Science Behind Revulsion* (Chicago: University of Chicago Press, 2013).

15 *The Ancient Emotion of Disgust*, ed. Donald Lateiner and Dimos Spatharas (Oxford: Oxford University Press, 2016).

16 Eleonora Joensuu, *A Politics of Disgust: Selfhood, World-Making, and Ethics* (New York: Routledge, 2020), chap. 3.

17 Zachary Samalin, *The Masses Are Revolting: Victorian Culture and the Political Aesthetics of Disgust* (Ithaca: Cornell University Press, 2021).

18 Luke F. Johnson, 'Foreign Food, Foreign Flesh: Apathetic Anthropophagy and Racial Melancholia in Houellebecq's *Submission*', *SubStance* 49.1 (2020): 25; Hannah Lee Rogers, 'Philosophy in Austen's Pump Room: How Enlightened Tolerance Became Disgust', *Eighteenth-Century Fiction* 32.2 (2020): 318; Neetu Khanna, 'Obscene Textures: The Erotics of Disgust in the Writings of Ismat Chughtai', *Comparative Literature* 72.4 (2020): 363.

19 Eve Kosofsky Sedgwick and Adam Frank, 'Shame in the Cybernetic Fold: Reading Silvan Tomkins', *Critical Inquiry* 21.2 (1995): 496–522; Sianne Ngai, *Ugly Feelings* (Cambridge: Cambridge University Press, 2005).

20 Sara Ahmed, *The Cultural Politics of Emotion* (Edinburgh: Edinburgh University Press, 2004), chap. 4.

21 Julia Kristeva, *Powers of Horror: An Essay on Abjection*, trans. Leon S. Roudiez (New York: Columbia University Press, 1982). (Originally published 1980.)

22 Mikhail Bakhtin, *Rabelais and His World*, trans. Hélène Iswolsky (Bloomington: Indiana University Press, 1984). For the grotesque in Renaissance England, see, for example, Willard Farnham, *The Shakespearean Grotesque: Its Genesis and Transformations* (Oxford: Clarendon Press, 1971); Neil Rhodes, *Elizabethan Grotesque* (London: Routledge, 1980); *Shakespeare and Carnival: After Bakhtin*, ed. Ronald Knowles (New York: St. Martin's Press, 1998); and the resources compiled in Liam E. Semler, *The Early Modern Grotesque: English Sources and Documents 1500–1700* (New York: Routledge, 2019).

23 Gail Kern Paster, *The Body Embarrassed: Drama and the Disciplines of Shame in Early Modern England* (Ithaca: Cornell University Press, 1993), 14.

24 Barbara Correll, *The End of Conduct: Grobianus and the Renaissance Text of the Subject* (Ithaca: Cornell University Press, 1996), 7.

25 Natalie K. Eschenbaum and Barbara Correll, eds., *Disgust in Early Modern English Literature* (New York: Routledge, 2016).

26 Benedict Robinson, 'Disgust c. 1600', *ELH* 81.2 (2014): 553–83; Natalie K. Eschenbaum and Barbara Correll, 'Introduction', in *Disgust in Early Modern English Literature*, 5. See also Zenón Luis-Martinez, '"A Weight of Carrion Flesh": Measuring Disgust, Shakespearean Mimesis', *European Journal of Anatomy* 24.Supplement 1 (2020): 51–62; I discovered this article after the book was completed, so I was not able to incorporate it into my analysis, but it still should be consulted as a brief study of disgust in Shakespeare. Finally, see my earlier analysis of disgust in chapter 1 of *Emotion in the Tudor Court*.

27 Eschenbaum and Correll, 'Introduction', 8.

28 Richard Meek and Erin Sullivan, 'Introduction', in *Renaissance of Emotion*, 6. Richard Strier was perhaps most critical of previous scholarship's focus on humoralism – see *The Unrepentant Renaissance: From Petrarch to Shakespeare to Milton* (Chicago: Chicago University Press, 2011), 7.

29 Literary and cultural scholars are, however, increasingly willing to incorporate this kind of scientific thought into their work; see *The Routledge Companion to Literature and Emotion*.

30 The most prominent constructivist scientist is Lisa Feldman Barrett, whose theory of 'psychological constructivism' is widely praised by historians of emotion. See Barrett, *How Emotions Are Made: The*

Secret Life of the Brain (New York: Houghton Mifflin Harcourt, 2017) and Bradley J. Irish, 'A Strategic Compromise: Universality, Interdisciplinarity, and the Case for Modal Emotions in History of Emotion Research', *Emotions: History, Culture, Society* 4.2 (2020): 235.

31 Paul Ekman, 'What Scientists Who Study Emotion Agree About', *Perspectives on Psychological Science* 11.1 (2016): 32.

32 See Stephen Greenblatt, *Learning to Curse: Essays in Early Modern Culture* (New York: Routledge, 1990), 222.

33 See Rob Boddice, *The History of Emotions* (Manchester: Manchester University Press, 2018), 158–9; Boddice, *A History of Feelings* (London: Reaktion Books, 2019), 64–5; Boddice and Mark Smith, *Emotion, Sense, Experience* (Cambridge: Cambridge University Press, 2020), 41.

34 For one account of a biocultural approach theorized by humanists, see Boddice and Smith, *Emotion, Sense, Experience*, 35. See also Irish, 'A Strategic Compromise', 233.

35 More specifically, both humanists and constructivist scientists sometimes have a 'cartoon' view of the universalist approach to emotion, such as in attitudes towards the much-maligned Basic Emotion Theory. See Michelle N. Shiota, 'Basic and Discrete Emotion Theories', in *The Routledge Handbook of Emotion Theory*, ed. Andrea Scarantino (forthcoming). Of course, this is not to imply that universalist scientists don't also distort the constructivist position.

36 See Ara Norenzayan and Steven J. Heine, 'Psychological Universals: What Are They and How Can We Know?' *Psychological Bulletin* 131.5 (2005): 763–84.

37 Richard A. Shweder, 'Relativism and Universalism', in *A Companion to Moral Anthropology*, ed. Didier Fassin (Chichester: John Wiley & Sons, 2012): 85–102. See also *Universalism Without Uniformity: Explorations in Mind & Culture*, ed. Julia L. Cassaniti and Usha Menon (Chicago: University of Chicago Press, 2017).

38 See Irish, 'A Strategic Compromise'.

39 See ibid. for my survey of Scherer's theory, and for a model of how it can be applied in humanities research.

40 Nor does it require embracing a vulgar form of evolutionary psychology, which has been rightly criticized by humanists. For a precise critique of evolutionary psychology, see Patrick Colm Hogan, *Cognitive Science, Literature, and the Arts: A Guide for Humanists* (New York: Routledge, 2003), Chap. 8.

41 Phyllis Gorfain, 'Toward a Theory of Play and the Carnivalesque in *Hamlet*', *Hamlet Studies* 13 (1991): 25.
42 See Hogan, *Literature and Emotion*, Introduction.
43 For a classic argument, see Patrick Colm Hogan, *What Literature Teaches Us About Emotion* (Cambridge: Cambridge University Press, 2011).

Chapter 1

1 Robinson, 'Disgust c. 1600', 553.
2 See Seger M. Breugelmans and Ype H. Poortinga, 'Emotion Without a Word: Shame and Guilt Among Rarámuri Indians and Rural Javanese', *Journal of Personality and Social psychology* 91.6 (2006): 1111–22.
3 Randle Cotgrave, *A Dictionarie of the French and English Tongues* (London, 1611), Bb.
4 Ibid., Aavi^v.
5 John Florio, *A Worlde of Wordes, or Most Copious, and Exact Dictionarie in Italian and English* (London, 1598), 370.
6 Thomas Wright, *A Treatise, Shewing the Possibilitie, and Conuieniencie of the Reall Presence of Our Sauior in the Blessed Sacrament* (London, 1596), fol. 118–118^v.
7 Anthony Copley, *Another Letter of Mr. A.C. to His Dis-Iesuited Kinseman* (London, 1602), 25.
8 Robinson, 'Disgust c. 1600', 558.
9 Richard J. McNally, 'Disgust Has Arrived', *Anxiety Disorders* 16 (2002): 561.
10 Search June 2022.
11 See Megan Oaten, Richard J. Stevenson and Trevor I. Case, 'Disgust as a Disease-Avoidance Mechanism', *Psychological Bulletin* 135.2 (2009): 307.
12 Charles Darwin, *The Expression of the Emotions in Man and Animals* (London: John Murray, 1872), 257–8.
13 Andras Angyal, 'Disgust and Related Aversions', *Journal of Abnormal and Social Psychology* 36.3 (1941): 394.
14 See, for example, Sigmund Freud, *Three Contributions to the Theory of Sex*, trans. A. A. Brill (New York, 1916), 16–17. On a different

note, the philosopher Aurel Kolnai wrote a short essay in disgust in 1927; in his account, 'the prototypical object of disgust is . . . the range of phenomena associated with putrefaction'. See Aurel Kolnai, *On Disgust*, ed. Barry Smith and Carolyn Korsmeyer (Chicago: Open Court, 2004), 53.

15 M. de L. Brooke, 'Is Eliciting Disgust Responses From Its Predators Beneficial for Toxic Prey?' *Animal Behaviour* 155 (2019): 225.

16 See, for example, the following exchange: Judith A. Toronchuk and George F. R. Ellis, 'Disgust: Sensory Affect or Primary Emotional System?' *Cognition & Emotion* 21.8 (2007): 1799–818; Judith A. Toronchuk and George F. R. Ellis, 'Criteria for Basic Emotions: Seeking DISGUST?' *Cognition & Emotion* 21.8 (2007): 1829–32; Jaak Panksepp, 'Criteria for Basic Emotions: Is DISGUST a Primary 'Emotion'?' *Cognition & Emotion* 21.8 (2007): 1819–28.

17 Paul Rozin, Jonathan Haidt and Clark McCauley, 'Disgust', in *Handbook of Emotions, Fourth Edition*, ed. Lisa Feldman Barrett, Michael Lewis and Jeannette M. Haviland-Jones (New York: Guilford Press, 2018), 815, for this and the next quotes on points of disgust agreement.

18 Trevor I. Case et al., 'The Animal Origins of Disgust: Reports of Basic Disgust in Nonhuman Great Apes', *Evolutionary Behavioral Sciences* 14.3 (2020): 231.

19 See Stephen Jay Gould, 'Exaptation: A Crucial Tool for Evolutionary Psychology', *Journal of Social Issues* 47 (1991): 43–65; and Stephen Jay Gould and Elisabeth S. Vrba, 'Exaptation - A Missing Term in the Science of Form', *Paleobiology* 8.1 (1982): 4–15.

20 See Caroline R. Amoroso et al., 'Disgust Theory Through the Lens of Psychiatric Medicine', *Clinical Psychological Science* 8.1 (2020): 3–24.

21 Ibid., 4.

22 Jonathan Haidt, Clark McCauley and Paul Rozin, 'Individual Differences in Sensitivity to Disgust: A Scale Sampling Seven Domains of Disgust Elicitors', *Personality and Individual Differences* 16.5 (1994): 712.

23 Ibid.

24 Edward B. Royzman, Robert F. Leeman and John Sabini, '"You Make Me Sick": Moral Dyspepsia as a Reaction to Third-Party Sibling Incest', *Motivation and Emotion* 32.2 (2008): 100.

25 Jonathan Haidt et al., 'Body, Psyche, and Culture: The Relationship between Disgust and Morality', *Psychology and Developing Societies* 9.1 (1997): 108.

26 Joshua M. Tybur, Debra Lieberman and Vladas Griskevicius, 'Microbes, Mating, and Morality: Individual Differences in Three Functional Domains of Disgust', *Journal of Personality and Social Psychology* 97.1 (2009): 103–22; Joshua M. Tybur et al., 'Disgust: Evolved Function and Structure', *Psychological Review* 120.1 (2013): 65–84; and Joshua M. Tybur and Debra Lieberman, 'Human Pathogen Avoidance Adaptations', *Current Opinion in Psychology* 7 (2016): 6–11.

27 Joshua M. Ackerman, Sarah E. Hill and Damian R. Murray, 'The Behavioral Immune System: Current Concerns and Future Directions', *Social and Personality Psychology Compass* 12.2 (2018): 1. See Valerie Curtis and Adam Biran, 'Dirt, Disgust, and Disease: Is Hygiene in Our Genes?' *Perspectives in Biology and Medicine* 44.1 (2001) 17–31; Val Curtis, Robert Aunger and Tamer Rabie, 'Evidence that Disgust Evolved to Protect From Risk of Disease', *Proceedings of the Royal Society B: Biological Sciences* 271 (2004): S131–3.

28 Tybur et al., 'Disgust', 69.

29 Ibid., 71–2.

30 Ibid., 74.

31 Darwin, *The Expression of the Emotions*, 258. For modern research on the disgust face, see Paul Ekman and Wallace V. Friesen, 'Constants Across Cultures in the Face and Emotion', *Journal of Personality and Social Psychology* 17.2 (1971): 124–9; Paul Rozin, Laura Lowery and Rhonda Ebert, 'Varieties of Disgust Faces and the Structure of Disgust', *Journal of Personality and Social Psychology* 66.5 (1994): 870–81; Sherri C. Widen and James A. Russell, 'Children's and Adults' Understanding of the "Disgust Face"', *Cognition & Emotion* 22.8 (2008): 1513–41; and Maren Westphal, George A. Bonanno and Anthony D. Mancini, 'Attachment and Attentional Biases for Facial Expressions of Disgust', *Journal of Social & Clinical Psychology* 33.2 (2014): 169–86.

32 Nina Strohminger, 'Disgust Talked About', *Philosophy Compass* 9.7 (2014): 479. As Strohminger explains, bitter taste receptors identify botanical toxins, while sour taste receptors identify the acids that reflect the bacterial metabolic cycle present in spoiling food.

33 Lisa S. Elwood and Bunmi O. Olatunji, 'A Cross-Cultural Perspective on Disgust', in *Disgust and its Disorders: Theory, Assessment, and Treatment Implications*, ed. Bunmi O. Olatunji and Dean McKay (Washington, DC: American Psychological Association, 2009), 116; 117.

34 See, for example, Joseph T. Pochedly, Sherri C. Widen and James A. Russell, 'What Emotion Does the "Facial Expression of Disgust" Express?' *Emotion* 12.6 (2012): 1315–19, and Ruth Leys, *The Ascent of Affect: Genealogy and Critique* (Chicago: University of Chicago Press, 2017), 106–14. For a recent analysis that complicates this account, see Shiota, 'Basic and Discrete Emotion Theories'.

35 Curtis, Aunger and Rabie, 'Evidence', S131; Elwood and Olatunji, 'A Cross-Cultural Perspective', 117.

36 Rozin, Haidt and McCauley, 'Disgust', 825. On disgust and the brain, see Bruno Wicker et al., 'Both of Us Disgusted in *My* Insula: The Common Neural Basis of Seeing and Feeling Disgust', *Neuron* 40.3 (2003): 655–64; Martin Kavaliers, Klaus-Peter Ossenkopp, and Elena Choleris, 'Social Neuroscience of Disgust', *Genes, Brain, and Behavior* 18.1 (2019): 1–13. For a caution, however, see Ruth Leys, '"Both of Us Disgusted in My Insula": Mirror Neuron Theory and Emotional Empathy', *Nonsite.org* 5 (2012): http://nonsite.org/article/%E2%80%9Cboth-of-us-disgusted-in-my-insula%E2%80%9D-mirror-neuron-theory-and-emotional-empathy.

37 Katherine Vytal and Stephan Hamann, 'Neuroimaging Support for Discrete Neural Correlates of Basic Emotions: A Voxel-based Meta-Analysis', *Journal of Cognitive Neuroscience* 22.12 (2010): 2980.

38 Kara A. Christensen and Matthew W. Southward, 'Habitual, But Not Momentary, Avoidance Strategy Use Moderates the Association Between Disgust Sensitivity and Affective Response To A Disgust-Inducing Film Clip', *Canadian Journal of Behavioural Science* 53.3 (2020): 254.

39 Simon Tobias Karg, Aaron Wiener-Blotner and Simone Schnall, 'Disgust Sensitivity is Associated with Heightened Risk Perception', *Journal of Risk Research* 22.5 (2019): 627.

40 See Josh M. Cisler, Bunmi O. Olatunji and Jeffrey M. Lohr, 'Disgust, Fear, and the Anxiety Disorders: A Critical Review', *Clinical Psychology Review* 29.1 (2009): 34–46; Kelly A. Knowles et al., 'Cognitive Mechanisms of Disgust in the Development and Maintenance of Psychopathology: A Qualitative Review and Synthesis', *Clinical Psychology Review* 69 (2019): 30–50.

41 See *The Revolting Self: Perspectives on the Psychological, Social, and Clinical Implications of Self-Directed Disgust,* ed. Philip A. Powell, Paul G. Overton and Jane Simpson (London: Karnac Books, 2015).

42 See, for example, Sheila R. Woody and Bethany A. Teachman, 'Intersection of Disgust and Fear: Normative and Pathological Views', *Clinical Psychology: Science and Practice* 7.3 (2000): 291–311;

Catherine Molho et al., 'Disgust and Anger Relate to Different Aggressive Responses to Moral Violations', *Psychological Science* 28.5 (2017): 609–19; Maria Miceli and Cristiano Castelfranchi, 'Contempt and Disgust: The Emotions of Disrespect', *Journal for the Theory of Social Behavior* 48 (2018): 205–29.

43 Craig N. Sawchuk, 'The Acquisition and Maintenance of Disgust: Developmental and Learning Perspectives', in *Disgust and its Disorders*, 77.

44 Rozin, Haidt and McCauley, 'Disgust', 823.

45 Sawchuk, 'The Acquisition and Maintenance', 79.

46 Rozin, Haidt and McCauley, 'Disgust', 822.

47 Ibid., 823.

48 Sawchuk, 'The Acquisition and Maintenance', 79.

49 Strohminger, 'Disgust Talked About', 483.

50 Sherri C. Widen and James A. Russell, 'Children's Recognition of Disgust in Others', *Psychological Bulletin* 139.2 (2013): 289.

51 Strohminger, 'Disgust Talked About', 482.

52 See Diana Santos Fleischman, 'Women's Disgust Adaptations', in *Evolutionary Perspectives on Human Sexual Psychology and Behavior*, ed. Viviana A. Weekes-Shackelford and Todd K. Shackelford (New York: Springer 2014), 277–96.

53 Jamilah R. George et al., 'Disgust Sensitivity Mediates the Effects of Race on Contamination Aversion', *Journal of Obsessive-Compulsive and Related Disorders* 19 (2018): 72–6.

54 Uri Berger and David Anaki, 'Demographic Influences on Disgust: Evidence from a Heterogeneous Sample', *Personality and Individual Differences* 64 (2014): 67.

55 Trevor I. Case, Betty M. Repacholi and Richard J. Stevenson, 'My Baby Doesn't Smell as Bad as Yours: The Plasticity of Disgust', *Evolution and Human Behavior* 27 (2006): 357; Carlota Batres and David I. Perrett, 'Pathogen Disgust Sensitivity Changes According to the Perceived Harshness of the Environment', *Cognition and Emotion* 34.2 (2020): 377.

56 Atilla Hoefling et al., 'When Hunger Finds No Fault With Moldy Corn: Food Deprivation Reduces Food-Related Disgust', *Emotion* 9.1 (2009): 50–8.

57 Curtis and Biran, 'Dirt, Disgust, and Disease', 21.

58 Strohminger, 'Disgust Talked About', 482.

59 Elwood and Olatunji, 'A Cross-Cultural Perspective on Disgust', 117; Haidt et al., 'Body, Psyche, and Culture', 125.

60 Alexander J. Skolnick and Vivian A. Dzokoto, 'Disgust and Contamination: A Cross-National Comparison of Ghana and the United States', *Frontiers in Psychology* 4 (2013): Article 91.

61 Haidt et al., 'Body, Psyche, and Culture', 118; 117.

62 On differences in disgust words, see Richard Firth-Godbehere, *A Human History of Emotion: How the Way We Feel Built the World We Know* (New York: Little, Brown Spark, 2021), 56.

63 Haidt et al., 'Body, Psyche, and Culture', 119.

64 Elwood and Olatunji, 'A Cross-Cultural Perspective on Disgust', 114.

65 Justin H. Park, Jason Faulkner and Mark Schaller, 'Evolved Disease-Avoidance Processes and Contemporary Anti-Social Behavior: Prejudicial Attitudes and Avoidance of People with Physical Disabilities', *Journal of Nonverbal Behavior* 27.2 (2003): 79.

66 Usha Menon and Julia L. Cassaniti, 'Introduction', in *Universalism Without Universality*, 4.

67 Herz, *That's Disgusting*, 57.

68 Firth-Godbehere, *A Human History of Emotion*, 259.

69 Ibid., 261.

70 Richard Sugg, *Mummies, Cannibals, and Vampires: The History of Corpse Medicine from the Renaissance to the Victorians* (New York: Routledge, 2011), 161.

71 Ibid., 162.

72 Immanuel Kant, *Critique of Judgment*, trans. Werner S. Pluhar (Cambridge: Hackett Publishing Company, 1987), 180.

73 See Menninghaus, *Disgust,* and Korsmeyer, *Savoring Disgust*.

74 On the motives behind watching horror films, see G. Neil Martin, '(Why) Do You Like Scary Movies? A Review of the Empirical Research on Psychological Responses to Horror Films', *Frontiers in Psychology* 10 (2019): Article 2298; for disgust in romance novels, see Lydia Kokkola and Elina Valovirta, 'The Disgust That Fascinates: Sibling Incest as a Bad Romance', *Sexuality & Culture* 21 (2017): 121–41.

75 See Paola Perone, D. Vaughn Becker and Joshua M. Tybur, 'Visual Disgust Elicitors Produce an Attentional Blink Independent of Contextual and Trait-Level Pathogen Avoidance', *Emotion* 21.4 (2021): 871–80.

76 Bridget Rubenking and Annie Lang, 'Captivated and Grossed Out: An Examination of Processing Core and Sociomoral Disgusts in Entertainment Media', *Journal of Communication* 64 (2014): 561.

77 Ibid., 543–4.
78 Korsmeyer, *Savoring Disgust*, 3. It should be noted, however, that not everyone agrees: Jenefer Robinson, for examples, argues that the inherently negative qualities of disgust preclude it from being a source of pleasure, suggesting instead that disgust can simply lead to a form of insight that contributes to aesthetic appreciation. See her 'Aesthetic Disgust?' *Royal Institute of Philosophy Supplement* 75 (2014): 51–84.
79 Matthew E. Ansfield, 'Smiling When Distressed: When a Smile Is a Frown Turned Upside Down', *Personality and Social Psychology Bulletin* 33.6 (2007): 764–75; Scott H. Hemenover and Ulrich Schimmack, 'That's Disgusting! . . . But Very Amusing: Mixed Feelings of Amusement and Disgust', *Cognition and Emotion* 21.5 (2007): 1102–13.
80 Strohminger, 'The Hedonics of Disgust', PhD Dissertation, The University of Michigan (2013), 86.
81 Ibid., 89.
82 Paul Rozin and Deborah Schiller, 'The Nature and Acquisition of a Preference for Chili Pepper by Humans', *Motivation and Emotion* 4 (1980): 77. On disgust as benign masochism, see Strohminger, 'The Hedonics of Disgust', 101.
83 Strohminger, 'The Hedonics of Disgust', 12.
84 Marvin Zuckerman, *Behavioral Expressions and Biosocial Bases of Sensation Seeking* (Cambridge: Cambridge University Press, 1994), 27; Cynthia M. King and Nora Hourani, 'Don't Tease Me: Effects of Ending Types on Horror Film Enjoyment', *Media Psychology* 9 (2007): 477; 478. See Martin, '(Why) Do You Like', 7.
85 Strohminger, 'The Hedonics of Disgust', 101.
86 Strohminger, 'Disgust Talked About', 487.
87 Ibid., 479.
88 Ibid., 480.
89 See Irish, 'A Strategic Compromise'.
90 In what follows I have consulted *The Harvard Concordance to Shakespeare*, ed. Marvin Spevack (Cambridge: Cambridge University Press, 1973).
91 OED, 'foul, *adj*', I.1.a.; II.13.a.
92 *OED*, 'vile, *adj., adv.,* and *n*', A.3.a; A.1.a.
93 OED, 'loathsome, *adj*', 1.a; b.
94 *OED*, 'filth, *n*', 1.b; 2.a.
95 *OED*, 'rotten, *adj., n.,* and *adv*', A.I.1.a; A.II.6.a.

Chapter 2

1 S. Clark Hulse, 'Wresting the Alphabet: Oratory and Action in *Titus Andronicus*', *Criticism* 21.2 (1979): 106.

2 Edward Ravenscroft, *Titus Andronicus, or, The Rape of Lavinia* (London, 1687), A2. Of course, modern research suggests that George Peele contributed extensively to the play's first act; see Bate's introduction to the revised Arden edition. My argument doesn't rest on authorship matters – and plenty of the play's gruesomeness is still Shakespeare's – so for convenience I refer to *Titus* as Shakespeare's play throughout.

3 William Hazlitt, *Characters of Shakespeare's Plays* (London: John Templeman, 1838), 317.

4 Farah Karim-Cooper, 'Introduction', in *Titus Andronicus: The State of Play*, ed. Farah Karim-Cooper (London: The Arden Shakespeare, 2020), 2.

5 Charles Spenser, '*Titus Andronicus*, Review', *The Telegraph* (2 May 2014): https://www.telegraph.co.uk/culture/theatre/theatre-reviews/10803436/Titus-Andronicus-review-a-dramatic-power-that-makes-the-stomach-churn-and-the-hands-sweat.html.

6 Hannah Furness, 'Globe Audience Faints at 'Grotesquely Violent' *Titus Andronicus*', *The Telegraph* (20 April 2014): https://www.telegraph.co.uk/culture/theatre/william-shakespeare/10798599/Globe-audience-faints-at-grotesquely-violent-Titus-Andronicus.html; Anna Dubuis, 'Shakespeare's *Titus Andronicus* Proves Too Much for Globe Crowd as Audience Members Faint During 'Grotesquely Violent' Scenes', *Evening Standard* (2 May 2014): https://www.standard.co.uk/news/london/shakespeare-s-titus-andronicus-proves-too-much-for-globe-crowd-as-audience-members-faint-during-grotesquely-violent-scenes-9315422.html.

7 Spenser, '*Titus Andronicus*, Review'.

8 Ian Hughes, 'Shakespeare Still Shocks, Research Reveals', *Stratford Observer* (27 October 2017): https://stratfordobserver.co.uk/news/shakespeare-still-shocks-research-reveals-2976.

9 Spenser, '*Titus Andronicus*, Review'. In a recent article, Thomas A. Oldham uses post-structuralist affect theory to argue that 'these violent stage effects were used to invite prolonged engagement with and meaningful consideration of Lavinia'; see 'The Affective Appeal of Violence and the Violent Appeal of Affect: *Titus Andronicus*, Lucy Bailey, and Shakespeare's Globe', *Shakespeare Bulletin*

40.1 (2022): 70. Oldham's essay appeared after this chapter was finalized, so I was not able to incorporate it more fully into my analysis.

10 Pascale Aebischer, *Shakespeare's Violated Bodies: Stage and Screen Performance* (Cambridge: Cambridge University Press, 2004), 52; quoted in ibid.

11 Ben Jonson, *Bartholmew Fayre* (London, 1631), A5ᵛ. On original performances of *Titus*, see G. Harold Metz, 'Stage History of *Titus Andronicus*', *Shakespeare Quarterly* 28.2 (1977): 154–6 and Roslyn L. Knutson and David McInnis, 'Lost Documents, Absent Documents, Forged Documents', in *Rethinking Theatrical Documents in Shakespeare's England*, ed. Tiffany Stern (London: The Arden Shakespeare, 2020), 241–59.

12 Cynthia Marshall, *The Shattering of the Self: Violence, Subjectivity, and Early Modern Texts* (Baltimore: Johns Hopkins University Press, 2002), 107.

13 Joel Elliot Slotkin, 'A Taste for Slaughter: Stephen Gosson, *Titus Andronicus*, and the Appeal of Evil', in *The Routledge Companion to Shakespeare and Philosophy*, ed. Craig Bourne and Emily Caddick Bourne (New York: Routledge, 2018), 495.

14 Marshall, *The Shattering of the Self*, 107.

15 Aebischer, *Shakespeare's Violated Bodies*, 52.

16 Ibid., 60.

17 Brian Cox, '*Titus Andronicus*', in *Players of Shakespeare 3*, ed. Russell Jackson and Robert Smallwood (Cambridge: Cambridge University Press, 1993), 186–7.

18 Pascale Aebischer, 'Vampires, Cannibals and Victim-Revengers: Watching Shakespearean Tragedy through Horror Film', *Shakespeare Jahrbuch* 143 (2007): 127–8.

19 Marshall, *The Shattering of the Self*, 110.

20 Cox, '*Titus Andronicus*', 175; 176.

21 Adele-France Jourdan, 'Grotesque Laughter as a Coping Mechanism in *Titus Andronicus*', in *Routledge Companion to Shakespeare and Philosophy*, 499.

22 Slotkin, 'A Taste for Slaughter', 485.

23 Joel Elliot Slotkin, *Sinister Aesthetics: The Appeal of Evil in Early Modern English Literature* (New York: Palgrave, 2017), 8.

24 Naomi Baker, *Plain Ugly: The Unattractive Body in Early Modern Culture* (Manchester: Manchester University Press, 2010), 1.

25 *Titus Andronicus,* ed. J. Dover Wilson (Cambridge: Cambridge University Press, 1948), xii.
26 Molly Smith, 'The Theater and the Scaffold: Death as Spectacle in *The Spanish Tragedy', SEL: Studies in English Literature, 1500–1900* 32.2 (1992): 217. See also ibid., 'Spectacles of Torment in *Titus Andronicus', Studies in English Literature 1500–1900* 36.2 (1996): 315–31; Christopher Pye, *The Regal Phantasm: Shakespeare and the Politics of Spectacle* (New York: Routledge, 1990), chap. 4; Susan Dwyer Amussen, 'Punishment, Discipline, and Power: The Social Meanings of Violence in Early Modern England', *Journal of British Studies* 34.1 (1995): 1–34; Mariangela Tempera, 'Body Parts on the Elizabethan Stage', *Textus* 13 (2000): 303–24.
27 Katherine Royer, *The English Execution Narrative, 1200–1700* (London: Pickering & Chatto, 2014), 9. Royer inspires my use of the term *spectacular disgust*.
28 Thomas Smith, *De Republica Anglorum* (London, 1583), 84; see Royer, *The English Execution Narrative,* 4.
29 Krista Kesselring, *Making Murder Public: Homicide in Early Modern England, 1480–1680* (Oxford: Oxford University Press, 2019), 122, for this and much of what follows in this paragraph. See also J. G. Bellamy, *Criminal Trial in Later Medieval England: Felony Before the Courts From Edward I to the Sixteenth Century* (Toronto: University of Toronto Press, 1998), Chap. 4.
30 For pirate executions, see Claire Jowitt, 'Scaffold Performances: The Politics of Pirate Execution', in *Pirates? The Politics of Plunder, 1550–1650,* ed. Claire Jowitt (New York: Palgrave, 2007), 151–68.
31 See Martin Ingram, 'Shame and Pain: Themes and Variations in Tudor Punishments', in *Penal Practice and Culture, 1500–1900: Punishing the English,* ed. Simon Devereux and Paul Griffiths (New York: Palgrave, 2004), 36–62.
32 John Harington, *Epigrams* (London, 1615), C4.
33 Smith, *De Republica Anglorum,* 84.
34 Raphael Holinshed, *The Chronicles* (London, 1577), fol. 107$^\text{v}$.
35 William Sanderson, *A Compleat History of the Life and Raigne of King Charles* (London, 1658), 124. See Bellamy, *Criminal Trial,* 154.
36 John Ward, *An Encovragement to Warre* (London, 1642), 9.
37 Philip Jenkins, 'From Gallows to Prison? The Execution Rate in Early Modern England', *Criminal Justice History* 7 (1986): 52.
38 Kesselring, *Making Murder Public,* 121.

39 See, for example, Peter Lake and Michael Questier, 'Agency, Appropriation and Rhetoric under the Gallows: Puritans, Romanists and the State in Early Modern England', *Past and Present* 153 (1996): 64–107; J. A. Sharpe, '"Last Dying Speeches": Religion, Ideology and Public Execution in Seventeenth-Century England', *Past and Present* 107 (1985): 144–67; Thomas W. Laqueur, 'Crowds, Carnival and the State in English Executions, 1604–1868', in *The First Modern Society: Essays in English History in Honour of Lawrence Stone*, ed. A. L. Beier, David Cannadine and James M. Rosenheim (Cambridge: Cambridge University Press, 1989), 305–55; Lorna Hutson, 'Rethinking the "Spectacle of the Scaffold": Juridical Epistemologies and English Revenge Tragedy', *Representations* 89.1 (2005): 30–58.

40 *Original Letters Relative to the English Reformation*, ed. Hastings Robinson (Cambridge: Cambridge University Press, 1846), 211; *Thomas Platter's Travels in England, 1599*, ed. Clare Williams (London: Jonathan Cape, 1937), 174.

41 Robert Whittington, *Vulgaria Roberti Whitintoni* (London, 1520), fol. 25v.

42 Williams, *Thomas Platter's Travels*, 155.

43 Henry Goodcole, *Heavens Speedie Hue and Cry* (London, 1615), C4v.

44 James Howell, *Therologia, The Parly of Beasts* (London, 1660), 8.

45 Michel de Montaigne, *The Essayes* (London, 1603), 248; 237 [misprint for 249].

46 Ibid., 237 [misprint for 249].

47 E. K. Chambers, *The Elizabethan Stage*, 4 vols. (Oxford: Oxford University Press, 1963), 2:396; John Stow, *Annales* (London, 1615), 749; 750.

48 Francis Barker, 'Treasures of Culture: *Titus Andronicus* and Death by Hanging', in *The Production of English Renaissance Culture*, ed. David Lee Miller, Sharon O'Dair and Harold Weber (Ithaca: Cornell University Press, 1994), 253.

49 Louise Noble, *Medicinal Cannibalism in Early Modern English Literature and Culture* (New York: Palgrave, 2011), 40; Louis Gernet, 'Capital Punishment', in *Athenian Democracy*, ed. P. J. Rhodes (Edinburgh: Edinburgh University Press, 2004), 154.

50 See Nadia Bishai, '"At the Signe of the Gunne": *Titus Andronicus*, the London Book Trade, and the Literature of Crime, 1590–1615', in *Titus Out of Joint: Reading the Fragmented Titus Andronicus*, ed.

Liberty Stanavage and Paxton Hehmeyer (Newcastle Upon Tyne: Cambridge Scholars Publishing, 2012), 7–48.

51 Kesselring, *Making Murder Public*, 130.
52 Anonymous, *Sundrye Strange and Inhumaine Murthers* (London, 1591), A4. I follow Bellamy's discussion of the pamphlet in *Strange, Inhuman Deaths*, 56–60.
53 See Owen Davies and Francesca Matteoni, *Executing Magic in the Modern Era: Criminal Bodies and the Gallows in Popular Medicine* (New York: Palgrave, 2017), 21–4.
54 Anonymous, *Sundrye Strange and Inhumaine Murthers*, B3^v.
55 Jonathan Sawday, *The Body Emblazoned: Dissection and the Human Body in Renaissance Culture* (New York: Routledge, 1995), Viii.
56 Hillary M. Nunn, *Staging Anatomies: Dissection and Spectacle in Early Stuart Tragedy* (New York: Routledge, 2016), 4.
57 Ibid., 2; *The Diary of Sir Simonds D'Ewes, 1622–1624*, ed. Elisabeth Bourcier (Paris: Didier, 1974), 128.
58 32 Henry VIII c. 42 in *Statutes of the Realm*, 11 vols. (London, 1810–28), 3:795.
59 *The Diary of Henry Machyn*, ed. John Gough Nichols (London, 1848), 251–2. See *OED*, 'notomy, n'.
60 Anonymous, *The Odcombian Banquet* (London, 1611), E3^v.
61 Noble, *Medicinal Cannibalism*, 26.
62 Quoted in *The Annals of the Barber-Surgeons* (London, 1890), 112.
63 The work on Lavinia is too numerous to mention, but see, for instance, Karen Cunningham, '"Scars Can Witness": Trials by Ordeal and Lavinia's Body in *Titus Andronicus*', in *Women and Violence in Literature*, ed. Katherine Anne Ackley (New York: Garland Publishing, Inc., 1990), 139–62; Robin L. Bott, '"O, Keep Me From Their Worse Than Killing Lust": Ideologies of Rape and Mutilation in Chaucer's *Physician's Tale* and Shakespeare's *Titus Andronicus*', in *Representing Rape in Medieval and Early Modern Literature*, ed. Elizabeth Robertson and Christine M. Rose (New York: Palgrave, 2001), 189–211; Deborah Willis, 'The Gnawing Vulture: Revenge, Trauma Theory, and *Titus Andronicus*', *Shakespeare Quarterly* 53.1 (2002): 21152; Bethany Packard, 'Lavinia as Coauthor of Shakespeare's *Titus Andronicus*', *SEL: Studies in English Literature 1500–1900* 50.2 (2010): 281–300; Donatella Pallotti, 'Maps of Woe: Narratives of Rape in Early Modern England', *Journal of Early Modern Studies* 2 (2013): 211–39; Sonya L. Brockman, 'Trauma and Abandoned Testimony in *Titus Andronicus* and *Rape of Lucrece*',

College Literature 44.3 (2017): 344–78; Alice Equestri, '"Rome's Rich Ornament": Lavinia, Commoditization, and the Senses in William Shakespeare's *Titus Andronicus*', in *Roman Women in Shakespeare and His Contemporaries*, ed. Domenico Lovascio (Berlin: De Gruyter, 2020), 19–37.

64 Jeffrey Jerome Cohen, 'Monster Culture (Seven Theses)', in *Monster Theory: Reading Culture*, ed. Jeffrey Jerome Cohen (Minneapolis: University of Minnesota Press, 1996), 6.

65 Mary Douglas, *Purity and Danger: An Analysis of Concepts of Pollution and Taboo* (New York: Routledge, 2001), 54.

66 Arnold I. Davidson, 'The Horror of Monsters', in *The Boundaries of Humanity: Humans, Animals, Machines*, ed. James J. Sheehan and Morton Sosna (Berkeley: University of California Press, 1991), 36.

67 Ambroise Paré, *Of Monsters and Marvels*, trans. Janis L. Pallister (Chicago: University of Chicago Press, 1982), 3. This translation uses the term *marvels* for the French *prodiges*, but the more usual term in monster studies is 'prodigies'. See Davidson, 'Horror', 65.

68 On monstrous births, see, for example, Stephen Pender, '"No Monster at the Resurrection": Inside Some Conjoined Twins', in *Monster Theory*, 143–67; Alan W. Bates, 'Good, Common, Regular, and Orderly: Early Modern Classifications of Monstrous Births', *Social History of Medicine* 18.2 (2005): 141–58; *Emblematic Monsters: Unnatural Conceptions and Deformed Births in Early Modern Europe* (Amsterdam: Rodopi, 2005); Julie Crawford, *Marvelous Protestantism: Monstrous Births in Post-Reformation England* (Baltimore: The Johns Hopkins University Press, 2005).

69 Crawford, *Marvelous Protestantism*, 3.

70 Lorraine Daston and Katharine Park, *Wonders and the Order of Nature, 1150–1750* (New York: Zone Books, 1998), 202; Anonymous, *Gods Handy-Worke in Wonders* (London, 1615), A3.

71 Pierre Boaistuau, *Certaine Secrete Wonders of Nature* (London, 1569), A4.

72 Daston and Park, *Wonders and the Order of Nature*, 193; 176–7.

73 Ibid., 176.

74 John Earle, *Micro-Cosmographie* (London, 1628), E10^v.

75 Thomas Bedford, *A True and Certaine Relation of a Strange-Birth* (London, 1635), 18; 14.

76 Mark Thornton Burnett, *Constructing 'Monsters' in Shakespearean Drama and Early Modern Culture* (New York: Palgrave, 2002), 13; Ben Jonson, *Workes* (London, 1616), 13.

77 Robert Chester, *Loves Martyr* (London, 1601), 174–5.
78 Alden T. Vaughan, 'Trinculo's Indian: American Natives in Shakespeare's England', in *The Tempest and Its Travels*, ed. Peter Hulme and William H. Sherman (London: Reaktion Books, 2000), 49–59.
79 Montaigne, *The Essayes*, 409.
80 Heather Dubrow, *Echoes of Desire: English Petrarchism and Its Counterdiscourses* (Ithaca: Cornell University Press, 1995), 163. This cultural discourse also activates the critical concerns of disability studies, which I discuss more in Chapter 7.
81 Shannon Kelley, 'Desire, a Crooked Yearning, and the Plants of *Endymion*', *Renaissance Drama* 44.1 (2016): 1; 6; Baker, *Plain Ugly*, 7.
82 Dubrow, *Echoes of Desire*, 164; Naomi Baker, '"To Make Love to a Deformity": Praising Ugliness in Early Modern England', *Renaissance Studies* 22.1 (2008): 98–9.
83 Baker, '"To Make Love to a Deformity"', 104.
84 J. B., *Anthropometamorphosis* (London, 1653), A1. For further discussion of these examples, see Baker, *Plain Ugly*, chapter 5, and Dubrow, *Echoes of Desire*, chapter 5.
85 John Lyly, *Endimion* (London, 1591), E2–E2^v.
86 James Shirley, *Poems* (London, 1646), 76.
87 George Gascoigne, *A Hundreth Sundrie Flowres* (London, 1573), 302; 306.
88 Barnabe Barnes, *Parthenophil and Parthenophe* (London, 1593), 9.
89 Sir Philip Sidney, *The Countesse of Pembrokes Arcadia* (London, 1590), 12^v.
90 Sir John Davies, *Epigrammes and Elegies* (London, 1599), C1.
91 Baker, *Plain Ugly*, 7.
92 Ibid.
93 Robert Burton, *The Anatomy of Melancholy* (London, 1621), 608–9.
94 Baker, *Plain Ugly*, 126.
95 Ibid., 131.
96 Kelley, 'Desire', 7.
97 Montaigne, *The Essayes*, 616–17. See Lawrence D. Kritzman, 'Representing the Monster: Cognition, Cripples, and Other Limp Parts in Montaigne's 'Des Boyteux', in *Monster Theory*, 168–82.

98 Quoted in Aebischer, *Shakespeare's Violated Bodies*, 39.

99 Ibid.

100 See, for example, Ann Christensen, '"Playing the Cook": Nurturing Men in *Titus Andronicus*', in *Shakespeare Yearbook* 6 (1996): 327–54; Birgit Walkenhorst, 'Substance Matters: Food Rites in *Titus Andronicus*', *Wissenschaftliches Seminar Online* 6 (2008): 11–19; Carol Mejia LaPerle, 'The Crime Scene of Revenge Tragedy: Sacrificial Cannibalism in Seneca's *Thyestes* and Shakespeare's *Titus Andronicus*', *Concentric* 38.1 (2012): 9–28; Natalia Brzozowska, 'Dangerous Feasts and the Social Appetite in *Macbeth* and *Titus Andronicus*', *Actes des Congrès de la Société Française Shakespeare* 29 (2012): 81–91; Gilberta Golinelli, '"Like a Cook, Placing the Dishes": Performance of "Eating" Practices in *Titus Andronicus*', *Textus* 31.3 (2018): 121–38.

101 Julia Kotzur, '"When We Have Stuffed These Pipes and These Conveyances of our Blood with Wine and Feeding": Sacramental Eating and Galenic Humourism in the Drama of William Shakespeare and Ben Jonson', PhD Thesis, University of Aberdeen (2016), 72; Elena Bonelli, 'Abject Bodies and Disseminated Remains in *Titus Andronicus*', *Proceedings of the Sixteenth International Conference on Literature and Psychoanalysis*, ed. Frederico Pereira (Lisbon: Instituto Superior de Psicologia Aplicada, 1999): 163.

102 David B. Goldstein, *Eating and Ethics in Shakespeare's England* (Cambridge: Cambridge University Press, 2013), 34; Daniel Cottom, *Cannibal and Philosophers: Bodies of Enlightenment* (Baltimore: John Hopkins University Press, 2001), 178; Maggie Kilgour, 'Foreword', in *Eating Their Words: Cannibalism and the Boundaries of Cultural Identity*, ed. Kristen Guest (Albany: SUNY Press, 2001), viii.

103 Matthew Sutcliffe, *An Abridgement or Suruey of Poperie* (London, 1606), 109 [misprint for 190]; Sebastian Münster, *A Treatyse of the Newe India* (London, 1553), G6^v.

104 Peter Martyr, *The Decades of the Newe Worlde* (London, 1555), 153.

105 Wendy Wall, *Staging Domesticity: Household Work and English Identity in Early Modern Drama* (Cambridge: Cambridge University Press, 2002), 197.

106 Folger Shakespeare Library, V.a.630, fol. 245; V.b.366, 36.

107 On early modern medical cannibalism, see Karl H. Dannenfeldt, 'Egyptian Mumia: The Sixteenth Century Experience and Debate', *The Sixteenth Century Journal* 16.2 (1985): 163–80; Karen Gordon-Grube, 'Anthropophagy in Post-Renaissance Europe: The Tradition of

Medical Cannibalism', *American Anthropologist* 90.2 (1988): 405–9; Richard Sugg, '"Good Physic but Bad Food": Early Modern Attitudes to Medicinal Cannibalism and its Suppliers', *Social History of Medicine* 19.2 (2006): 225–40; *Mummies, Cannibals, and Vampires*; Noble, *Medicinal Cannibalism*. The examples in the paragraphs that follow largely come from these sources. See also Sarah-Maria Schober, 'Muck, Mummies and Medicine: Disgust in Early Modern Science', *Emotions: History, Culture, Society* 4.1 (2020): 43–65, which I discovered after the completion of this chapter, and which has affinity with my argument more broadly.

108 Henrich von Staden, 'Women and Dirt', *Helios* 19.1/2 (1992): 7; 16.

109 Douglas, *Purity and Danger*, 160.

110 Ibid., 162.

111 John Gerard, *The Herball or Generall Historie of Plantes* (London, 1633), 1563.

112 Dannenfeldt, 'Egyptian Mumia', 163, for this and the next quote.

113 John Hall, *A Most Excellent and Learned Woorke of Chirurgerie* (London, 1565), 73.

114 Oswald Croll, *Bazilica Chymica* (London, 1670), 155.

115 Noble, *Medicinal Cannibalism*, 3–4; quoted in ibid., 25.

116 Samuel Pepys, *The Diary of Samuel Pepys*, ed. Ernest Rhys, 2 vols. (London: J.M. Dent & Co., 1906), 2:507.

117 Sugg, '"Good Physic but Bad Food"', 225.

118 Cited in Owsei Temkin, *The Falling Sickness: A History of Epilepsy from the Greeks to the Beginnings of Modern Neurology* (Baltimore: The Johns Hopkins University Press, 1971), 23.

119 Thomas Moffett, *Healths Improvement* (London, 1655), 139; 140.

120 Cited in Lynn Thorndike, *A History of Magic and Experimental Science,* 8 vols. (New York: Columbia University Press, 1923–1958), 8:414; Richard Hakluyt, *The Principal Nauigations, Voyages, Traffiques and Discoveries of the English Nation* (London, 1600), 201.

121 Ambroise Paré, *The Workes of that Famous Chirurgion Ambrose Parey* (London, 1634), 448.

122 Quoted in Dannenfeldt, 'Egyptian Mumia', 176.

123 Montaigne, *The Essayes*, 104.

124 Louise Christine Noble, '"And Make Two Pasties of Your Shameful Heads": Medicinal Cannibalism and Healing the Body Politic in *Titus Andronicus*', *ELH* 70.3 (2003): 678.

Chapter 3

1 Aisha Egolf, Michael Siegrist and Christina Hartmann, 'How People's Food Disgust Sensitivity Shapes Their Eating and Food Behaviour', *Appetite* 127 (2018): 28.

2 Laith Al-Shawaf et al., 'Mating Strategy, Disgust, and Food Neophobia', *Appetite* 85 (2015): 30; see also Çağla Çınar, Annika K. Karinen and Joshua M. Tybur, 'The Multidimensional Nature of Food Neophobia', *Appetite* 162 (2021): Article 105177.

3 Ruth Aharoni and Marianne M. Hertz, 'Disgust Sensitivity and Anorexia Nervosa', *European Eating Disorders Review* 20 (2012): 106.

4 Katrijn Houben and Remco C. Havermans, 'A Delicious Fly in the Soup: The Relationship between Disgust, Obesity, and Restraint', *Appetite* 58 (2012): 827.

5 Alia Aleshaiwi and Tim Harries, 'A Step in the Journey to Food Waste: How and Why Mealtime Surpluses Become Unwanted', *Appetite* 158 (2021): Article 105040; Sean T. Hingston and Theodore J. Noseworthy, 'On the Epidemic of Food Waste: Idealized Prototypes and the Aversion to Misshapen Fruits and Vegetables', *Food Quality and Preference* 86 (2020): Article 103999.

6 Aisha Egolf, Christina Hartmann and Michael Siegrist, 'When Evolution Works against the Future: Disgust's Contributions to the Acceptance of New Food Technologies', *Risk Analysis* 39.7 (2019): 1546.

7 See Joshua M. Tybur et al., 'How Pathogen Cues Shape Impressions of Foods: The Omnivore's Dilemma and Functionally Specialized Conditioning', *Evolution and Human Behavior* 37 (2016): 376–86.

8 See Francesco La Barbera et al., 'Understanding Westerners' Disgust for the Eating of Insects: The Role of Food Neophobia and Implicit Associations', *Food Quality and Preference* 64 (2018): 120–5.

9 Christina Hartmann and Michael Siegrist, 'Development and Validation of the Food Disgust Scale', *Food Quality and Preference* 63 (2018): 38.

10 Caroline F. E. Spurgeon, *Shakespeare's Imagery and What It Tells Us* (Cambridge: Cambridge University Press, 1935), 121.

11 See, for instance, Amy L. Tigner and Allison Carruth, *Literature and Food Studies* (New York: Routledge, 2018); *Critical Perspectives in Food Studies, Third Edition*, ed. Mustafa Koç, Jennifer Sumner and Anthony Winson (Oxford: Oxford University Press, 2021).

12 Ken Albala, *Eating Right in the Renaissance* (Berkeley: University of California Press, 2002); Robert Appelbaum, *Aguecheek's Beef, Belch's Hiccup, and Other Gastronomic Interjections: Literature, Culture, and Food Among the Early Moderns* (Chicago: University of Chicago Press, 2006); Joan Fitzpatrick, *Food in Shakespeare: Early Modern Dietaries and the Plays* (Burlington: Ashgate, 2007).

13 On Shakespeare and food broadly, see Peter Holland, 'Feasting and Starving: Staging Food in Shakespeare', *Shakespeare Jahrbuch* 145 (2009): 11–28; David B. Goldstein, 'Shakespeare and Food: A Review Essay', *Literature Compass* 6.1 (2009): 153–74; Joan Fitzpatrick, '"I Must Eat My Dinner": Shakespeare's Foods from Apples to Walrus', in *Renaissance Food from Rabelais to Shakespeare: Culinary Readings and Culinary Histories*, ed. Joan Fitzpatrick (Burlington: Ashgate, 2010), 127–43; 'Reading Early Modern Food: A Review Article', *Literature Compass* 8.3 (2011): 118–29; 'Bodily Health and Spiritual Wealth (1550–1650)', in *A History of Food in Literature: From the Fourteenth Century to the Present*, ed. Charlotte Boyce and Joan Fitzpatrick (New York: Routledge, 2017), 63–113; Ken Albala, 'Shakespeare's Culinary Metaphors: A Practical Approach', *Shakespeare Studies* 42 (2014): 63–74; Diane Purkiss, 'The Masque of Food: Staging and Banqueting in Shakespeare's England', *Shakespeare Studies* 42 (2014): 91–105; *Culinary Shakespeare: Staging Food and Drink in Early Modern England*, ed. David B. Goldstein and Amy L. Tigner (Pittsburgh: Duquesne University Press, 2016).

14 Chris Meads, *Banquets Set Forth: Banqueting in English Renaissance Drama* (Manchester: Manchester University Press, 2001), 1.

15 Carolin Biewer, 'Dietetics as a Key to Language and Character in Shakespeare's Comedy', *English Studies* 90.1 (2009): 17. See also Stephanie Chamberlain, 'Fatal Indulgences: Gertrude and the Perils of Excess in Early Modern England', *Journal of the Wooden O* 13 (2013): 25–33; and Joan Fitzpatrick, 'Diet and Identity in Early Modern Dietaries and Shakespeare: The Inflections of Nationality, Gender, Social Rank, and Age', *Shakespeare Studies* 42 (2014): 75–90.

16 Kimberly Anne Coles and Gitanjali Shahani, 'Introduction to Special Forum: Diet and Identity in Shakespeare's England', *Shakespeare Studies* 42 (2014): 22.

17 Darwin, *The Expression of the Emotions*, 258.

18 Christoph A. Becker et al., 'Neural Correlates of the Perception of Spoiled Food Stimuli', *Frontiers in Human Neuroscience* 10 (2016): Article 302, 1; Carmelo M. Vicario et al., 'Pictures of Disgusting Foods and Disgusted Facial Expressions Suppress the Tongue Motor Cortex', *Social Cognition and Affective Neuroscience* 12.2 (2017): 352.

19 A *tallow-catch* is a 'receptacle that would catch the animal fat while cooking'; see Joan Fitzpatrick, *Shakespeare and the Language of Food: A Dictionary* (London: Continuum, 2011), 397.
20 Colleen E. Kennedy, '"Qualmish at the Smell of Leek": Overcoming Disgust and Creating the Nation-State in *Henry V*', in *Disgust in Early Modern English Literature*, 124.
21 Many of the examples in this paragraph are drawn from Spurgeon, *Shakespeare's Imagery*, 117–23.
22 *OED*, 'surfeit, *n.*', 4.a.
23 Robert Lipscomb, 'Caesar's Same-Sex-Food-Sex Dilemma', *Early English Studies* 2 (2009): 1.
24 Peter A. Parolin, '"Cloyless Sauce": The Pleasurable Politics of Food in *Antony and Cleopatra*', in *Antony and Cleopatra: New Critical Essays*, ed. Sara M. Deats (New York: Routledge, 2004), 213.
25 Matt Williamson, '"Strange Flesh": Hunger and Appetite in Shakespeare's Rome', *Shakespeare* 15.4 (2019): 320; *The Second Tome of Homilees* (London, 1571), 206.
26 Thomas Elyot, *The Boke Named the Gouernour* (London 1537), 214ᵛ. See Williamson, '"Strange Flesh"', 317.
27 Lipscomb, 'Caesar's Same-Sex-Food-Sex Dilemma', 1.
28 Pompa Banerjee, 'Cosmopolitanism and "Strange Flesh"', *Antony and Cleopatra*, *Parergon* 35.1 (2018): 126.
29 Lipscomb, 'Caesar's Same-Sex-Food-Sex Dilemma', 4.
30 *OED*, 'cloy, *v.1*', 7.a; 8.
31 Parolin, '"Cloyless Sauce"', 214.
32 Plutarch, *The Lives of the Noble Grecians and Romanes*, 977–8.
33 Ibid. Arthur L. Little, Jr. notes that 'the exigent and collective carnivorism in Plutarch's text becomes Antony's singular cannibalistic indulgence'; see *Shakespeare Jungle Fever: National-Imperial Re-Visions of Race, Rape, and Sacrifice* (Stanford: Stanford University Press, 2001), 138.
34 *OED*, 'flesh, *n.*', 4.d.

Chapter 4

1 For the discussion of both the dating of the play and the dynamics of the Shakespeare/Middleton collaboration, see the intro to Anthony B. Dawson and Gretchen E. Minton's Arden edition. (They settle on a

probably date of 1607, but note that it could be slightly earlier.) I am interested in how disgust manifests in the play broadly, so neither the precise year of the play nor the specifics of which author composed which particular scene are relevant to my discussion.

2 Jodie Austin, '"Be as a Planetary Plague": Pestilence and Cure in *Timon of Athens*', *HLQ* 82.2 (2020): 273.

3 Ibid., 271. See also Keir Elam, '"I'll Plague Thee For That Word": Language, Performance, and Communicable Disease', *Shakespeare Survey* 50 (1997): 19–27; Rebecca Totaro, *Suffering in Paradise: The Bubonic Plague in English Literature from More to Milton* (Pittsburgh: Duquesne University Press, 2005), chap. 4; Darryl Chalk, '"A Nature But Infected": Plague and Embodied Transformation in *Timon of Athens*', *EMLS* Special Issue 19 (2009): 9.1–28; and Hristomir A. Stanev, 'Infectious Purgatives and Loss of Breath in *Timon of Athens*', *ANQ* 26.3 (2013): 150–6.

4 Philip Brockbank, *On Shakespeare: Jesus, Shakespeare and Karl Marx, and Other Essays* (Oxford: Basil Blackwell, 1989), 10.

5 Fitzpatrick, *Food in Shakespeare*, 113.

6 Daniel W. Ross, '"What A Number of Men Eats Timon": Consumption in *Timon of Athens*', *Iowa State Journal of Research* 59.3 (1985): 274.

7 M.B., *The Triall of True Friendship* (London, 1596), B3. See Austin, '"Planetary Plague"', 278.

8 Ross, '"What A Number"', 276.

9 Ibid., 277.

10 Ibid., 273.

11 Keri Sanburn Behre, 'Renaissance Fare: Appetite and Authority on the Early Modern English Stage', Ph.D. Dissertation, University of Kansas (2011), 122.

12 Fitzpatrick, *Food in Shakespeare*, 116.

13 Maria Teresa Micaela Prendergast, *Railing, Reviling, and Invective in England Literary Culture, 1588–1617* (Burlington: Ashgate, 2012), 107. See also Davide Del Bello, 'Poisonous Language: *Timon of Athens* and the Scope of Invective', *Memoria di Shakespeare* 5 (2018): 69–101.

14 As he digs, he says 'Earth, yield me roots. / Who seeks for better of thee, sauce his palate / With thy most operant poison' (23–5). See Elam, '"I'll Plague Thee For That Word"', 23.

15 Ross, '"What A Number"', 281.

16 Austin, '"Be as a Planetary Plague"', 271.
17 Robert S. Miola, 'Timon in Shakespeare's Athens', *Shakespeare Quarterly* 31.1 (1980): 22. Miola's analysis cites many of the examples in what follows.
18 Ibid.; Plutarch, *The Philosophie, Commonlie Called, The Morals* (London, 1603), 373.
19 Claudius Aelian, *A Registre of Hystories* (London, 1576), fol. 17^v; Erasmus, *Apophthegmes* (London, 1542), fol. 15^v.
20 Aelian, *Registre of Hystories*, fol. 19.
21 Isocrates, *A Perfite Looking Glasse* (London, 1580), fol. 8^v; Demosthenes, *The Three Orations* (London, 1570), 6.
22 Aelian, *Registre of Hystories*, fol. 58^v.
23 Ibid., fol. 43; 136^v.
24 Ibid., fol. 154^v; John Lyly, *Campaspe* (London, 1584), D4.
25 Cesare Cuttica and Markku Peltonen, '"Gone Missing": Democracy and Anti-Democracy in Seventeenth Century England', in *Democracy and Anti-Democracy in Early Modern England, 1603–1689,* ed. ibid. (Leiden: Brill, 2019), 1; 11. See also Cuttica, 'The Spectre Haunting Early Seventeenth Century England (ca. 1603–1649): Democracy at Its Worst', in ibid., 132–51.
26 Aristotle, *Aristotles Politiques* (London, 1598).
27 Ibid., 151.
28 Anonymous, *The Treasurie of Auncient and Moderne Times* (London, 1613), 816.
29 Ibid., 818.
30 Marchamont Nedham, *A Plea for the King and Kingdom* (London, 1648), 26. For Nedham, see Markku Peltonen, '"All Government is In the People, From The People, and For the People": Democracy in the English Revolution', in *Democracy and Anti-Democracy in Early Modern England*, 79–84.
31 Aristotle, *Aristotles Politiques*, 154.
32 Anonymous, *Treasurie of Auncient and Moderne Times*, 816.
33 Pedro Mexía, *The Foreste or Collection of Histories* (London, 1571), fol. 69^v.
34 Peltonen, '"All Government is In the People, From the People, and For the People"', 84.
35 Aristotle, *Aristotles Politiques,* 164.
36 Plutarch, *The Lives of the Noble Grecians and Romanes*, 216.

37 Adam Hansen, 'London and Its "Others" in *Timon of Athens'*, *Shakespeare Jahrbuch* 147 (2011): 53; 54. Hansen's work greatly informs what follows.

38 Anonymous, *Greuous Grones for the Poore* (London, 1621), B-B^v. See *Rogues and Early Modern English Culture*, ed. Craig Dionne and Steve Mentz (Ann Arbor: The University of Michigan Press, 2004). Early modern texts on this subject have been collected in *The Elizabethan Underworld: A Collection of Tudor and Early Stuart Tracts and Ballads*, ed. A. V. Judges (London: Routledge, 1965) and *Rogues, Vagabonds, and Sturdy Beggars*, ed. Arthur Kinney (Amherst: The University of Massachusetts Press, 1990).

39 J. Thomas Kelly, *Thorns on the Tudor Rose: Monks, Rogues, Vagabonds, and Sturdy Beggars* (Jackson: University of Mississippi Press, 1977), Appendix 3.

40 Linda Woodbridge, *Vagrancy, Homelessness, and English Renaissance Literature* (Urbana: University of Illinois Press, 2001), 2; William C. Carroll, *Fat King, Lean Beggar: Representations of Poverty in the Age of Shakespeare* (Ithaca: Cornell University Press), 36.

41 Bronislaw Geremek, *Poverty: A History* (Cambridge: Blackwell, 1994), 190.

42 Robert Sanderson, *XXXVI Sermons* (London, 1686), 213; Richard Johnson, *Looke on Me London* (London, 1613), B4^v; Samuel Rid, *The Art of Iugling or Legerdemaine* (London, 1612), B. See Adam Hansen, 'Sin City and the "Urban Condom": Rogues, Writing and the Early Modern Urban Environment', in *Rogues and Early Modern English Culture,* 221.

43 Robert Greene, *The Second Part of Conny-Catching* (London, 1591), C3; *A Notable Discouery of Coosenage* (London, 1592), C2^v. See Hansen, 'London and Its "Others"', 65.

44 Woodbridge, *Vagrancy,* 187.

45 *Tudor Royal Proclamations,* ed. Paul L. Hughes and James F. Larkin, 3 vols. (New Haven: Yale University Press, 1969), 2:47.

46 Claire S. Schen, 'Constructing the Poor in Early Seventeenth-Century London', *Albion* 32.3 (2000): 453; Linda Bradley Salamon, 'Vagabond Veterans: The Roguish Company of Martin Guerre and Henry V', in *Rogues and Early Modern English Culture,* 262.

47 John Awdelay, *The Fraternitye of Uacabondes* (London, 1575), A2.

48 Hughes and Larkin, *Tudor Royal Proclamations,* 3:82.

49 Thomas Nashe, *Pierce Penilesse His Supplication to the Diuell* (London, 1592), fol. 25^v.

50 Barnabe Rich, *A Souldiers Wishe to Britons Welfare* (London, 1604), 62.
51 Hansen, 'London and Its "Others"', 62.
52 Hansen, 'Sin City', 221.
53 Plutarch, *The Lives of the Noble Grecians and Romanes*, 1003.
54 John Marston, *The Scourge of Villanie* (London, 1598), F1^v; Plutarch, *The Philosophie, Commonlie Called, The Morals*, 934. For Apemantus as a dog, see, for example, 1.1.204; 1.1.279; 2.2.87; 4.3.366.
55 Jean de L'Espine, *A Very Excellent and Learned Discourse* (London, 1592), 37^v. See Robert B. Pierce, 'From Anecdotal Philosophy to Drama: Shakespeare's Apemantus as Cynic', *Classical and Modern Literature* 25.2 (2005): 77–88; Frances K. Barasch, 'Performing Apemantus in Shakespeare's *Timon of Athens*', in *Acts of Criticism: Performance Matters in Shakespeare and His Contemporaries*, ed. Paul Nelsen and June Schlueter (Madison: Fairleigh Dickinson University Press, 2006), 111–25; and David Hershinow, 'Diogenes the Cynic and Shakespeare's Bitter Fool: The Politics and Aesthetics of Free Speech', *Criticism* 56.4 (2014): 807–35.
56 See John Leon Lievsay, 'Some Renaissance Views of Diogenes The Cynic', in *John Quincy Adams Memorial Studies*, ed. James G. McManaway, Giles E. Dawson and Edwin E. Willoughby (Washington, DC: The Folger Shakespeare Library, 1948), 449.
57 Barasch, 'Performing Apemantus', 114. See also Lievsay, 'Some Renaissance View'; Hershinow, 'Diogenes the Cynic'; Daniel Kinney, 'Heirs of the Dog: Cynic Selfhood in Medieval and Renaissance Culture', in *The Cynics: The Cynic Movement in Antiquity and it's Legacy*, ed. R. Bracht Branham and Marie-Odile Goulet-Cazé (Berkeley: University of California Press, 1996), 294–328; David Mazella, *The Making of Modern Cynicism* (Charlottesville: University of Virginia Press, 2007), chap. 2.
58 Anonymous, *A Breefe Discourse, Declaring and Approuing the Necessarie and Inuiolable Maintenance of the Laudable Customes of London* (London, 1584), 24.
59 Derek Krueger, 'The Bawdy and Society: The Shamelessness of Diogenes in Roman Imperial Culture', in *Cynics*, 225; Lancelot Andrewes, *Apospasmatia Sacra* (London, 1657), 331; Erasmus, *The Apophthegmes of Erasmus: Literally Reprinted From the Scarce Edition of 1564* (Boston, 1877), 100.
60 Kruegar, 'Bawdy and Society', 227.
61 Paster, *The Body Embarassed*, 164.

62 Johannes Ferrarius, *A Worke of Ioannes Ferrarius Montanus* (London, 1559), 85ᵛ; Thomas Rogers, *A Philosophicall Discourse, Entituled, The Anatomie of the Minde* (London, 1576), fol. 82ᵛ; Alexander Le Sylvain, *The Orator* (London, 1596), 364.

63 Nicolas Caussin, *The Holy Court in Five Tomes* (London, 1650), 83; William Bates, *The Harmony of the Divine Attributes* (London, 1674), 358.

64 Erasmus, *Apophthegmes* (1877), 172, for this and the next two quotes.

65 Richard Younge, *The Drunkard's Character* (London, 1638), 418.

66 Erasmus, *Apophthegmes* (1877), 82; Jeremias Drexel, *A Right Intention The Rule of All Mens Actions* (London, 1655), 141.

67 Erasmus, *Apophthegmes* (1877), 78.

68 John Hudson, *A Sermon Preached At Paules Crosse* (London, 1584), E8v-F.

69 Erasmus, *Apophthegmes* (1877), 121.

70 Dio Chrysostom, *Discourses 1–11*, trans. J. W. Cohoon (Cambridge, MA: Harvard University Press, 1932), 399.

71 Erasmus, *Apophthegmes* (1877), 148.

72 Scipion Dupleix, *The Resoluer* (London, 1635), 19.

73 Plutarch, *The Philosophie, Commonlie Called, The Morals*, 1069.

74 Montaigne, *The Essayes*, 340; Marston, *The Scourge of Villanie*, C6; Cotgrave, *Dictionarie*, Nniv.

75 Hugh Roberts, 'Cynic Shamelessness in Late Sixteenth-Century French Texts', *Modern Language Review* 99.3 (2004): 595.

76 Ibid., 596.

77 Montaigne, *The Essayes*, 165.

78 For the distinction between Timon and Apemantus, see Barasch, 'Performing Apemantus'.

79 Peter Sloterdijk, *Critique of Cynical Reason*, trans. Michael Eldred (Minneapolis: University of Minnesota Press, 1987), 4.

80 Dawson and Minton raise this possibility in the note to 1.1.61–4.

Chapter 5

1 Oaten, Stevenson and Case, 'Disgust as a Disease-Avoidance Mechanism', 303.

2 Ackerman, Hill and Murray, 'The Behavioral Immune System: Current Concerns and Future Directions', 1.
3 Mark Schaller, 'Parasites, Behavioral Defenses, and the Social Psychological Mechanisms Through Which Cultures Are Evoked', *Psychological Inquiry* 17.2 (2006): 96.
4 Ibid., 97; Lene Aarøe, Michael Bang Petersen and Kevin Arceneaux, 'The Behavioral Immune System Shapes Political Intuitions: Why and How Individual Differences in Disgust Sensitivity Underlie Opposition to Immigration', *American Political Science Review* 111.2 (2017): 278.
5 Mark Schaller and Justin H. Park, 'The Behavioral Immune System (and Why It Matters)', *Current Directions in Psychological Science* 20.2 (2011): 100.
6 Damian R. Murray and Mark Schaller, 'The Behavioral Immune System: Implications for Social Cognition, Social Interaction, and Social Influence', *Advances in Experimental Social Psychology* 53 (2016): 115; Debra Lieberman and Carlton Patrick, 'Are the Behavioral Immune System and Pathogen Disgust Identical?' *Evolutionary Behavioral Sciences* 8.4 (2014): 244.
7 Isabel Kusche and Jessica L. Barker, 'Pathogens and Immigrants: A Critical Appraisal of the Behavioral Immune System as an Explanation of Prejudice Against Ethnic Outgroups', *Frontiers in Psychology* 10 (2019): Article 2412, 2; Aarøe, Petersen and Arceneaux, 'Behavioral Immune System', 279.
8 Randolph M. Nesse, 'The Smoke Detector Principle: Signal Detection and Optimal Defense Regulation', *Evolution, Medicine, & Public Health* 2019.1 (2019): 1, for this and the next quotation.
9 Justin H. Park, Mark Schaller and Christian S. Crandall, 'Pathogen-Avoidance Mechanism and the Stigmatization of Obese People', *Evolution and Human Behavior* 28 (2007): 410.
10 David M. Bergeron, 'Sickness in *Romeo and Juliet*', *CLA Journal* 20.3 (1977): 356.
11 Jennifer Richards, 'Diagnosing the Body Politic: Shakespeare's *Henry IV, Part Two*', in *Medieval and Early Modern Literature, Science and Medicine*, ed. Rachel Falconer and Denis Renevey (Tübingen: Narr Verlag, 2013), 225.
12 William Spates, 'Shakespeare and the Irony of Early Modern Disease Metaphor and Metonymy', in *Rhetorics of Bodily Disease and Health in Medieval and Early Modern England*, ed. Jennifer C. Vaught (New York: Routledge, 2010), 158.

13 While I obviously did not focus on disease in *Titus*, see Catherine Belling, 'Infectious Rape, Therapeutic Revenge: Bloodletting and the Health of Rome's Body', in *Disease, Diagnosis, and Cure on the Early Modern Stage*, ed. Stephanie Moss and Kaara L. Peterson (New York: Routledge, 2004), 113–32; and Jennifer Feather, 'Contagious Pity: Cultural Difference and the Language of Contagion in *Titus Andronicus*', in *Contagion and the Shakespearean Stage*, 169–87.

14 Darryl Chalk and Mary Floyd-Wilson, 'Introduction: Beyond the Plague', in *Contagion and the Shakespearean Stage*, 3. See also Angelique Marie Wheelock, '"Passion is Catching": Emotional Contagion and Affective Action in Select Works by Shakespeare', PhD Dissertation, University of Maryland, College Park (2011).

15 Chalk, '"A Nature But Infected"', Paragraph 2; John Rainolds, *Th' Overthrow of Stage-Playes* (London, 1599), 162–3; 36–7.

16 Julia D. Staykova, '"We Sit In The Chaire of Pestilence": The Discourse of Disease in the Anti-Theatrical Pamphlets, 1570s–1630s', in *Medieval and Early Modern Literature, Science and Medicine*, 208.

17 Nat Wayne Hardy, 'Anatomy of Pestilence: The Satiric Disgust of Plague in Early Modern London (1563–1625)', PhD Dissertation, University of Alberta (2000), n.p.

18 Bergeron, 'Sickness in *Romeo and Juliet*', 358. On plague and illness in *Romeo and Juliet*, see also 'Shakespeare's Dual Lexicons of Plague: Infections in Speech and Space', in *Representing the Plague in Early Modern England*, ed. Rebecca Totaro and Ernest B. Gilman (New York: Routledge, 2010), 150–68; Mary Floyd-Wilson, '"Angry Mab with Blisters Plague": The Pre-Modern Science of Contagion in *Romeo and Juliet*', in *The Palgrave Handbook of Early Modern Literature and Science*, ed. Evelyn Tribble and Howard Marchitello (New York: Palgrave Macmillan, 2017), 401–22; Kathryn Schwarz, 'Held in Common: *Romeo and Juliet* and the Promiscuous Seductions of Plague', in *Queer Shakespeare: Desire and Sexuality*, ed. Goran Stanivukovic (London: Bloomsbury, 2017), 245–61.

19 Ian Frederick Moulton, 'Catching the Plague: Love, Happiness, Health, and Disease in Shakespeare', in *Disability, Health, and Happiness in the Shakespearean Body*, ed. Sujata Iyengar (New York: Routledge, 2014), 215; 214.

20 Alanna Skuse, 'The Worm and the Flesh: Cankered Bodies in Shakespeare's Sonnets', in *Disability, Health, and Happiness*, 240–59.

21 Bryan Adams Hampton, 'Purgation, Exorcism, and the Civilizing Process in *Macbeth*', *SEL: Studies in English Literature 1500–1900* 51.2 (2011): 328. On disease in the play, see also Christine Couche, 'A Mind Diseased: Reading Lady Macbeth's Madness', in *Word and Self Estranged in English Texts, 1550–1660*, ed. L. E. Semler and Philippa Kelly (New York: Routledge, 2010), 135–48; Allison P. Hobgood, 'Feeling Fear in *Macbeth*', in *Shakespearean Sensations: Experiencing Literature in Early Modern England*, ed. Katharine A. Craik and Tanya Pollard (Cambridge: Cambridge University Press, 2013), 29–46.

22 Bard C. Cosman, '*All's Well That Ends Well*: Shakespeare's Treatment of Anal Fistula', *The Upstart Crow* 19 (1999): 83; Jeremy Lopez, 'Text as Performance as Text: The King's Disease in *All's Well That Ends Well*', in *Shakespeare In the Light: Essays in Honor of Ralph Alan Cohen*, ed. Paul Menzer and Amy R. Cohen (Lanham: Fairleigh Dickinson University Press, 2019), 21.

23 Sujata Iyengar, '"Handling Soft the Hurts": Sexual Healing and Manual Contact in *Orlando Furioso*, *The Faerie Queene*, and *All's Well That Ends Well*', in *Sensible Flesh: On Touch in Early Modern Culture*, ed. Elizabeth D. Harvey (Philadelphia: University of Pennsylvania Press, 2003), 53; Cosman, '*All's Well That Ends Well*', 78; Lopez, 'Text as Performance as Text', 21.

24 Richards, 'Diagnosing the Body Politic', 223–4.

25 See Sarah Clara Dodson, 'The Northumberland of Shakespeare and Holinshed', *Studies in English* 19 (1939): 74–85.

26 Pauline Ellen Reid, 'Giddy Lies the Head that Wears the Crown: Apoplexy and Political Spectacle in 2 Henry IV', *Early Modern Literary Studies* 19.1 (2016): 5: https://extra.shu.ac.uk/emls/journal/index.php/emls/article/view/96.

27 Spates, 'Shakespeare and the Irony of Early Modern Disease', 160.

28 Pliny, *The Historie of the World* (London, 1634), 131; George Stradling, *Sermons and Discourses* (London, 1692), 520.

Chapter 6

1 Stanley Cavell, *Disowning Knowledge In Six Plays of Shakespeare* (Cambridge: Cambridge University Press, 1987), 146.

2 *Coriolanus*, ed. R. B. Parker (Oxford: Oxford University Press, 1994), 77–81.

3 For a discussion of the play's relevant imagery, see Gail Kern Paster, 'To Starve with Feeding: The City in *Coriolanus*', *Shakespeare Studies* 11 (1978): 123–44.

4 Michael D. Bristol, 'Lenten Butchery: Legitimation Crisis in *Coriolanus*', in *Shakespeare Reproduced*, ed. Jean E. Howard and Marion F. O'Connor (New York: Methuen, 1987), 215.

5 Zvi Jagendorf, '*Coriolanus*: Body Politic and Private Parts', *Shakespeare Quarterly* 41.4 (1990): 458.

6 Kenneth Burke, *Language as Symbolic Action: Essays on Life, Literature, and Method* (Berkley: University of California Press, 1966), 96.

7 See Paster, 'To Starve With Feeding', 123.

8 See Arthur Riss, 'The Belly Politic: Coriolanus and the Revolt of Language', *ELH* 59.1 (1992): 53–75; Nate Eastman, 'The Rumbling Belly Politic: Metaphorical Location and Metaphorical Government in *Coriolanus*', *EMLS* 13.1 (2007): http://purl.oclc.org/emls/13-1/eastcori.htm.

9 Plutarch, *The Lives of the Noble Grecians and Romanes*, 239.

10 On the play's biopolitics, see James Kuzner, 'Unbuilding the City: *Coriolanus* and the Birth of Republican Rome', *Shakespeare Quarterly* 58.2 (2007): 174–99.

11 James Holstun, 'Tragic Superfluity in *Coriolanus*', *ELH* 50.3 (1983): 487; Riss, 'Belly Politics', 62.

12 Frank Whigham, 'Reading Social Conflict in the Alimentary Tract: More on the Body in Renaissance Drama', *ELH* 55.2 (1988): 333. See also Bruce Thomas Boehrer, *The Fury of Men's Gullets: Ben Jonson & The Digestive Canal* (Philadelphia: University of Pennsylvania Press, 1997).

13 Anny Crunelle, '*Coriolanus*: The Smiling Belly and the Parliament Fart', *ANQ* 22.3 (2009): 11.

14 Jonathan Goldberg, *Shakespeare's Hand* (Minneapolis: University of Minnesota Press, 2003), 177.

15 Peter Holland, '"Musty Superfluity": *Coriolanus* and the Remains of Excess', in *Shakespeare et l'excès*, ed. Pierre Kapitaniak and Jean-Michel Déprats (Paris: Société Française Shakespeare, 2007), 94.

16 See note 20.

17 See the Introduction, especially the work of Paster.

18 Thomas Thomas, *Dictionarium Linguae Latinae et Anglicanae* (London, 1587), Kkk iiij^v-v.

19 Jorge Moll et al., 'The Moral Affiliations of Disgust: A Functional MRI Study', *Cognitive and Behavioral Neurology* 18.1 (2005): 69.
20 Pliny, *The Historie of the World*, 2 vol., 2.46.
21 Thomas Cooper, *Thesaurus Linguae Romanae & Britannicae* (London, 1578), T.i.
22 William Bullein, *Bulleins Bulwarke of Defence Against All Sicknesse, Soarenesse, and Woundes That Doe Dayly Assaulte Mankinde* (London, 1579), fol. 2$^{v.}$
23 See *OED*, 'quarry, *n*.:' 'A collection or heap of all the deer or other game killed during a hunt.'
24 Holland, 'Musty Superfluity', 93.
25 Goldberg notes that Coriolanus experiences the words of plebeians 'as shit hurled at him' (*Shakespeare's Hand*, 178).
26 Plutarch, *The Lives of the Noble Grecians and Romanes*, 243.
27 Richard Perceval, *A Dictionarie in Spanish and English* (London, 1599), 125.
28 Bakhtin, *Rabelais and his World*, 29.
29 On concepts of the foreign body, see Jonathan Gil Harris, *Foreign Bodies and the Body Politic: Discourses of Social Pathology in Early Modern England* (Cambridge: Cambridge University Press, 1998).
30 See, for example, Coppélia Kahn, *Man's Estate: Masculine Identity in Shakespeare* (Berkeley: University of California Press, 1981); Sean Benson, '"Even to the Gates of Rome": Grotesque Bodies and Fragmented Stories in *Coriolanus*', *Comitatus* 30.1 (1999): 95–113.
31 Plutarch, *The Lives of the Noble Grecians and Romanes*, 244.
32 Paster observers that, in this scene, the play allows no distinction 'between new and old wounds, between flowing blood and healed-over scars'; see *The Body Embarrassed*, 97.
33 Paster, 'To Starve with Feeding', 137.
34 Miller, *The Anatomy of Disgust*, 99.

Chapter 7

1 James J. Gross, 'Antecedent- and Response-Focused Emotion Regulation: Divergent Consequences for Experience, Expression, and Physiology', *Journal of Personality and Social Psychology* 74.1 (1998): 227.

2 Haidt, McCauley and Rozin, 'Individual Differences in Sensitivity to Disgust', 702.
3 Ibid., 712.
4 See, for example, Kumaran Shanmugarajah et al., 'The Role of Disgust Emotions in the Observer Response to Facial Disfigurement', *Body Image* 9 (2012): 460.
5 Nicholas Burden et al., 'Prothesis Use is Associated With Reduced Physical Self-Disgust in Limb Amputees', *Body Image* 27 (2018): 109.
6 Amitai Shenhav and Wendy Berry Mendes, 'Aiming for the Stomach and Hitting the Heart: Dissociable Triggers and Sources for Disgust Reactions', *Emotion* 14.2 (2014): 301.
7 Justin H. Park, Jason Faulkner and Mark Schaller, 'Evolved Disease-Avoidance Processes and Contemporary Anti-Social Behavior: Prejudicial Attitudes and Avoidance of People with Physical Disabilities', *Journal of Nonverbal Behavior* 27.2 (2003): 65.
8 Park, Schaller and Crandall, 'Pathogen-Avoidance Mechanism', 410.
9 Stephen Ryan et al., 'Facial Disfigurement is Treated Like an Infectious Disease', *Evolution and Human Behavior* 33 (2012): 639.
10 Megan Oaten, Richard J. Stevenson and Trevor I. Case, 'Disease Avoidance as a Functional Basis for Stigmatization', *Philosophical Transactions of the Royal Society B* 366 (2011): 3438.
11 Caroline Karschney and Leah Shaffner, 'Rehumanization as an Intervention for Disgust-Based Prejudice: The Case of Ableism', Honors Thesis, Whitman College (2019), v.
12 Andrew C. Page and Benjamin J. Tan, 'Disgust and Blood-Injury-Injection Phobia', in *Disgust and Its Disorders,* 191; 194.
13 Burden et al., 'Prosthesis Use', 109; Ryan et al., 'Facial Disfigurement', 639.
14 Caley Tapp et al., 'Is Obesity Treated Like a Contagious Disease?' *Journal of Applied Social Psychology* 50 (2020): 211.
15 Burden et al., 'Prothesis Use', 109.
16 See Natalie L. Wilver et al., 'An Initial Investigation of the Unique Relationship between Disgust Propensity and Body Dysmorphic Disorder', *Psychiatry Research* 269 (2018): 237–43.
17 Burden et al., 'Prothesis Use', 114.
18 Gabriella Bottini, Peter Brugger and Anna Sedda, 'Is the Desire for Amputation Related to Disturbed Emotion Processing? A Multiple Case Study Analysis in BIID', *Neurocase* 21.3 (2015): 394.

19 S. Gaind, A. Clarke and P. E. M. Butler, 'The Role of Disgust Emotions in Predicting Self-Management in Wound Care', *Journal of Wound Care* 20.7 (2011): 346–50.
20 Yanfei Jin, 'Development and Psychometric Evaluation of the Colostomy Disgust Scale in Patients with Colostomy', *European Journal of Cancer Care* 29.6 (2020): 1–12; Elaine N. Clarke, Andrew R. Thompson and Paul Norman, 'Depression in People with Skin Conditions: The Effects of Disgust and Self-Compassion', *British Journal of Health Psychology* 25 (2020): 540–57.
21 Ronan E. O'Carroll et al., 'The "Ick" Factor, Anticipated Regret, and Willingness to Become an Organ Donor', *Health Psychology* 30.2 (2011): 244.
22 Sarah Bonell et al., 'When (Fake) Beauty Turns Ugly: Plastic Surgery as a Moral Violation', *Current Psychology* (2020): 1: https://doi.org/10.1007/s12144-020-01060-0.
23 Jeffrey R. Wilson, 'The Trouble with Disability in Shakespeare Studies', *Disability Studies Quarterly* 37.2 (2017): https://dsq-sds.org/article/view/5430/4644.
24 For work in early modern disability studies, see, for example, *Recovering Disability in Early Modern England*, ed. Allison P. Hobgood and David Houston Wood (Columbus: Ohio State University Press, 2013); David Houston Wood, 'Staging Disability in Renaissance Drama', in *A New Companion to Renaissance Drama*, ed. Arthur F. Kinney and Thomas Warren Hopper (Hoboken: John Wiley & Sons, Inc., 2017), 487–500; Genevieve Love, *Early Modern Theatre and the Figure of Disability* (London: Bloomsbury Publishing, 2018); Lindsey Row-Heyveld, *Dissembling Disability in Early Modern English Drama* (New York: Palgrave, 2018); *Performing Disability in Early Modern English Drama*, ed. Leslie C. Dunn (New York: Palgrave, 2020); Katherine Schaap Williams, *Unfixable Forms: Disability, Performance, and the Early Modern English Theater* (Ithaca: Cornell University Press, 2021).
25 Wilson has created a website (https://wilson.fas.harvard.edu/stigma-in-shakespeare) that extensively documents instances of stigma in Shakespeare; this resource has greatly informed the rest of this chapter. See also his 'The Figure of Stigma in Shakespeare's Drama', *Genre* 51.3 (2018): 237–66.
26 For the history of Richard III in disability studies, see the discussion in Katherine Schaap Williams, 'Enabling Richard: The Rhetoric of Disability in *Richard III*', *Disability Studies Quarterly* 29.4 (2009): https://dsq-sds.org/article/view/997/1181.
27 On this speech, see Katherine Schapp Williams, 'Demonstrable Disability', *Early Theatre* 22.2 (2019): 188–91.

28 On Falstaff in terms of grotesqueness, see Jonathan Hall, 'The Evacuations of Falstaff *(The Merry Wives of Windsor)*, in Knowles, *Shakespeare and Carnival*, 125–51; in terms of disability, see Royce Best, 'Making Obesity Fat: Crip Estrangement in Shakespeare's *Henry IV, Part 1*', *Disability Studies Quarterly* 39.4 (2019): https://dsq-sds.org/article/view/7149/5470.

29 Samuel Johnson, ed., *The Plays of William Shakespeare, Volume the Seventh* (Dublin, 1766), 418; John D. Staines, 'Radical Pity: Responding to Spectacles of Violence in *King Lear*', in *Staging Pain, 1580–1800: Violence and Trauma in British Theater*, ed. James Robert Allard and Matthew R. Martin (Burlington: Ashgate, 2009), 75.

30 Robert B. Pierce, '"I Stumbled When I Saw": Interpreting Gloucester's Blindness in *King Lear*', *Philosophy and Literature* 36.1 (2012): 157.

31 Jay Halio, 'Gloucester's Blinding', *Shakespeare Quarterly* 43.2 (1992): 221–3; *Certayne Sermons, Or Homelies Appoynted by The Kynges Maiestie* (London, 1547), W4^v.

32 On Shylock's nose, see Jeffrey R. Wilson, 'Hath Not A Jew a Nose? Or, The Danger of Deformity in Comedy', in *New Readings of the Merchant of Venice*, ed. Horacio Sierra (Newcastle upon Tyne: Cambridge Scholars Publishing, 2013): 131–59.

33 Clayton Koelb, 'The Bonds of Flesh and Blood: Having it Both Ways in *The Merchant of Venice*', *Cardozo Studies in Law and Literature* 5.1 (1993): 107.

34 James Shapiro, *Shakespeare and the Jews* (New York: Columbia University Press, 2016), 114.

35 François-Xavier Gleyzon, 'Opening the Sacred Body or the Profaned Host in *The Merchant of Venice*', *English Studies* 94.7 (2013): 821.

36 David S. Katz, 'Shylock's Gender: Jewish Male Menstruation in Early Modern England', *The Review of English Studies* 50.200 (1999): 460.

37 On Caesar as disabled, see Allison P. Hobgood, 'Caesar Hath the Falling Sickness: The Legibility of Early Modern Disability in Shakespearean Drama', *Disability Studies Quarterly* 29.4 (2009): https://dsq-sds.org/article/view/993/1184.

38 Maurice Charney, *Shakespeare's Roman Plays: The Function of Imagery in the Drama* (Cambridge, MA: Harvard University Press, 1961), 48.

39 Gail Kern Paster, '"In the Spirit of Men There Is No Blood": Blood as a Trope of Gender in *Julius Caesar*', *Shakespeare Quarterly* 40.3 (1989): 285, for this and the next quote.

Chapter 8

1 Though PCRS is becoming the most common designation, the field is also sometimes referred to as early modern critical race studies, or more specifically, Shakespeare critical race studies. Margo Hendricks set out an agenda for PCRS in her important talk 'Coloring the Past, Rewriting Our Future: RaceB4Race', lecture delivered at the Folger Institute and the Arizona Center for Medieval and Renaissance Studies 'Race and Periodization' symposium, Folger Shakespeare Library, Washington, DC, September 2019 (https://www.folger.edu/institute/scholarly-programs/race-periodization/margo-hendricks [accessed 12 May 2022]); she has recently elaborated this talk in 'Coloring the Past, Considerations on Our Future: RaceB4Race', *New Literary History* 52.3–4 (2021): 365–84. See also Dorothy Kim, 'Introduction to Literature Compass Special Cluster: Critical Race and the Middle Ages', *Literature Compass* 16 (2019): 1–16. Arthur L. Little, Jr. deploys both 'early modern critical race studies' and 'Shakespeare critical race studies' in 'Critical Race Studies', in *The Arden Research Handbook of Contemporary Shakespeare Criticism*, ed. Evelyn Gajowski (London: Bloomsbury, 2021), 139–58. Little notes that while 'critical Shakespeare and early modern race work is by no means univocal and involves a diversity of approaches and informed perspectives', there are nonetheless certain foundational approaches and outlooks that tend to guide scholars working within the broad boundaries of the field (139).

2 Although valuable research in early modern race studies has been under way for at least three decades, there has been a particular surge of interest in the past few years, especially as such scholarship has increasingly incorporated the insights of critical race theory. For recent overviews of race (and race studies) in early modern England, see Margo Hendricks, 'Race and Nation', in *The Cambridge Guide to the Worlds of Shakespeare*, ed. Bruce R. Smith, 2 vols. (Cambridge: Cambridge University Press, 2016), 1:663–8; Peter Erickson and Kim F. Hall, '"A New Scholarly Song": Rereading Early Modern Race', *Shakespeare Quarterly* 67.1 (2016): 1–13 [the rest of this issue is devoted to race]; Jason Demeter and Ayanna Thompson, 'Shakespeare and Early Modern Race Studies: An Overview of the Field', *The Shakespearean World*, ed. Jill L. Levenson and Robert Ormsby (London: Routledge, 2017), 574–89; Urvashi Chakravarty, 'The Renaissance of Race and the Future of Early Modern Race Studies', *English Literary Renaissance* 50.1 (Winter 2020): 17–24; Ayanna Thompson (ed.), *The Cambridge Companion to Shakespeare and Race* (Cambridge: Cambridge University Press, 2021). For some

notable precursors, see Margo Hendricks and Patricia Parker, eds., *Women, 'Race', and Writing in the Early Modern Period* (New York: Routledge, 1994); Kim F. Hall, *Things of Darkness: Economies of Race and Gender in Early Modern England* (Ithaca: Cornell University Press, 1996); Little, *Shakespeare Jungle Fever*; Joyce Green MacDonald, *Women and Race in Early Modern Texts* (Cambridge: Cambridge University Press, 2002); Ania Loomba, *Shakespeare, Race, and Colonialism* (Oxford: Oxford University Press, 2002); and Imtiaz H. Habib, *Black Lives in the English Archives, 1500–1677: Imprints of the Invisible* (Burlington: Ashgate, 2008).

3 Carol Mejia LaPerle (ed.), *Race and Affect in Early Modern English Literature* (Tempe: ACMRS Press, 2022). See also Mejia LaPerle's 'Race and Affect: Pleasurable Mixing in Ben Jonson's *The Masque of Blackness*', *The Ben Jonson Journal* 26.1 (2019): 1–20 and '"If I Might Have My Will": Aaron's Affect and Race in *Titus Andronicus*', in *Titus Andronicus: The State of Play*, ed. Farah Karim-Cooper (London: Bloomsbury, 2019), 135–56. For an early work on race and emotion in the early modern period, see Mary Floyd-Wilson's *English Ethnicity and Race in Early Modern Drama* (Cambridge: Cambridge University Press, 2003).

4 Mira 'Assaf Kafantaris, 'Desire, Disgust, and the Perils of Strange Queenship in Edmund Spenser's *The Faerie Queene*', in *Race and Affect*, 23–40; Gitanjali G. Shahani, *Tasting Difference: Food, Race, and Cultural Encounters in Early Modern Literature* (Ithaca: Cornell University Press, 2020), Chap. 4; Ian Smith, 'We are Othello: Speaking of Race in Early Modern Studies', *Shakespeare Quarterly* 67.1 (2016): 110.

5 There is, of course, a wealth of recent criticism on race (and racial violence) in *Othello*. See, for example, Ian Smith, 'Othello's Black Handkerchief', *Shakespeare Quarterly* 64.1 (2013): 1–25, and 'Seeing Blackness: Reading Race in *Othello*', in *The Oxford Handbook of Shakespearean Tragedy*, ed. Michael Neill and David Schalkwyk (Oxford: Oxford University Press, 2016). 405–20; Dennis Austin Britton, *Becoming Christian: Race, Reformation, and Early Modern English Romance* (New York: Fordham University Press, 2014) and '*Contaminatio*, Race, and Pity in *Othello*', in *Rethinking Shakespeare Source Study: Audiences, Authors, and Digital Technologies*, ed. Dennis Austin Britton and Melissa Walter (New York: Routledge, 2018), 46–64; Ambereen Dadabhoy, 'Two Faced: The Problem of Othello's Visage', in *Othello: The State of Play*, ed. Lena Cowen Orlin (London: Bloomsbury 2014), 121–47; Imtiaz Habib, 'The Black Alien in Othello: Beyond the European Immigrant', in *Shakespeare and Immigration*,

ed. Ruben Espinosa and David Ruiter (Burlington: Ashgate, 2014), 135–58; Matthieu Chapman, *Anti-Black Racism in Early Modern English Drama: The Other 'Other'* (New York: Routledge, 2017), chap. 5; Justin Shaw, '"Rub Him about the Temples": *Othello*, Disability, and the Failures of Care', *Early Theatre* 22.2 (2019): 171–83; Joyce Green MacDonald, *Shakespearean Adaptation, Race and Memory in the New World* (New York: Palgrave Macmillan, 2020), chaps. 2 and 5; Matthew Dimmock, 'Experimental *Othello*', in *The Cambridge Companion to Shakespeare and Race*, 93–107; and Eric Brinkman, 'Iago as the Racist-Function in *Othello*', *Shakespeare Bulletin* 40.1 (2022): 23–44. For recent treatments of *Othello* and emotion, see Toria Johnson, 'Fear: *Macbeth, Othello*', in *Shakespeare and Emotion*, 199–210 and Cora Fox, 'Othello's Unfortunate Happiness', in *Race and Affect*, 187–204.

6 Because my analysis centres on the affective underpinnings of racial violence, it is vital to acknowledge Hendricks's comments on anti-Blackness in early modern race studies. While noting that 'race equaling anti-Blackness is still a jumping-off point for . . . premodern critical race studies' (and suggesting that 'we need to not let go of that'), she also emphasizes that a focus on anti-Blackness can reinforce and sustain white supremacist discourses ('Coloring the Past'). With Hendricks's caution in mind, I see the current essay as aligned with Little's observation that one of central 'affirmative arguments' of early modern critical race studies is that 'race (as an assemblage of racialized processes) is very much founded on endlessly mutable acts of social and political violence' ('Critical Race Studies', 139). By deconstructing this violence, I hope to contribute to the field's ongoing interest in how 'Shakespeare and his early modern English contemporaries sought to reinvent, delimit and theorize about the humanity of themselves, especially in relationship to the humanity of others' (Little, 'Critical Race Studies', 140).

7 Little, 'Critical Race Studies', 139 (emphasis in original); Hendricks, 'Coloring the Past'. See also Ruben Espinosa's recently released *Shakespeare on the Shades of Racism* (New York: Routledge, 2021), which considers Shakespeare and many forms of modern racism.

8 Michael Bang Petersen, 'How and Why Disgust Responses Underlie Prejudice: Evidence from the Field', *Politics and the Life Sciences* 38.1 (2019): 64. As Petersen discusses, though much prejudice and disgust research has focused on Western, white subjects, scholars are increasingly discovering that there seems to be a 'cross-culturally robust pattern to the association between disgust sensitivity and indicators of prejudice such as traditional values and opposition to immigration' (65).

9   Gordon Hodson and Kimberly Costello, 'Interpersonal Disgust, Ideological Orientations, and Dehumanization as Predictors of Intergroup Attitudes', *Psychological Science* 18.8 (2007): 691.
10 Maayan Katzir, Matan Hoffmann and Nira Liberman, 'Disgust as an Essentialist Emotion That Signals Nonviolent Outgrouping With Potentially Low Social Costs', *Emotion* 19.5 (2019): 841.
11 Ibid., 843; 841.
12 Kathleen Taylor, 'Disgust is a Factor in Extreme Prejudice', *British Journal of Social Psychology* 46 (2007): 613.
13 Erin E. Buckels and Paul D. Trapnell, 'Disgust Facilitates Outgroup Dehumanization', *Group Processes & Intergroup Relations* 16.6 (2013): 772.
14 Ibid.; Hodson and Costello, 'Interpersonal Disgust'.
15 Nick Haslam, 'Dehumanization: An Integrative Review', *Personality and Social Psychology Review* 10.3 (2006): 252; Carlos David Navarrete and Daniel M. T. Fessler, 'Disease Avoidance and Ethnocentrism: The Effects of Disease Vulnerability and Disgust Sensitivity on Intergroup Attitudes', *Evolution and Human Behavior* 27.4 (2006): 271. See also the discussions of anti-immigrant sentiment throughout Espinosa, *Shakespeare on the Shades of Racism*.
16 Thomas Browne, *Pseudodoxia Epidemica* (London, 1646), 334; 336. For discussion, see Ian Smith, 'White Skin, Black Masks: Racial Cross-Dressing on the Early Modern Stage', *Renaissance Drama* 32 (2003): 51–2.
17 *OED,* 'fuliginous, *adj.*', 2.a.
18 Douglas, *Purity and Danger*, 36.
19 Benjamin Minor and Ayanna Thompson, '"Edgar I Nothing Am": Blackface in *King Lear*', in *Staged Transgression in Shakespeare's England*, ed. Rory Loughnane and Edel Semple (New York: Palgrave Macmillan, 2013), 153–64.
20 William Worship, *The Christians Iewell* (London, 1617), 210. On this proverb, see Morris Palmer Tilley, *A Dictionary of the Proverbs in England in the Sixteenth and Seventeenth Centuries* (Ann Arbor: University of Michigan Press, 1950), E186.
21 Hall, *Things of Darkness*, 114.
22 Jonathan Gil Harris, 'Shakespeare and Race', in *The New Cambridge Companion to Shakespeare,* ed. Margreta De Grazia and Stanley Wells (Cambridge: Cambridge University Press, 2010), 209.
23 George Best, *A True Discourse of the Late Voyages of Discouerie* (London, 1578), 30.

24 John Josselyn, *An Account of Two Voyages to New-England* (London, 1674), 187.
25 Best, *A True Discourse*, 31.
26 Sujata Iyengar, *Shades of Difference: Mythologies of Skin Color in Early Modern England* (Philadelphia: University of Pennsylvania Press, 2005), 9.
27 Joyce Green MacDonald, 'The Force of Imagination: The Subject of Blackness in Shakespeare, Jonson, and Ravenscroft', *Renaissance Papers* (1991), 58.
28 Shahani, *Tasting Difference*, 115.
29 Ibid., 116; 117.
30 Smith, 'White Skin, Black Masks', 44; see also ibid., 'Seeing Blackness', 409–10.
31 The National Archives, SP 14/12, fol. 8ᵛ; Memorials of Affairs of State in the Reigns of Q. Elizabeth and K. James I, 3 vols. (London, 1725), 2:44.
32 Hardin Aasand, '"To Blanch an Ethiop, and Revive a Corse"; Queen Anne and The Masque of Blackness', *Studies in English Literature 1500–1900* 32.2 (1992): 273.
33 Mejia LaPerle, 'Race and Affect'; Bernadette Andrea, 'Black Skin, The Queen's Masques: Africanist Ambivalence and Feminine Author(ity) in the Masques of *Blackness* and *Beauty*', *English Literary Renaissance* 29.2 (1999): 271–85.
34 Smith, 'Seeing Blackness', 409.
35 Nancy W. Thornhill et al., 'Evolutionary Theory and Human Social Institutions: Psychological Foundations', in *Human By Nature: Between Biology and the Social Sciences*, ed. Peter Weingart et al. (London: Lawrence Erlbaum Associates, 1997), 201–52.
36 Patricia Akhimie, *Shakespeare and the Cultivation of Difference: Race and Conduct in the Early Modern World* (New York: Routledge, 2018), 64; 53.
37 Nick Haslam, Steve Loughnan and Pamela Sun, 'Beastly: What Makes Animal Metaphors Offensive?' *Journal of Language and Social Psychology* 30.3 (2011): 323; Haslam, 'Dehumanization', 258.
38 Indeed, as Michael Neill has shown, anxiety about Othello and Desdemona's relationship has marked the play's reception and performance history; see 'Unproper Beds: Race, Adultery, and the Hideous in *Othello*', *Shakespeare Quarterly* 40.4 (1989): 383–412.
39 Allison L. Skinner and Caitlin M. Hudac, '"Yuck, You Disgust Me!" Affective Bias against Interracial Couples', *Journal of Experimental Social Psychology* 68 (2017): 75.

40 Ben Saunders, 'Iago's Clyster: Purgation, Anality, and the Civilizing Process', *Shakespeare Quarterly* 55.2 (2004): 154. (Italics in original.) Despite the fact that purgation and disgust are related concepts, this quotation is the only time that Saunders mentions disgust in his essay.

41 Paul Cefalu, 'The Burdens of Mind Reading in Shakespeare's *Othello*: A Cognitive and Psychoanalytic Approach to Iago's Theory of Mind', *Shakespeare Quarterly* 64.3 (2013): 276; 272.

42 Cristina León Alfar, *Women and Shakespeare's Cuckoldry Plays: Shifting Narratives of Marital Betrayal* (New York: Routledge, 2017), 143.

43 Britton, '*Contaminatio*, Race, and Pity in *Othello*', 54.

44 Dadabhoy, 'Two Faced', 139.

45 Neill, 'Unproper Beds', 383.

46 Edward Berry, 'Othello's Alienation', *SEL: Studies in English Literature, 1500–1900* 30.2 (1990): 320.

47 Saunders, 'Iago's Clyster', 167.

48 Mary Janell Metzger, 'Interpreting Shakespeare as Historical Reckoning: A Qualities of Mercy Dispatch', *The Sundial* (August 2020): https://medium.com/the-sundial-acmrs/interpreting-shakespeare-as-historical-reckoning-a-qualities-of-mercy-dispatch-a94ad1b1c4e3, n.p; Ruben Espinosa, 'Chicano Shakespeare: The Bard, The Border, and the Peripheries of Performance', in *Teaching Social Justice Through Shakespeare: Why Renaissance Literature Matters Now*, ed. Hillary Eklund and Wendy Beth Hyman (Edinburgh: Edinburgh University Press, 2019), 79. For structures of racism in historical England, see Emily Weissbourd, '"Those in Their Possession": Race, Slavery, and Queen Elizabeth's "Edicts of Expulsion"', *Huntington Library Quarterly* 78.1 (2015): 1–19.

49 Smith, 'We Are Othello', 104; Shaw, '"Rub Him About the Temples"', 171. See also the discussion of police violence throughout Espinosa, *Shakespeare on the Shades of Racism*.

50 'Assaf Kafantaris, 'Desire, Disgust', 38.

51 Haylie Jones, 'Disgust as a Predictor of Shooter Bias', MS thesis, Texas Woman's University (2019).

Chapter 9

1 Stephen D. Reicher et al., 'Core Disgust Is Attenuated by Ingroup Relations', *PNAS* 113.10 (2016): 2631–5.

2 Navarrete and Fessler, 'Disease Avoidance and Ethnocentrism', 270.
3 Lene Aarøe, Mathias Osmundsen and Michael Bang Petersen, 'Distrust As A Disease Avoidance Strategy: Individual Differences in Disgust Sensitivity Regulate Generalized Social Trust', *Frontiers in Psychology* 7 (2016): Article 1038, 12.
4 Schaller and Park, 'Behavioral Immune System', 101.
5 John A. Terrizzi, Jr., Natalie J. Shook and Michael A. McDaniel, 'The Behavioral Immune System and Social Conservatism: A Meta-Analysis', *Evolution and Human Behavior* 34 (2013): 99.
6 Gordon Hodson et al., 'The Role of Intergroup Disgust in Predicting Negative Outgroup Evaluations', *Journal of Experimental Social Psychology* 49 (2013): 196–7.
7 Petersen, 'How and Why', 68–9.
8 Kusche and Barker, 'Pathogens and Immigrants', 3.
9 See Carol Mejia LaPerle, 'An Unlawful Race: Shakespeare's Cleopatra and the Crimes of Early Modern Gypsies', *Shakespeare* 13.3 (2017): 226–38; Melissa E. Sanchez, 'Was Sexuality Racialized for Shakespeare? *Antony and Cleopatra*', in *The Cambridge Companion to Shakespeare and Race*, 123–38.
10 Imtiaz Habib, 'Elizabethan Racial Medical Psychology, Popular Drama, and the Social Programming of the Late-Tudor Black: Sketching an Exploratory Postcolonial Hypothesis', in *Disease, Diagnosis, and Cure on the Early Modern Stage*, ed. Stephanie Moss and Kaara L. Peterson (Burlington: Ashgate, 2004), 94.
11 Brett D. Hirsch, 'Judaism and Jews', in *Cambridge Guide*, 1:712. This essay informs the next two paragraphs.
12 Ibid., 709.
13 Erasmus, *The First Tome or Volume of the Paraphrase of Erasmus vpon the Newe Testamente* (London, 1548), fol. 34; Anonymous, *All The Famous Battels That Haue Bene Fought In Our Age* (London, 1578), 133; Daniel Dyke, *The Mystery of Selfe-Deceiuing* (London, 1614), 94.
14 Joseph Hall, *Pharisaisme and Christianity Compared* (London, 1608), 41; Thomas Adams, *A Commentary or Exposition Vpon the Diuine Second Epistle Generall* (London, 1633), 78; Cristóbal de Fonseca, *Deuout Contemplations* (London, 1629), 220.
15 See Hirsch, 'Judaism and Jews', 712.
16 John Foxe, *Actes and Monuments* (London, 1570), 410.

17 Daniel Dyke, *Sixe Evangelical Histories* (London, 1617), 268.
18 Peter Heylyn, *Keimēlia 'Ekklēsiastika* (London, 1681), 394.
19 Hirsch, 'Judaism and Jews', 712; see also Drew Daniel, 'Early Modern Affect Theory, Racialized Aversion, and the Strange Case of *Foetor Judaicus*', in *Race and Affect*, 57–78.
20 Browne, *Pseudodoxia Epidemica*, 201; Thomas Fitzherbert, *The First Part of a Treatise Concerning Policy* (London, 1606), 187; John Weemes, *A Treatise of the Foure Degenerate Sonnes* (London, 1636), 330.
21 Weems, *A Treatise*, 330; 329.
22 Robert Heath, *Paradoxical Assertions and Philosophical Problems* (London, 1659), 2 (of *Philosophical Problems*).
23 Edward Kellett, *Tricoenivm Christi* (London, 1641), 142.
24 Hirsch, 'Judaism and Jews', 712.
25 Thomas Nashe, *The Vnfortunate Traueller* (London, 1594), N1.
26 For a recent treatment of race in *Merchant*, see Dennis Austin Britton, 'Flesh and Blood: Race and Religion in *The Merchant of Venice*', in *The Cambridge Companion to Shakespeare and Race*, 108–22.

Chapter 10

1 A. C. Bradley, *Shakespearean Tragedy* (London: Macmillan and Co., 1904), 112, for this and the next quote.
2 G. Wilson Knight, *The Wheel of Fire: Interpretations of Shakespearean Tragedy* (New York: Routledge, 1989), 24.
3 William Tanner, 'To Kill a King in the Malcontent *Hamlet*', *Shakespeare Quarterly* 70.2 (2019): 136.
4 Elemér Hankiss, 'Shakespeare's Hamlet: The Tragedy in the Light of Communication Theory', *Acta Litteraria Academiae Scientiarum Hungaricae* 12 (1970): 299.
5 See Gorfain, 'Toward a Theory of Play and the Carnivalesque in *Hamlet*', 25–49; Michael D. Bristol, '"Funeral Bak'd Meats": Carnival and the Carnivalesque in *Hamlet*', in *Hamlet*, ed. Susanne L. Wofford (New York: Bedford, 1994), 348–67; Dominick M. Grace, 'The Anti-Carnivalesque Hamlet', *Atenea* 21 (2001): 101–8; Zita Turi, 'Fasting and Feasting in *Hamlet*: A Carnivalesque Interpretation', *The AnaChronisT* 15 (2010): 27–42; Chikako D. Kumamoto, 'Gertrude,

Ophelia, Ghost: Hamlet's Revenge and the Abject', *Journal of the Wooden O Symposium* 6 (2006): 48–64; Duncan A. Lucas, *Affect Theory, Genre, and the Example of Tragedy: Dreams We Learn* (New York: Palgrave, 2018), 201.

6 See Irish, *Emotion in the Tudor Court*, Chap 4.

7 Bradley J. Irish, '"Something After"?: *Hamlet* and Dread', in *Hamlet and Emotions*, 229–49.

8 Sheldon Solomon, Jeff Greenberg and Tom Pyszczynski, 'The Cultural Animal: Twenty Years of Terror Management Theory and Research', in *Handbook of Experimental Existential Psychology*, ed. Jeff Greenberg, Sander L. Koole and Tom Pyszczynski (New York: Guilford, 2004), 16. For the background of TMT, see Irish, *Emotion in the Tudor Court*, 141–3 and Irish, '"Something After"?', 232–4.

9 Jamie L. Goldenberg et al., 'I Am *Not* An Animal: Mortality Salience, Disgust, and the Denial of Human Creatureliness', *Journal of Experimental Psychology* 130.3 (2001): 428; Solomon, Greenberg and Pyszczynski, 'The Cultural Animal', 16.

10 Goldenberg et al., 'I Am *Not* An Animal', 428; Jamie Goldenberg et al., 'Of Mice and Men, and Objectified Women: A Terror Management Account of Infrahumanization', *Group Processes & Intergroup Relations* 12.6 (2009): 765.

11 Brian L. Burke, Andy Martens and Erik H. Faucher, 'Two Decades of Terror Management Theory: A Meta-Analysis of Mortality Salience Research', *Personality and Social Psychology Review* 14.2 (2010): 185.

12 Jeff Greenberg and Spee Kosloff, 'Terror Management Theory: Implications for Understanding Prejudice, Stereotyping, Intergroup Conflict, and Political Attitudes', *Social and Personality Psychology Compass* 2.5 (2008): 1883.

13 Goldenberg et al., 'I Am *Not* An Animal', 430.

14 Haidt, McCauley and Rozin, 'Individual Differences in Sensitivity to Disgust', 711.

15 Goldenberg et al., 'I Am *Not* An Animal', 429, for this and the next quote.

16 Ibid., 430; Cathy R. Cox et al., 'Disgust, Creatureliness and the Accessibility of Death-Related Thoughts', *European Journal of Social Psychology* 37 (2007): 504.

17 Goldenberg et al., 'I Am *Not* An Animal', 432.

18 Derek Traversi, *An Approach to Shakespeare*, 2 vols. (New York: Doubleday, 1969), 2:33; Eric S. Mallin, *Inscribing the Time:*

Shakespeare and the End of Elizabethan England (Berkeley: University of California Press, 1995), 65.

19 Spurgeon, *Shakespeare's Imagery*, 133.
20 Unless otherwise noted, I quote from Q2.
21 See, for example, in *OED*, 'gross, *adj.* and *n.*4', A.I.2.b ('Overfed, bloated with excess, unwholesomely or repulsively fat or corpulent'), and A.I.4 ('Glaring, flagrant, monstrous'). On early modern usage of the word, see Katherine Walker, '"Palpable to Thinking": *Othello* and Gross Conceits', *ELR* 52.2 (2022): 1–25.
22 Michael Cameron Andrews, '"Foul Play" in *Hamlet*', *Hamlet Studies* 16 (1994): 79.
23 Patrick Colm Hogan, 'The Brain in Love: A Case Study in Cognitive Neuroscience and Literary Theory', *Journal of Literary Theory* 1.2 (2007): 348.
24 Piotr Sadowski, '"Foul, Strange and Unnatural": Poison as a Murder Weapon in English Renaissance Drama', *Mosaic* 53.3 (2020): 140.
25 Linda Bamber, *Comic Women, Tragic Men: A Study of Gender and Genre in Shakespeare* (Stanford: Stanford University Press, 1982), 71. As far as I've been able to locate, the first use of the term *sex nausea* in Shakespeare is J. Dover Wilson, *The Essential Shakespeare: A Biographical Adventure* (Cambridge: Cambridge University Press, 1932), 118, but the concept predates this.
26 Sigmund Freud, *The Basic Writings of Sigmund Freud,* trans. A. A. Brill (New York: Random House, 1938), 314.
27 Frank Harris, *The Man Shakespeare and His Tragic Life-Story* (New York: Mitchell Kennerley, 1909), 264.
28 Ernest Jones, *A Psycho-Analytic Study of Hamlet* (London, 1922), 61.
29 T. S. Eliot, *Selected Essays, 1917–1932* (London: Faber and Faber, 1932), 125.
30 Bradley, *Shakespearean Tragedy,* 117–18.
31 Ibid., 118–19.
32 Celia R. Daileader, 'Thomas Middleton, William Shakespeare, and the Masculine Grotesque', in *The Oxford Handbook of Thomas Middleton*, ed. Gary Taylor and Trish Thomas Henley (Oxford: Oxford University Press, 2012), 454.
33 Karl P. Wentersdorf, 'Animal Symbolism in Shakespeare's *Hamlet*: The Imagery of Sex Nausea', *Comparative Drama* 17.4 (1983–84): 351.

34 Janet Adelman, *Suffocating Mothers: Fantasies of Maternal Origin in Shakespeare's Plays, Hamlet to The Tempest* (New York: Routledge, 1992), 15.

35 Mark King, 'The Theatricality of Rot in Thomas Middleton's *The Revenger's Tragedy* and William Shakespeare's *Hamlet*', *The Upstart Crow* 20 (2000): 59.

36 Wentersdorf, 'Animal Symbolism', 354.

37 Jamie L. Goldenberg et al., 'Fleeing The Body: A Terror Management Perspective on the Problem of Human Corporeality', *Personality and Social Psychology Review* 4.3 (2000): 206.

38 Jamie L. Goldenberg et al., 'Understanding Human Ambivalence about Sex: The Effects of Stripping Sex of Meaning', *The Journal of Sex Research* 39.4 (2002): 319; 'The Body Stripped Down: An Existential Account of the Threat Posed by the Physical Body', *Current Directions in Psychological Science* 14.4 (2005): 225.

39 Jamie L. Goldenberg et al., 'Death, Sex, Love, and Neuroticism: Why Is Sex Such a Problem?' *Journal of Personality and Social Psychology* 77.6 (1999): 1184.

40 Goldenberg et al., 'Fleeing The Body', 208; Goldenberg et al, 'Death, Sex, Love, and Neuroticism', 1176.

41 See W. F. Bynum and Michael Neve, 'Hamlet on the Couch', *American Scientist* 74.4 (1986): 390–6.

42 Jacqueline Rose, 'Sexuality in the Reading of Shakespeare: *Hamlet* and *Measure for Measure*', in *Alternative Shakespeares*, ed. John Drakakis (New York: Routledge, 2002), 99.

43 See Goldenberg et al., 'Understanding Human Ambivalence'.

44 Richard Levin, 'Gertrude's Elusive Libido and Shakespeare's Unreliable Narrators', *SEL: Studies in English Literature 1500–1900* 48.2 (2008): 323.

45 See Karen Raber, 'Vermin and Parasites: Shakespeare's Animal Architectures', in *Ecocritical Shakespeare*, ed. Lynne Bruckner (Burlington: Ashgate, 2011), 13–32.

46 Susan Dunn-Hensley, 'Whore Queens: The Sexualized Female Body and the State', in *High and Mighty Queens of Early Modern England: Realities and Representations*, ed. Carole Levin, Jo Eldridge Carney and Debra Barrett-Graves (New York: Palgrave, 2003), 102.

47 On incest in the play, see, for example, Charles R. Forker, '"A Little More Than Kin, and Less Than Kind": Incest, Intimacy, Narcissism,

and Identity in Elizabethan and Stuart Drama', *Medieval & Renaissance Drama in England* 4 (1989): 13–51; Lisa Jardine, '"No Offence I' Th' World": Hamlet and Unlawful Marriage', in *Uses of History: Marxism, Postmodernism and the Renaissance,* ed. Francis Barker, Peter Hulme and Margaret Iversen (Manchester: Manchester University Press, 1991), 123–39; Richard A. McCabe, *Incest, Drama and Nature's Law: 1550–1700* (Cambridge: Cambridge University Press, 1993), 162–71.

48 Forker, '"A Little More Than Kin"', 26.
49 Bradley, *Shakespearean Tragedy*, 119.
50 For this and the next quotations, see Luis De Granada's *Of Prayer, and Meditation* (London, 1582), fol. 201ᵛ; 192. On the text as a possible source, see Randall Martin, 'Ecology, Evolution, and *Hamlet*' in *Renaissance Shakespeare: Shakespeare Renaissances,* ed. Martin Procházka et al. (Newark: University of Delaware Press, 2014), 40.
51 See Martin, 'Ecology, Evolution, and *Hamlet*', 38. On worms in *Hamlet* see also Amanda Bailey, '*Hamlet* Without Sex: The Politics of Regenerate Loss', in *Sexuality and Memory in Early Modern England: Literature and the Erotics of Recollection,* ed. John S. Garrison and Kyle Pivetti (New York: Routledge, 2016), 221; and Ian MacInnes, 'The Politic Worm: Invertebrate Life in the Early Modern English Body', *The Indistinct Human in Renaissance Literature,* ed. Jean E. Feerick and Vin Nardizzi (New York: Palgrave, 2012), 253–73.
52 John Hunt, 'A Thing of Nothing: The Catastrophic Body in *Hamlet*', *Shakespeare Quarterly* 39.1 (1988): 44; 38.
53 On skulls in this scene, and more generally in early modern culture, see Roland Mushat Frye, 'Ladies, Gentlemen, and Skulls: *Hamlet* and the Iconographic Traditions', *Shakespeare Quarterly* 30.1 (1979): 15–28; Andrew Sofer, 'The Skull on the Renaissance Stage: Imagination and the Erotic Life of Props', *ELR* 28.1 (1998): 47–74; Gail Kern Paster, 'The Pith and Marrow of Our Attribute: Dialogue of Skin and Skull in *Hamlet* and Holbein's *The Ambassadors*', *Textual Practice* 23.2 (2009): 247–65.
54 Susan Zimmerman, *The Early Modern Corpse and Shakespeare's Theatre* (Edinburgh: Edinburgh University Press, 2005), 2.
55 *The Bible: Translated According to the Ebrew and Greeke* (London, 1611).
56 Bradley, *Shakespearean Tragedy,* 145.
57 Burke, Martens and Faucher, 'Two Decades of Terror Management Theory', 155.

Chapter 11

1 Darrell Figgis, *Shakespeare: A Study* (New York: Mitchell Kennerley, 1912), 284.
2 Wilson, *The Essential Shakespeare*, 118.
3 Charmaine Borg and Peter J. de Jong, 'Feelings of Disgust and Disgust-Induced Avoidance Weaken following Induced Sexual Arousal in Women', *PLoS ONE* 7.9 (2012): e44111: 1.
4 Tybur et al., 'Disgust', 71, for this and the next quote.
5 Rozin, Haidt and McCauley, 'Disgust', 821.
6 Tybur et al., 'Disgust', 71.
7 Borg and de Jong, 'Feelings of Disgust', 1.
8 Charmaine Borg et al., 'The Influence of Olfactory Disgust on (Genital) Sexual Arousal in Men', *PLoSONE* 14.2 (2019): e0213059: 1.
9 Ibid.; Richard J. Stevenson, Trevor I. Case, Megan J. Oaten, 'Effect of Self-Reported Sexual Arousal On Responses to Sex-Related and Non-Sex Related Disgust Cues', *Archives of Sexual Behavior* 40 (2011): 79–85.
10 Laith Al-Shawaf, David M. G. Lewis and David M. Buss, 'Disgust and Mating Strategy', *Evolution and Human Behavior* 36 (2015): 205.
11 Ellen M. Lee, James K. Ambler and Brad J. Sagarin, 'Effects of Subjective Sexual Arousal on Sexual, Pathogen, and Moral Disgust Sensitivity in Women and Men', *Archives of Sexual Behavior* 43 (2014): 1115.
12 See Laith Al-Shawaf et al., 'Mating Strategy'.
13 Ibid., 32.
14 See Peter J. de Jong and Madelon L. Peters, 'Sex and the Sexual Dysfunctions: The Role of Disgust and Contamination Sensitivity', in *Disgust and Its Disorders*, 253–70; Mark van Overveld et al., 'The Sexual Disgust Questionnaire; a Psychometric Study and a First Exploration in Patients with Sexual Dysfunctions', *Journal of Sexual Medicine* 10.2 (2013): 396–407.
15 Goldenberg et al., 'Fleeing The Body', 205.
16 See Mark J. Kiss, Melanie A. Morrison and Todd G. Morrison, 'A Meta-Analytic Review of the Association Between Disgust and Prejudice Toward Gay Men', *Journal of Homosexuality* 67.5 (2020): 690.

17 Jarret T. Crawford, Yoel Inbar and Victoria Maloney, 'Disgust Sensitivity Selectively Predicts Attitudes Toward Groups That Threaten (or Uphold) Traditional Sexual Morality', *Personality and Individual Differences* 70 (2014): 218–23.

18 Bunmi O. Olatunji, 'Disgust, Scrupulosity and Conservative Attitudes About Sex: Evidence For A Mediational Model Of Homophobia', *Journal of Research in Personality* 42 (2008): 1364.

19 Breanna Maureen O'Handley, Karen L. Blair and Rhea Ashley Hoskin, 'What Do Two Men Kissing and a Bucket of Maggots Have in Common? Heterosexual Men's Indistinguishable Salivary α-amylase Responses to Photos of Two Men Kissing and Disgusting Images', *Psychology and Sexuality* 8.3 (2017): 173.

20 Olatunji, 'Disgust, Scrupulosity', 1368.

21 Jonathan Gil Harris, *Sick Economies: Drama, Mercantilism, and Disease in Shakespeare's England* (Philadelphia: University of Pennsylvania Press, 2003), 29.

22 John J. Ross, 'Shakespeare's Chancre: Did the Bard Have Syphilis?' *Clinical Infectious Diseases* 40.3 (2005): 399. For syphilis in Shakespeare and the early modern period, see, for example, Francis R. Packard, 'References to Syphilis in the Plays of Shakespeare', *Annals of Medical History* 6 (1924): 194–200; Aubrey C. Kail, *The Medical Mind of Shakespeare* (Sydney: Williams & Wilkins, 1986); Johannes Fabricius, *Syphilis in Shakespeare's England* (London: Jessica Kingsley Publishers, 1994); Mickey Wadia, '"Most Infectious Pestilence": A Shakespearean Treatment of Syphilis', *Tennessee Philological Bulletin* 37 (2000): 25–42; Margaret Healy, *Fictions of Disease in Early Modern England* (New York: Palgrave, 2001); William W. E. Slights, 'Contagion and Blame in Early Modern England: The Case of the French Pox', *Literature and Medicine* 22.1 (2003): 1–24; Frédérique Fouassier-Tate, '"The 'French Disease" in Elizabethan and Jacobean Drama', in *Representing France and the French in Early Modern English Drama,* ed. Jean-Christophe Mayer (Newark: University of Delaware Press, 2008), 193–206.

23 Margaret Healy, *'Pericles* and the Pox', in *Shakespeare's Late Plays: New Readings,* ed. James Knowles and Jennifer Richards (Edinburgh: Edinburgh University Press, 1999), 95.

24 Fabricius, *Syphilis in Shakespeare's England,* 197.

25 R. W. McConchie, '"Foul Sin Gathering Head": Venereal Disease in Shakespeare's *Henry the Fourth, Part 2*', *Parergon* 32 (1982): 33.

26 The Q and F both print 'Doll' at 5.1.82 but some editors (like T. W. Craik's Arden edition) accept Johnson's emendation of 'Nell'.

Ultimately it doesn't matter to my argument; the theme of syphilis is furthered through either reading.
27 Fabricius, *Syphilis in Shakespeare's England*, 200. Fabricius's analysis of Falstaff informs what follows.
28 See ibid., Chapter 2, for syphilis treatments.
29 Ibid., 202.
30 Gillian M. E. Alban, 'What Makes the Sexually Fraught Play *Measure for Measure* More Tragical than Comical?' in *Tribute to Professor Oya Basak: (Re)Reading Shakespeare in Text and Performance*, ed. Ash Tekinay (Istanbul: Bogaziçi University Press, 2005), 150–60; Marilyn French, *Shakespeare's Division of Experience* (New York: Summit Books, 1981), 182.
31 See Emily A. Detmer-Goebel, 'Shakespeare's Bed-tricks: Finding Justice in Lies?' in *Justice, Women, and Power in English Renaissance Drama*, ed. Andrew J. Majeske and Emily Detmet-Goebel (Madison: Fairleigh Dickinson University Press, 2009), 118–39; Laura Kolb, 'The Very Modern Anger of Shakespeare's Women: What *Measure for Measure* Means to Us in 2019', *Electric Lit* (6 February 2019): https://electricliterature.com/the-very-modern-anger-of-shakespeares-women/; and Nora J. Williams, 'Incomplete Dramaturgies', *Shakespeare Bulletin* 40.1 (2022): 1–22.
32 Carolyn E. Brown, 'The Homoeroticism of Duke Vincentio: "Some Feeling of the Sport"', *Studies in Philology* 94.2 (1997): 188.
33 Catherine I. Cox, '"Lord Have Mercy upon Us": The King, the Pestilence, and Shakespeare's *Measure for Measure*', *Exemplaria* 20.4 (2008): 433.
34 Fabricius, *Syphilis in Shakespeare's England*, 234.
35 Cited in Albert Hunt and Geoffrey Reeves, *Peter Brook* (Cambridge: Cambridge University Press, 1995), 221.
36 See Edward L. Hart, '"War and Lechery": Thematic Unity of *Troilus and Cressida*', *The Bulletin of the Rocky Mountain Modern Language Association* 27.3 (1973): 181–6.
37 Marvin Krims, 'Misreading Cressida', *Psychoanalytic Review* 89 (2002): 239.
38 Joseph Lenz, 'Base Trade: Theater as Prostitution', *ELH* 60.4 (1993): 846.
39 Wilson, *The Essential Shakespeare*, 118.
40 See, for example, Robert H. West, 'Sex and Pessimism in *King Lear*', *Shakespeare Quarterly* 11.1 (1960): 55–60; Peter L. Rudnytsky, '"The

Darke and Vicious Place": The Dread of the Vagina in *King Lear*', *Modern Philology* 96.3 (1999): 291–311.
41 West, 'Sex and Pessimism in *King Lear*', 56.
42 See *OED*, 'fie, *int*'. ('An exclamation expressing, in early use, disgust or indignant reproach') and 'pah, *int*. and *adj*'. ('Expressing disgust or disdain'.)

INDEX

Page numbers followed with "n" refer to endnotes.

Aasand, Hardin   153
adaptationist model of disgust   23, 99, 195
Adelman, Janet   182
Aebischer, Pascale   39, 55
aesthetic disgust   32
affective sciences   7, 10, 18–33
affect theory   209 n.6
Akhimie, Patricia   154
Alban, Gillian M. E.   200
Alcibiades (character)   74, 77, 79, 80, 82, 84, 85, 87–9
Alfar, Cristina León   158
ambivalence   33
anal fistula   103–4
anatomical dissection   48, 49
Andrea, Bernadette   153
Andrews, Michael Cameron   179
Angyal, Andras   19
animalistic dehumanization   154, 171
animalization   162, 170
animal-reminder disgust   22, 23, 135, 136, 176, 195
anti-Blackness   248 n.6
anti-Semitism   168–70
anxiety   183, 188–9, 192, 193
Apemantus (character)   74, 76–8, 82, 89, 90, 94–6
Aristotle   84
'Assaf Kafantaris, Mira   163
Athenian democracy   84–5

Austin, Jodie   74
avoidance response   137

Baker, Naomi   41, 53–5
Bakhtin, Mikhail   112, 122, 126
Bamber, Linda   180
Banerjee, Pompa   68
banishment   106, 132
    Alcibiades (character)   82, 85, 88
    Martius, Caius   121, 125, 130, 132
Barker, Francis   46
Barnes, Barnabe   54
beauty   54–5
Bedford, Thomas   52
behavioural immune system (BIS)   99–100, 165–6, 197
Behre, Keri Sanburn   78
benign masochism   32
Bergeron, David M.   100
Berry, Edward   161
Best, George   151, 152
BIID. *See* body integrity identity disorder (BIID)
BII phobia. *See* blood-injury-injection (BII) phobia
Biran, Adam   27
BIS. *See* behavioural immune system (BIS)
Bishai, Nadia   46

Blackness 151, 152, 155, 156, 160, 161
Black racial outsiders 150
Black skin 151–5
  Othello (Shakespeare) 154
blood 128, 135–7, 140–3
blood-injury-injection (BII) phobia 137
Boaistuau, Pierre 51
Boddice, Rob 8
bodily integrity 141
bodily metaphors 131
body envelope
  disgust 137–8, 140, 141
    Coriolanus (Shakespeare) 135
    Henry VI, Part 2 (Shakespeare) 139
    Julius Caesar (Shakespeare) 142–5
    King John (Shakespeare) 139–40
    King Lear (Shakespeare) 140
    The Merchant of Venice (Shakespeare) 141–2
    The Tempest (Shakespeare) 139
    Titus Andronicus (Shakespeare) 135, 140
    Twelfth Night (Shakespeare) 139
  Jews 141–2
  violations 135–6, 140–2
body integrity identity disorder (BIID) 137
body-politic 101, 103, 106–8, 120–2, 125, 130, 131, 150
Bradley, A. C. 173, 181, 185, 193
Brasavola, Antonio 58
Bristol, Michael D. 112
Britton, Dennis Austin 159
Brockbank, Philip 74
Brown, Carolyn E. 200
Browne, Sir Thomas 150, 169
Burke, Kenneth 113
Burnett, Mark Thornton 52
Burton, Robert 54

Canibales 56
cannibalism 56–60, 77–8, 113, 120
capital punishment 42, 44, 46, 52, 60
Carleton, Dudley 153
Carroll, William C. 86
Cassaniti, Julia L. 29
Cavell, Stanley 111
Cefalu, Paul 158
Chalk, Darryl 102
Cham 152
Charney, Maurice 142
choler 117–18
cholera 117
Cohen, Jeffrey Jerome 50
Coles, Kimberly Anne 65
Company of Barber-Surgeons 48, 49
contagion 95, 102, 122
Copley, Anthony 18
corpse 42–9, 58–60, 142, 145, 189–92
  medicine 58–60
corruption 82, 83, 89, 94, 101, 104, 106, 107
Cottom, Daniel 56
The Countess of Pembroke's Arcadia 54
Cox, Brian 39, 40
critical race studies 246 n.1, 248 n.6
critical race theory 153, 162
Croll, Oswald 58

cross-cultural research on
    disgust 27–9
Crunelle, Anny 115
cultural evolution model of
    disgust 21–3
culture of dissection 48
Curtis, Valerie 23, 27, 30
Cuttica, Cesare 83
Cynic body 94
Cynicism 90–6
Cynick friction 93
Cynic shamelessness 94

Dadabhoy, Ambereen 160
Daileader, Celia R. 181
Daniell, David 144, 145
Dannenfeldt, Karl H. 58
Darwin, Charles 19, 24, 66
Daston, Lorraine 51, 52
Davidson, Arnold I. 50
Davies, John 54
Dawson, Anthony B. 73, 78
death 174–8, 182, 183, 187–90, 192, 193
    and disgust 173–94
    of Hamlet (character) 177–9, 183
    inevitability of 191
debased eating 76, 77
deformed mistress tradition 53, 54
dehumanization 150, 154, 170
Dekker, Thomas 2
democracy 84–5
D'Ewes, Simonds 48
digestion 66, 115–17, 119
Diogenes 90–6
dirt 151
discrimination 150, 154
    racial 148, 149
disease disgust
    All's Well That Ends Well
        (Shakespeare) 103
    Coriolanus (Shakespeare) 102

Hamlet (Shakespeare) 102
Henry IV, Part 1 (Shakespeare) 104
Henry IV, Part 2 (Shakespeare) 104–8
Macbeth (Shakespeare) 103
Romeo and Juliet
    (Shakespeare) 102
Th' Overthrow of Stage-Playes
    (Rainolds) 102
Troilus and Cressida
    (Shakespeare) 103
disgust 2–3, 12–14, 50
    attentional bias 32
    as avoidance response 22, 24
    Black skin and 151
    body envelope (*see* body envelope: disgust)
    in children 26
    cross-cultural research 27–9
    cultural evolution model of 21
    death and 173–94
    disease (*see* disease disgust)
    early modern usage of 18
    emotion of 19–21, 24, 25, 30, 111, 137, 150, 154
    extreme 24
    facial expression 24, 26, 123
    food 63–7, 152, 167, 178
    historical approach 6
    imaging research 25
    and indignation 124
    as messy emotion 33
    origin 17
    psychological research 32–3
    psychopathologies 25
    racial (*see* racial disgust)
    racism and 166
    sensitivity 25–7, 138, 149, 150, 196, 197
    sex (*see* sex disgust)
    sociomoral 28, 29, 112, 120, 123, 152

symbolic   151, 179
theory   21–4
as universal emotion   8, 9, 31
visceral   28, 29, 112, 118, 120, 122, 123, 178, 179
in women   26–7
work on   4–6
disgust face   24, 26, 123
dissection of bodies   48, 49
Douglas, Mary   50, 57, 151
Dreckapotheke   57
Dubrow, Heather   53
Dyke, Daniel   169

Earle, John   52
early modern critical race studies   248 n.6
early modern England   41, 42, 65, 86, 87, 151
Egyptian mummies   58
Eliot, T. S.   181
Espinosa, Ruben   162
ethnographic disgust   152
exaptation. *See* preadapation
exile   81, 82, 84, 85, 89
Exostracisme   85

Fabricius, Johannes   199, 200
The Faerie Queene (Spenser)   163
Falstaff   66, 67, 105–6, 140, 199, 200
female sexuality   182, 185
filth/filthy   35, 36, 57
Firth-Godbehere, Richard   30
Fitzpatrick, Joan   75
food
    neophobia   196
    studies   65
food disgust   63–6
    Aguecheek's Beef, Belch's Hiccup, and Other Gastronomic Interjections (Appelbaum)   65

in *Antony and Cleopatra* (Shakespeare)   67–71
The Castel of Health (Elyot)   65
Compendious Regiment or a Dietary of Health (Boorde)   65
Eating Right in the Renaissance (Albala)   65
Food in Shakespeare (Fitzpatrick)   65
The Merry Wives of Windsor (Shakespeare)   67
Midsummer Night's Dream (Shakespeare)   67
Othello (Shakespeare)   67
The Rape of Lucrece (Shakespeare)   67
Romeo and Juliet (Shakespeare)   67
Timon of Athens (Middleton and Shakespeare)   75–8
Titus Andronicus (Shakespeare)   63, 66
Troilus and Cressida (Shakespeare)   67
Twelfth Night (Shakespeare)   67
Food Disgust Scale   64
food rejection system of distaste   20–2
Forker, Charles R.   185
foul/foulness   34, 36, 155, 159, 179, 202
French, Marilyn   200
Fuchs, Leonhart   60

Gascoigne, George   54
Gernet, Louis   46
Gleyzon, François-Xavier   141
Goldberg, Jonathan   115
Goldenberg, Jamie L.   176
Goldstein, David B.   56

INDEX

Granada, Luis De 190
Greene, Robert 87

Habib, Imtiaz 168
Haidt, Jonathan 21, 22, 28
Halio, Jay 140
Hall, John 58
Hall, Kim F. 151
Hamlet (character)
  death of 177–9, 183
  disgust 180–1
  misogynistic anti-carnality 181
  mortality 191–3
  sex nausea 180–3, 185–7
Hampton, Bryan Adams 103
hangings 42–4, 46
Hansen, Adam 85, 88
Harington, John 43
Harris, Jonathan Gil 151, 198
Healy, Margaret 199
Heath, Robert 169
hedonic disgust 32
Hendricks, Margo 149, 246 n.1, 248 n.6
Henry V 106–9
Herz, Rachel 30
Hirsch, Brett D. 168, 169
Histoires Prodigieuses (Boaistuau) 51
Hogan, Patrick Colm 179
Holland, Peter 115, 119
homophobic disgust 197
Houlston, James 115
A Human History of Emotion (Firth-Godbehere) 30
A Hundreth Sundrie Flowres (Gascoigne) 54
Hunt, John 191

indignation 117, 118, 122–4, 133
  of Martius, Caius 118, 123

intergroup disgust sensitivity 166
internalized racism 160
interpersonal disgust 22
Iyengar, Sujata 152

Jagendorf, Zvi 112
jealousy 156, 158, 159
Jews 141, 168–70
Johnson, Richard 86
Johnson, Samuel 140, 161
Jones, Ernest 181
Jonson, Ben 38
Jourdan, Adele-France 40
judicial killings 42–4

Kant, Immanuel 31
Katz, David S. 141
Kellett, Edward 169
Kelley, Shannon 55
Kelly, Thomas J. 86
Kennedy, Colleen E. 66
Kesselring, Krista 43, 44, 46
Kilgour, Maggie 56
King, Mark 182
Knight, Wilson G. 173
Knowell, Edward 52
Koelb, Clayton 141
Korsmeyer, Carolyn 4, 32
Kotzur, Julia 56
Krims, Marvin 201
Krueger, Derek 90

Leigh, Vivian 55
Lenz, Joseph 201
Levin, Richard 184
Lipscomb, Robert 68–9
Little, Arthur L. Jr. 149
loathsome 35, 36, 152, 169, 180
lovesickness 103

McCauley, Clark 21, 22
Machyn, Henry 49
McNally, Richard J. 18

Mallin, Eric S.   177
Marshall, Cynthia   38–40
Marston, John   52, 93
Martin, Randall   190
Martius, Caius   1, 12, 111, 114, 115, 118–28, 130
  banishment   121, 125, 130, 132
  indignation of   118, 123
Martyr, Peter   57
The Masque of Blackness (Jonson)   153
medicinal cannibalism   57–9
Mejia LaPerle, Carol   148, 153
Menon, Usha   29
Metzger, Mary Janell   162
Middleton, Thomas   73, 74, 88, 90, 92–4
Minor, Benjamin   151
Minton, Gretchen E.   73, 78
Miola, Robert S.   82
misanthropy   78, 79, 94
Moffett, Thomas   59
monsters/monstrosity   49–53
Montaigne, Michel de   45, 52–3, 55, 60, 93, 95
moral
  disgust   22, 23, 28–9, 112, 118, 122, 151, 178, 197
  dyspepsia   22
  revulsion   179, 182
mortality   175–8, 180, 182–4, 187, 189–93
Moulton, Ian Frederick   103
Mummy (Egyptian)   58, 59
Mundella, Aloysius   59
murder   178–9
murder pamphlets   47–8

nature   51
Nedham, Marchamont   84
Neill, Michael   161
neuroticism   182–3

Noble, Louis   46, 60
Nunn, Hillary M.   48
nunnery   186

omnivore's dilemma   26
Ostracisme   85
outgroup disgust   149, 156, 165
outgroup prejudice   166

Paré, Ambroise   51, 60
Park, Justin H.   29, 100
Park, Katharine   51, 52
Parker, R. B.   112
Parolin, Peter A.   67
Paster, Gail Kern   130, 142
pathogen avoidance   20, 99, 129, 166
patricians   114, 116, 117, 119, 120, 125, 126
PCRS. *See* premodern critical race studies (PCRS)
Peltonen, Markku   83, 84
Pierce, Robert B.   140
plague   74, 80, 81, 97, 102, 124
plebeians   114, 119–26, 129, 130, 133
Plutarch   1, 70, 83, 85, 90, 114, 119, 129
Politics (Aristotle)   84
Porter, Roy   2
preadapation   20, 22
premodern critical race studies (PCRS)   148, 149, 163, 246 n.1
Prendergast, Maria Teresa Micaela   79
profane feeding   75–8, 81
prostitution   182, 186, 201
Pseudodoxia Epidemica (Browne)   169
public executions   42, 44, 46, 52

rabble 122, 129, 130
race/racial
    animalization 170
    discourse of 161
    discrimination 148, 149
    and emotion 148
    meaning 162
    otherness 162, 168
    outsiders 150, 154, 159, 167, 170
    violence 148, 248 n.6
racial disgust 148–9, 152, 153, 167–8, 170, 171
    Antony and Cleopatra (Shakespeare) 167
    Henry V (Shakespeare) 167
    Love's Labour's Lost (Shakespeare) 167
    The Merchant of Venice (Shakespeare) 168–71
    A Midsummer Night's Dream (Shakespeare) 167
    Othello (Shakespeare) 154–63
    The Tempest (Shakespeare) 167–8
    Titus Andronicus (Shakespeare) 167
    The Unfortunate Traveller (Nashe) 179
racism 153–4, 157, 160, 162, 166
Rainolds, John 102
rank 108, 159, 178
Reid, Pauline Ellen 106
revulsion 21, 55, 112, 153–6, 161, 163, 166–7, 176, 179
    moral 179, 182
    sexual 181, 186, 201
Richard II (King of England, character) 106, 109

Richard III (King of England, character) 138–9
Rid, Samuel 86
Riss, Arthur 115
Roberts, Hugh 93
Robinson, Benedict 17, 18
romanticizing of sex 184
Rose, Jacqueline 183
Ross, Daniel W. 76
rottenness 35–6
Royer, Katherine 42
Rozin, Paul 21, 22

Sadowski, Piotr 179
Salamon, Linda Bradley 87
Sanderson, Robert 86
Saunders, Ben 157, 162
scabs 129
Schaller, Mark 100
Schen, Claire S. 87
self-disgust 137
sensation seeking 33
sex disgust 23, 195–7
    The Comedy of Errors (Shakespeare) 198
    Hamlet (Shakespeare) 195
    King Lear (Shakespeare) 202–4
    Measure for Measure (Shakespeare) 200–3
    The Merry Wives of Windsor (Shakespeare) 199–200
    Much Ado About Nothing (Shakespeare) 199
    Pericles (Shakespeare) 199
    sensitivity 197
    Troilus and Cressida (Shakespeare) 201–2
sex/sexual 156, 162, 181–4, 186, 192, 196, 200–1
    arousal 196
    aversion 181, 187
    jealousy 156

morality 197
and mortality 183
nausea 180, 182, 183, 185–7, 195, 198, 200, 202
revulsion 181, 186, 201
romanticizing of 184
Shahani, Gitanjali G. 65, 148, 152
Shakespeare, William
   All's Well That Ends Well 103
   Antony and Cleopatra 67–71, 167
   As You Like It 199, 207
   The Comedy of Errors 54, 198
   Coriolanus 1–2, 12, 111–33
   disgust 9, 10, 13–14, 31, 34, 36, 108, 167
   drama of sickness 101
   early modern medical discourse 101
   Hamlet 173
      death and disgust 173–94
      Terror Management Theory (TMT) 177–8, 182–4, 187–90, 193, 194
   Henry IV, Part 1 104
   Henry IV, Part 2 104–8, 199
   Henry V 199
   historicist treatment of 7
   Julius Caesar 35, 68–70, 102, 142–5
   King John 139–40
   King Lear 140, 151, 202–4
   Love's Labour's Lost 167
   Macbeth 103
   Measure for Measure 200–3
   The Merchant of Venice 141–2, 162, 168–71
   The Merry Wives of Windsor 67, 199–200
   A Midsummer Night's Dream 67, 83, 103, 167, 199
   Much Ado About Nothing 199
   Othello 67, 154, 166, 168
      animalization of 155
      internalized racism 160
      racial disgust 153–63
      racial violence 148–9
   Pericles 199
   racial disgust 168
   The Rape of Lucrece 35, 67
   Romeo and Juliet 35, 67, 102
   sex nausea 200
   The Tempest 52, 167–8
   Timon of Athens 73–97
      cannibalism 77–8
      disease 78–81
      eating process 75–8
      food disgust 75–8
      profane feeding 75–8, 81
      sexual infection 80
      Timon in 74–90, 92, 94–6
   Titus Andronicus 13, 37–61, 63, 66, 135, 140, 167, 173
      bloody contents of 46
      judicial killings 42–4
      monstrosity 49–50
      rape-revenge narrative 39
      review 38
      sinister aesthetics 40
      theatrical killings 46
      violence in 37–42
   Troilus and Cressida 67, 103, 201–2
   Twelfth Night 67, 139, 207
   The Two Noble Kinsmen 205
   use of disgusting terms 34–6
   work on food disgust 67
shamelessness 93–4
Shapiro, James 141
Shaw, Justin 163
Shirley, James 54
Shweder, Richard A. 8

sinister aesthetics 40
Sir Tophas 53
Skuse, Alanna 103
Sloterdijk, Peter 95
Slotkin, Joel Elliot 38, 40
Smith, Ian 148, 153, 163
Smith, Thomas 42
Smoke Detector Principle 100
sociomoral disgust 28, 29, 112, 120, 123, 152
sociomoral violation 28, 171
Spates, William 101, 108
spectacular disgust 41
Spenser, Edmund 163
Spurgeon, Caroline 64, 177
Staden, Heinrich von 57
Staines, John D. 140
stigmatization 138
stomach 114–18
Stow, John 46
Strohminger, Nina 27, 33
Sugg, Richard 31, 59
Sundrye Strange and Inhumaine Murthers (1591) 47–8
symbolic disgust 151, 179
syphilis 79, 81, 102–3, 198–201

Tanner, William 173
Terror Management Theory (TMT) 12, 13, 174–7, 195
  Hamlet (Shakespeare) 177–8, 182–4, 187–90, 193, 194
theatrical killings 46
Thompson, Ayanna 151
Timon (character) 74–90, 92, 94–6
Timon of Athens (Middleton and Shakespeare) 73–97
  cannibalism 77–8
  disease 78–81
  eating process 75–8
  food disgust 75–8
  profane feeding 75–8, 81
  sexual infection 80
  Timon in 74–90, 92, 94–6
Traversi, Derek 177
tribunes 121–5
Tybur, Joshua M. 21–3, 42, 43
  evolutionary adaptationist model 99, 195

Udall, Nicolas 91, 92
ugliness/ugly body 54–5
ugly beauty 53
The Unfortunate Traveller (Nashe) 170
universal emotion 7–9
universalism without the uniformity (Menon and Cassaniti) 29
universality 8

Vaughan, Alden T. 52
vent 119
vile 35, 36, 180
violence 37–42, 150
  racial 148–9
visceral disgust 28, 29, 112, 118, 120, 122, 123, 178, 179
Volscian 127, 128, 131, 132
  assault 119, 121
vomit 75, 76, 79

Wall, Wendy 57
Weemes, John 169
Wentersdorf, Karl P. 181
West, Robert H. 202
Western medicine 57
Whigham, Frank 115
Williamson, Matt 68
Wilson, Dover J. 42
Wilson, Jeffrey R. 138
Woodbridge, Linda 86, 87
Wright, Thomas 18

Zimmerman, Susan 191

www.ingramcontent.com/pod-product-compliance
Lightning Source LLC
Chambersburg PA
CBHW052218300426
44115CB00011B/1744